British Journal of **Educational Psychology**
Monograph Series II: Psychological Aspects of Education – Current Trends

Number 2

Development and Motivation: Joint Perspectives

Edited by
Leslie Smith, Colin Rogers and **Peter Tomlinson**

Dedication

PAUL PINTRICH [1953–2003]

As this volume was going to press, we learned the tragic news of Paul's unexpected and all too early death on 12 July 2003. We value his contributions at our conference, both his invited paper and his participation in formal discussions and informally. All were testimony to his erudition and personal charm – it was a delight to be with him. We dedicate this volume to Paul and trust that the ideas and evidence that he has left us – both here and elsewhere in his prodigious output – will live on.

Leslie Smith
Colin Rogers
Peter Tomlinson

Published in 2003 by The British Psychological Society, St Andrews House, 48 Princess Road East, Leicester LE1 7DR, UK.

ISSN 1476–9808 Monograph Series II: Psychological Aspects of Education–Current Trends
ISBN 1–85433–393–3 Development and Motivation

To order, please contact the Commercial Sales Department, The British Psychological Society, St Andrews House, 48 Princess Road East, Leicester LE1 7DR. Tel: +44 (0)116 252 9551, Fax: +44 (0)116 247 0787, Email: sarsta@bps.org.uk.

www.bps.org.uk

Typeset by YHT Ltd, London
Printed in Great Britain by Cambrian Printers, Aberystwyth

Contents

www.bps.org.uk

v   Series preface
        Peter Tomlinson

1   Introduction
        Leslie Smith and Colin Rogers

13   Ability conceptions, motivation and development
        Carol S. Dweck

29   Morals, motives and actions
        Elliot Turiel

41   An integration of motivation and cognition
        Mark H. Bickhard

57   Interest and human development: An educational-psychological perspective
        Andreas Krapp

85   Developmental regulation across the life span: A control-theory approach and implications
        for secondary education
        Jutta Heckhausen and Susan P. Farruggia

103   Two motivational systems that shape development: Epistemic and self-organizing
        Kurt W. Fischer and Michael W. Connell

125   Taking agency seriously in the theories-of-mind enterprise: Exploring children's
        understanding of interpretation and intention
        Bryan W. Sokol and Michael J. Chandler

137   Multiple goals and multiple pathways in the development of motivation and self-regulated
        learning
        Paul R. Pintrich

155   Achievement motivation in real contexts
        Julian Elliott and Neil Hufton

173   Towards a model that integrates motivation, affect and learning
        Monique Boekaerts

191   Conclusion
        Colin Rogers and Leslie Smith

Series preface

www.bps.org.uk

The origin of this new series of BJEP monographs lies in a striking but lamentable paradox. Its positive strand is well instanced and articulated by the influential recent volume: *How people learn: Brain, mind, experience, and school* (1999), edited by John Bransford, Anne Brown and Rodney Cocking on behalf of the Committee on Developments in the Science of Learning of the US National Research Council. As the first chapter tells us:

> Thirty years ago, educators paid little attention to the work of cognitive scientists, and researchers in the nascent field of cognitive science worked far removed from classrooms. [...] The story we can now tell about learning is far richer than ever before, and it promises to evolve dramatically in the next generation. (Bransford, Brown, & Cocking, 1999, p. 3.)

The remainder of the book then provides an extremely readable and balanced review of what is currently known about learners and learning, focusing subsequently on implications of this research for the design of effective learning environments, including roles for technology and emphasizing the key role of teachers. As a widely accessible positive indication of, so to speak, 'what psychology now offers to education', it would be hard to better.

In the UK, on the one hand, there has been a welcome, if gradual, shift of concern from specification of national curricular goals, through assessment of their achievement, towards more recent emphasis on promoting such achievement through effective pedagogy (cf. Barber, 1998; Leach & Moon, 1999; Mortimore, 1999). On the other hand, by contrast, the paradox is that over precisely the same few decades, the UK education system has been rapidly losing touch with the psychological insights our American colleagues (and Europeans and Australasians and others worldwide) have been increasingly celebrating as relevant to teaching. In particular, a variety of influences have led directly or indirectly to the initial teacher preparation sector in UK universities and colleges steadily losing precisely those staff whose psychological qualifications would enable it to be kept critically aware of these resources—in spite of efforts by the British Psychological Society to argue the case (see Tomlinson, Edwards, Finn, Smith, & Wilkinson, 1992).

If the idea for the present series arose from the BJEP Editorial Board's desire to play some small part in ameliorating the situation just described, its conception and realization were due to a stroke of financial good fortune whose provenance deserves recognition. Namely, although this Journal is now fully owned by the British Psychological Society, it was in fact published from 1935 onwards by an independent company, *British Journal of Educational Psychology Ltd*. Only in 1995 did the directors of that company decide to wind it up and to donate it and its considerable assets to the Society.

Acting according to the terms of this transfer, the Editorial Board of BJEP decided that in the face of the situation described above, it would be worthwhile to spend some of the funds at its disposal to mount a series of annual conferences in the UK on psychological aspects of education, in which world-leading researchers would be assembled to provide inputs on the latest cutting-edge advances in their fields. Access to these inputs, particularly for educationists, would be maximized by making these conference events free of charge and by publishing the papers as a corresponding series of monographs. The Journal had already published a series of edited monographs in the 1980s, so it was decided that these collections of conference papers would comprise a new *British Journal of Educational Psychology Monograph Series II: Psychological Aspects of Education—Current Trends*.

At the time of writing, the first and second conferences have been held, and a third is in preparation. Beyond these, this will be a rolling programme, but there seems little doubt, given the considerable recent expansion of psychological research in, or of relevance to, education, that over the coming decade we shall be able to hold events and publish monographs in many major areas and aspects of educational interest. So whilst the original impetus for the series was admittedly local, the monographs in the new series should, in return, offer useful resources to the international community of those concerned with the psychological aspects of education.

References

Barber, M. (1998). *The learning game*. London: Fontana.

Bransford, J. D., Brown, A. L., & Cocking, R. R. (Eds.) (1999). *How people learn: Brain, mind, experience, and school*. Committee on Developments in the Science of Learning of the US National Research Council. Washington, DC: National Academy Press.

Leach, J., & Moon, R. (Eds.) (1999). *Learners and pedagogy*. London: Paul Chapman in association with The Open University.

Mortimore, P. (Ed.) (1999). *Understanding pedagogy and its impact on learning*. London: Paul Chapman.

Tomlinson, P. D., Edwards, A., Finn, G., Smith, L., & Wilkinson, J. E. (1992). *Psychological aspects of beginning teacher competence. A submission by the British Psychological Society to the Council for the Accreditation of Teacher Education*. Leicester: British Psychological Society.

PETER TOMLINSON (University of Leeds, UK)

Development and Motivation, 1–11
BJEP Monograph Series II, 2
© 2003 The British Psychological Society
www.bps.org.uk

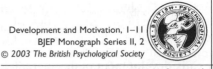

Introduction

Leslie Smith* and Colin Rogers

Lancaster University, UK

> When April with its sweet showers has pierced the drought of March to the root, and
> bathed every vein of earth with that liquid by whose power the flowers are engendered
> ... then, as the poet Geoffrey Chaucer observed many years ago, folk long to go on
> pilgrimages. Only, these days, professional people call them conferences.
>
> David Lodge (1984) *Small world.*

This monograph had its origin in a conference with the same name. The conference was a pilgrimage in two respects. First, speakers were international, drawn from mainland Europe and the USA to the English Lake District in April 2002. More relevant here is an intellectual journey central to the aims of the conference, the journey from motivation to development and back again. This intellectual journey should seemingly be quite easy to make. Unfortunately, this is not the case. To see why, we need to take three steps. One is recognition of the mismatch between common sense and psychology, another is analysis of the guiding principles in past models, and a third is a brief outline of pathways ahead. These pathways will be re-visited in our conclusion.

Mismatch between common sense and psychology

At the common-sense level, development and motivation are interlinked. The phenomena are clear enough. Thus Sir Edmund Hillary after his successful ascent of Mt Everest in 1953 was invited to engage in fund-raising with the authorities in New Zealand for a trip to the Antarctic:

> initially I had no plans to go south myself, but as I did what I could to motivate the
> powers that be, I started almost unconsciously to develop an enthusiasm for the idea.
> (Hillary, 1999)

Hillary's own motivation to be an active member of the Antarctic expedition had been externally produced through his official invitation. His fund-raising activities had led to the development of his own enthusiasm for this project. And Sir Edmund reckoned that his own motivation had itself undergone development. The converse also occurs. Soon

---

Requests for reprints should be addressed to Leslie Smith, Department of Educational Research, Lancaster University, Lancaster, LA1 4YL, UK (e-mail: l.smith@lancaster.ac.uk).

after graduation, Peter Cook had meteoric success with *Beyond the Fringe* in London and New York. But 30 years later, he offered this verdict:

> there is only one depressing side effect of re-reading the text—I may have done some other things as good but I am sure none better. I haven't matured, progressed, grown, become deeper, wiser, or funnier. But then I thought I never would. (Cook, 1987)

The early development of this incredible talent did not lead to better things, or so Peter Cook confessed.

A comparable link is typically manifest in students' thinking about psychology and education. Motivational models central to a course in the Social Psychology of Education often lead students to ask questions about the implications of these models for children's development. There is nothing wrong in that except for two things. One is that the very same students raise the counterpart question about the implications for motivation of developmental models on their completion of a course on Children's Development and Schooling. Apparently, this rather obvious question about interlinkage had not been as well investigated on these courses with an exclusive focus on developmental models, or on motivational models, but not on both. And this leads to the second reason as to what is odd here. These students' own thinking tracked the coverage given on their courses, which in turn tracked research in these areas, research on motivation in one, and research on development in the other, but not on both at once! Here are some interesting manifestations, interesting because they are explicit statements about *omissions* in current research to be remedied in research in the twenty-first century.

> A theory of motivation must include the full range of cognitive processes. (Weiner, 1992)

> Emotional, motivational, attitudinal, cultural, and other affective and social factors operate simultaneously with cognitive factors and play a critical role in determining what is learned. (Shuell, 1996)

> The motivation researcher with a developmental focus needs to take into account [the fact that the motivational] models elaborated for 'adults' may not fit childhood. (Graham & Weiner, 1996)

> We have said nothing, however, about why the sensori-motor or any subsequent cognitive system should ever operate in the first place, nor about the circumstances under which it would be most likely to operate with maximum intensity and persistence. What needs to be added is an account of cognitive motivation—that is, of the factors and forces that activate or intensify human cognitive processing. (Flavell et al., 1993)

> Although cognitive psychologists have long posited a relationship between learning and motivation, they have paid little attention to the latter, despite its vital interest to teachers [which will require new steps in research the aims of which are to] make a commitment to basic research programs in cognition, learning, and teaching [and to] investigate the interaction between cognitive competence and motivational factors. (Bransford, Brown, & Cocking, 2001)

> Motivation theorists increasingly are interested in the ways in which motivation and cognition work together ... although various models are flourishing, there is a need for theoretical integration. (Eccles & Wigfield, 2002)

These statements by leading researchers in these areas amount to the stark reminder that quite a lot has still to be done in the articulation of a joint model of motivation and development. And this means that the common-sense view about the interlinkage of development and motivation remains indeterminate in psychology. The main omission is plain to see as the lack of an inclusive focus which gives joint attention to development and motivation in a unitary account.

Three caveats should be entered here. Firstly, a joint account and an account with joint implications are not the same thing. It is one thing for a developmental model to have implications for motivation, or for a motivational model to have implications for development. But it is something else again for there to be a joint account which sets out a coherent integration of both. It is a joint account which is lacking in current research-based models in psychology and education. Secondly, a division of labour is always in the reckoning: everybody cannot do everything all of the time. In scientific research, an exclusive focus on development alone or on motivation alone is not in itself misguided. On the contrary, this is generally the royal road to scientific advance whereby a complex problem—How does the human mind work?—is broken down into its constituent parts for finer interpretation. During the last century, psychology has advanced through its ABC of associationism, behaviourism, and the cognitive revolution. The division of labour in this area is taken up later in our conclusion. Thirdly, a tendency is not an invariance. There are exceptions, and these include work by contributors to this monograph as well as others (for example, Brown, 2003; Demetriou & Kazi, 2001; Shayer & Adey, 2002).

In the past, there have been many false starts. Right now, it will be instructive to take a look backwards for guidance about pathways ahead: *reculer pour mieux sauter*.

Guiding principles in past models

The retrospective review that now follows sets out three principles for use in an inclusive study of the interlinkage of motivation and development in one joint account. These three principles will be individually reviewed, but they have a common focus which is how to answer a question posed two millennia ago in the *De Anima* by Aristotle (1987; para. 432a, pp. 23–24).

How many parts are there to the human mind?

If a model of the mind locates motivation 'in one part' and development 'in another part', then that account faces a dilemma. If these parts are independent, this means that both parts may be activated together, or that either part may be activated without the other, or that neither part may be activated. Applied to the mind, the latter of these alternatives is fair enough (sleep, coma). But the three other alternatives lead to questions such as 'By recourse to which criteria and under what conditions are both parts, or this part, or that part activated?' An answer could arise in two ways, one external and the other internal to the mind. If activation was comprehensively external, then mental activation would be due to non-mental factors. Factors in nature and nurture have long been the usual suspects. But this type of answer exacts a high price, namely that the major factors—genome, culture—activating the mind would not themselves be intrinsically mental. Yet motivation and development fit the lives of autonomous individuals in social worlds. To leave the mind out would be a cavalier disregard. The other alternative is to link the parts in a joint model of the mind. This could be done in several ways: locate motivation and development as constituents in the same part; show how the separate parts intersect; specify a bridging mechanism.

This type of answer has the great merit that, firstly it is not exclusive of the external factors, and secondly, at least one of the factors activating the mind would be itself mental. The three following arguments demonstrate why this second alternative is to be preferred. These arguments concern belief, desire and action; maximal and human rationality; human judgment, knowledge and action. Their implications for current research are taken up in the conclusion.

Belief, desire, action

Human actions are due to the agent's motivational state whose members are beliefs, desires, preferences, evaluations, realizations, and many more (Williams, 2001). An adequate account of human action should be assessed through its capacity to present all of the operative members of an agent's motivational state and their corresponding actions in one mental account. This argument is long-standing (see Bickhard, Chapter 4). It is stated here in two steps, with attention to two outstanding problems known to Aristotle.

The first step concerns the demarcation of living from non-living things. Aristotle's answer was in terms of the presence of the 'anima' in living, and its absence in non-living, things.[1] In the twenty-first century, this looks like a pseudo-answer. Not so. Recall that the English word 'animated' has the same origin, and that our intuitions enable us to distinguish (1) Hamlet's animated performance in his duel with Laertes, (2) Ophelia's non-animate corpse, and (3) the inanimate castle walls at Elsinore. Aristotle went on to argue that a living mind is stocked with beliefs and desires which are central to human action.[2] What 'moves' living beings, what 'makes' them act, what 'causes' them to do one thing on one occasion but not on another are the beliefs and desires in the agent's motivational state. So interpreted, this account includes both cognitive and motivational elements. Indeed, Aristotle's is the first statement of the view that beliefs and desires 'move' people to act. As such, this is now the classical model (Searle, 2001); a classical model but also a complex one (Millgram, 2001). The obvious way is to interpret the relation of beliefs and desires to action as (efficient) causality. But Aristotle realized that this cannot be right. In many cases, actions follow on from the agent's beliefs and desires. But, in otherwise similar cases, the same beliefs and desires do not issue in the same action.[3] Examples are easy to find. Liking bagels and croissants equally for breakfast, and with exactly similar prior desires and beliefs for both, why did Sam have a croissant—not a bagel—for breakfast yesterday, and a bagel—not a croissant— today? Buridan's ass starved to death through a complete incapacity to make a choice between exactly equivalent bales of hay (Clark, 2002). But Sam is not an ass; Sam does have a human capacity for free choice. Exercises of this capacity mean that the relation between beliefs and desires as the motivational states of action is not causality in the Humean sense whereby the conditional link between a cause *C* and its effect *E* requires their regular co-instantiation, such as a sub-zero air temperature causing the freezing of

---

[1] 'Anima', or 'mind alive'. For Aristotle (1987, De Anima, 415b, pp. 8–13), this is operative in human action in three ways: (1) the generative factor in bodily movement, (2) the goal for the sake of which it occurs, and (3) the raison d'être *of any embodied mind. The possessor of a living mind has the capacity to 'live and perceive and think' (De Anima, 414a, pp. 13–14) in that non-living things are not alive, they do not perceive, nor do they think.*
[2] *See Aristotle (1987, Movement of animals, 700b, pp. 17–18): 'now we see that the movers of the animal are reasoning and phantasia [imagination] and choice and wish and appetite. And all of these can be reduced to thought and desire' [such that with regard to the motivation of human action] 'the first mover is the object of desire and also of thought'.*
[3] *See Aristotle (1987, Movement of animals, 701a, pp. 6–7): 'but how does it happen that thinking is sometimes accompanied by action and sometimes not?'*

water. One problem, then, is to explain what the relation is and so show how beliefs and desires are related to action. This continues to be at the forefront of current research (see Sokol & Chandler, Chapter 8).

The second step follows on. Is one mind one, or does it have parts, and if so, how many parts are there? Minds seem to have many parts. There are many reasons why, but here are two. One reason is that beliefs have a mind–world direction of fit which is the converse of a world–mind direction of fit for desires (Searle, 2001). This difference can be interpreted as the location of mental elements with opposing properties in different parts of the mind. A second reason is more general, in that a modular account of the mind strictly requires there to be as many parts to the mind as there are discrete modules (Fodor, 1983). Independence is written into modularity. But this cannot be the whole story. If it were, information arising from one module could not have any bearing on information arising from any other. Indeed, Fodor (2000) has now acknowledged this, specifically mentioning an argument due to Aristotle.[4] If sensory module M_1 serves in the detection of whiteness and sensory module M_2 in the detection of sweetness, then the independent use of these modules would be insufficient to classify and differentiate sugar (white and sweet), salt (white but not sweet), honey (sweet but not white) and pepper (neither white nor sweet). M_1 would be active in the first two cases, and inactive—and so 'blind'—in the last two cases. M_2 would be active in the first and third cases, and inactive—and so 'blind'—in the second and fourth cases. Yet plainly, sugar, salt, honey and pepper are different, and this means something other than these sensory modules is at work. What is required instead are cross-modular mental capacities covering human judgments across the range (see Pintrich, Chapter 9).

So one guiding principle is this. If human actions are motivated by beliefs and desires, these require common capacities for judgment in any 'mind alive'. This argument makes it an explicit requirement that one account should cover all aspects of motivation, including beliefs and desires along with the other diverse elements of the human psyche (see Dweck, Chapter 2). What is left open is the contribution made by development, which is taken up next.

Maximal and human rationality

If beliefs and desires provide motivating reasons for human action, then that action is rational. Crucially, there are degrees or levels of rationality. It is just possible that all agents enjoy maximal rationality. Equally, many other possibilities of sub-maximal rationality are in the reckoning. A denial of maximal rationality can take two forms. One is phylogenetic: maximal rationality is unequally distributed across populations whereby the members of a specified population (such as the 'master race', *Homo sapiens*, or whatever) are maximally rational, whilst agents in other populations are not. The other denial is ontogenetic: rationality is unequally distributed within any population, for example in the case of the human life span, where the rationality of children is not that of adults.

Rousseau (1974) was at pains to point out that children are not miniature adults.[5] The implication is that an account of childhood should shift from a focus on 'being' to

---

[4] See Aristotle (1987, De Anima, 426b, pp. 17–18, 24): 'nor indeed is it possible to judge by separate means that sweet is different from white ... [rather one and the same part of the mind] must assert that they are different'.

[5] See the Preface to Rousseau's (1974) Emile: 'the wisest writers devote themselves to what a man ought to know, without asking what a child is capable of learning. They are always looking for the man in the child, without considering what he is before he becomes a man'.

'becoming', taking on board the sequences and mechanisms by which children become adults. To see Rousseau's point, recall the definition of man as a rational animal.[6] In this context, the term *man* was used in the traditional sense to cover all humans regardless of sex and age. Rousseau's point was that this definition does not fit the facts. We are not born rational, but rather and at best we become rational. In line with this claim, Rousseau (1974, p. 71) used an arresting analogy that 'childhood is the sleep of reason'. The states *being asleep* and *being awake* are opposites. From this it follows that if adult reason amounts to being fully awake with a lively mind in action, there are other states contrary to this, such as fast asleep, half asleep, half awake and so on. These latter states will be sub-maximal, rationally speaking. According to Rousseau, it is these states which fit childhood. This position leaves open actual levels of children's human rationality which could be at zero, minimal or some better level other than maximal rationality.[7]

Three implications may be noticed. One is the methodological principle that developmental similarities and differences should be investigated empirically and systematically.[8] This is something that Rousseau did not do. His case study of the development of Emile scored well on imagination, and hardly at all on scientific value. Even so, a developmental door had been opened, and others have taken on what was left unexplored (see Fischer & Connell, Chapter 7). A second implication concerns education, whose function for Rousseau was to assist children in 'waking up'. In his Preface, Rousseau (1974) specifically denied that he would endorse current educational thinking and practice. His main reason was that he considered successful educational applications to be inherently problematic due to their dependence on given conditions in the prevailing contingencies. In his view, these contingencies vary indefinitely, and resist generalization. This was a stark statement of educational scepticism. Others have taken a more positive stance (see Boekaerts, Chapter 11). A third implication concerns a joint account of development and motivation. Rousseau did not provide such an account. One of his successors was Piaget, whose starting-point in his first book, *Recherche*, took this on.[9] Moreover, Piaget's (1995) socially constituting model of human development required there to be a socially constituting contribution by interacting agents in the individualization of knowledge and values. This position assigned prime place to autonomy in the motivation of human judgment. True: Piaget

---

[6] Aristotle (1987, Nichomachean Ethics, 1098a, pp. 4–8).

[7] Cohen (1986) has argued that adult rationality could not be at the zero level and Cherniak (1986) that, the way things are, it could not be maximal. The implication is that human rationality falls somewhere on a scale between 0 and 1; zero and maximal rationality. But the jury is still out. Gigerenzer and Selten (2001) have argued that notions of maximal rationality are in fact dispensable in the interpretation of the rationality of adults, in contrast to Goswami's (2002) argument that some versions of rational competence have their origin in early childhood.

[8] See Vygotsky (1994, p. 344): 'one and the same event occurring at different ages of the child is reflected in his consciousness in a completely different manner and has an entirely different meaning for the child'.

[9] Recherche means search. For Piaget (1918, pp. 21, 98–99, 155–157), human development is the search for an objective means by which we can evaluate the competing claims of science–faith, facts–norms, knowledge–values. The motivational consequences were put like this in his Sorbonne lectures (Piaget, 1981, pp. 1–2): 'it is impossible to find behaviour arising from affectivity alone without any cognitive elements. It is equally impossible to find behaviour composed only of cognitive elements ... For a student to solve an algebra problem or a mathematician to discover a theorem, there must be intrinsic, extrinsic interest, or a need at the beginning'. See also Piaget (1995, pp. 98–110; for commentary, see Brown, 2002; Mischel, 1971).

did not always follow through the implications of his position for motivation.[10] Others have set out to remedy this omission (see Krapp, Chapter 5).

So the second guiding principle is this. There are two respects in which human reasons are important in the context of agency (Hookway, 2000). One is normative: How are action and thought rational? The other is motivational: Why perform an action, why believe a thought? Psychology can make a contribution to answering both through a unitary focus on the development of the normativity of these reasons with a motivating force from childhood to adulthood.

Human judgment, knowledge and action
A third principle is due to Kant's account of the human mind. His detailed account is notoriously complex, but its outlines are clear enough. For Kant, the human mind is marked by two fundamental powers or capacities for judgment (Longuenesse, 1998). One is the intellectual capacity for understanding, i.e. gaining true knowledge. The other is the practical capacity for willing and the production of free action.[11] These capacities have two important features. First, they are non-reducible. Actions do not have truth-values; nor is knowing a matter of willing. Kant's account secures their non-reducibility. Second, both capacities are subject to internal regulation in being rule-governed. This means that the use of either capacity in a causal context may be governed by rules which are normative in character. The normative regulation of human action and thought is tied to the reasons expressed in judgments. Action due to judgment may be charged with obligation; thought due to judgment may be bound by necessitation. This occurs through the use of rules covering 'what has to be done' and 'what has to be'. However, in that case, there must be a unitary system so that a rational action and a rational thought can be judged by one and the same individual. To Aristotle's question 'How many parts are there to the human mind?', Kant's answer was 'two parts'. But these two parts are parts of one and the same system, otherwise all of 'my' knowledge would not be mine; nor would all of 'my' actions be mine, and therefore neither my own knowledge nor my own actions would be my own.[12]

---

[10] *This omission surfaced in an exchange between Piaget and his colleague Alina Szeminska at his official retirement. Szeminska (1976, p. 119) asked the question: [in situations where a child has already constructed several action-schemes] 'why is such-and-such a scheme activated, and not another?' Piaget's answer was by reference to cognitive repression: 'an observable previously neglected tends both to impose itself and to penetrate consciousness sooner or later'. But this reply has two weaknesses. First, Szeminska (pp. 121–22) pointed out that it is one thing for the apprehension of an object to be blocked by countervailing factors, and something else for it not to be comprehended at all. Second, the reference to 'sooner or later' is notoriously problematic (Smith, 1993, p. 148).*

[11] *See Kant (1997, p. 41): 'logic gives us rules in regard to the use of understanding, and practical philosophy in regard to the use of willing, which are the two powers from which everything in our minds arises'. For Kant, both forms of human rationality are regulated by logical laws which are necessary in character: 'the exercise of our own faculties takes place also according to certain rules [and] understanding, in particular, is governed in its actions by rules which we can investigate [and these are] the necessary laws of understanding and reason generally' (Kant, 1972, paras 170–171). Note that it is one thing to characterize human capacities in this way; it is something else again to claim that all displays of these capacities are similarly so characterized. There is nothing in Kant's account to exclude dual-processing (Sloman, 1996), and quite a lot which requires mental mediation in terms of 'normative facts' (Smith, 2002).*

[12] *See Kant (1933, B131): 'it must be possible for the "I think" to accompany all my representations for otherwise something would be represented in me which could not be thought at all, and that is equivalent to saying that the representation would be impossible, or at least would be nothing to me'. This insight was characterized as 'the transcendental unity of apperception' (Kant, 1933, A107) and it generalizes to the practical capacity for human action. Searle (2001) has ironically noted that this label attests Kant's proclivity for catchy aphorisms. True: this does not trip easily off the tongue. But its main thrust is a commitment to constructivism: whatever is constructed can be preserved by the constructing system. This is because 'I exist as an intelligence which is conscious solely of its power of combination' (Kant, 1933, B158). This 'power of combination' is the capacity for the construction of true knowledge in the theoretical sphere and the production of free action in the practical sphere.*

So interpreted, Kant's account secures a link between action and thought, between motivation, cognition and morality. Less clear is where and how development fits in. The apparent difficulty is due to Kant's (1972, para. 171), commitment to the a priori nature of normative rules; a priori and so valid independently of experience. This commitment seems to be incompatible with human development altogether. This difficulty continues to be regarded as decisive. It led to introspectionism in psychology and eventually to the unsuccessful search for 'imageless thought' (Humphrey, 1963). Latterly, it has been argued that human thought is never a priori, due to its situated origin in social contexts (Kitcher, 1983). Even so, this difficulty is more apparent than real. First, Kant (1933, A1) was careful to note that even though all knowledge has its 'debut' in experience, this does not mean that its 'derivation' is in experience. The 'debut' amounts to the denial of innate knowledge. The 'derivation' is the denial of the sufficiency of experience for the rationality of action and thought. Secondly, this is because the same experience is compatible with different normative properties. In the moral domain, an action in compliant conformity with a rule is not thereby an action obliged in full conscience by that rule. Similarly, in learning arithmetic, believing that 7 and 5 'make' 12 is not the same knowing that $7 + 5 = 12$, still less judging this to be true, and necessarily so. The difference between behavioural compliance and action charged with obligation, between correct thinking and necessary thought is well founded.[13] Thirdly, much less clear is how such advances are made. The question of whether knowledge can be a priori is one thing; quite another is the question about how *in fact* the advance from empirical experience could be made. These questions were run together in Kant's account. But they are separable, as is attested in commentaries on the learning paradox (Moravcsik, 1992). The diversity of modal phenomena attests the importance of these advances.

Social accounts are especially interesting in this respect. According to von Wright (1983), social learning and training are typically marked by 'normative pressure' in that the 'norms', such as rules, directives and values, used by the older members of one society are made available by 'pressure' to younger members of the next generation. The investigation of social norms in this sense is empirical, not a priori, in covering motivation and development across the life span (see Heckhausen & Farrnggia, Chapter 6) as well as cross-culturally (see Elliott & Hufton, Chapter 10). Heteronomous transmission such as this is as essential as it is important. Even so, it is importantly different from the autonomous formation and acceptance of norms. Adapting an example due to Mele (1995), a coin which is a perfect counterfeit thereby has all of the physical properties of legal tender. Even so, there is one crucial difference in normative origin. A valid coin is legal tender due to the normative process of its construction, unlike counterfeit coins whose origin is invalid. Similarly, action or thought whose origin is heteronomous and due to 'normative pressure' is thereby not autonomous action or thought. The outstanding problems here are as complex as they are central to current perspectives (see Turiel, Chapter 3).

In short, a family of distinctions have a common element in normativity. It is the advance from causality to normativity which is implicated in both developmental and

---

[13] *Normativity has modal properties (Smith, 1993, 2002). Like Monsieur Jourdain, we make modal judgments in everyday life, often without realizing this. Compare the modality of action in Luther 'Here I stand. I can't do anything else' (contrast, 'I am not doing anything else'). Similarly, logical judgments in ordinary life can be necessary, such as the modality of thought in Gershwin's* Porgy and Bess *'It ain't necessarily so' (contrast 'It is not so'). The difference is in the modality of the judgment, i.e. the mode or manner in which it is made. Kant's account has the signal virtue that it gives centre stage to modal phenomena whilst giving other actors equal prominence—the Prince of Denmark is not alone in his* Hamlet.

motivational models. The presence of normativity provides a link between motivation, cognition and development. And so this is a third guiding principle for a unitary account of motivation and development in psychology.

Fixing the frame for a jointly motivational and developmental model

Three guiding principles from past models for the joint study of motivation and development in one account were set out in the previous section:

- human actions with motivating reasons in beliefs and desires require common capacities for judgment in any 'mind alive';
- these judgments based on reasoning develop with a motivating force from childhood to adulthood;
- human minds have twin capacities for action and understanding under the normative regulation central to human judgments made in causal contexts.

These principles are not intended to be exhaustive. They are, however, presented as being influential and continue to attract sponsorship as well as critical discussion. Crucially, however, these arguments have been influential in philosophy. And there's the rub. When psychology emerged as an empirical science in the nineteenth century, the temptation to cut its links with its antenatal life proved to be strong. Macnamara (1994) astutely noted that the severance was mutual in that philosophers were slamming the door just at the point when the psychologists were running away. But this takes the argument back to the first section. During the twentieth century, psychology tended to have a mono-focus, and it was precisely because development and motivation were severally rather than jointly investigated in contemporary psychology that the present excursion was taken.

The chapters which follow are intended to present:

- perspectives on human development applied to motivation;
- perspectives on motivation applied to human development;
- perspectives on both human development and motivation;
- perspectives on human development and motivation applied to education.

It is these questions which were part of the motivation of the conference 'Development and motivation', and it is the chapters in this monograph which we believe may well make an instructive contribution to the development of a joint model.

References

Aristotle (1987). In J. Ackrill (Ed.), *A new Aristotle reader*. Oxford: Oxford University Press.

Bransford, J., Brown, A., & Cocking, R. (2001). *How people learn*. Washington, DC: National Academy Press.

Brown, T. (2002). In T. Brown & L. Smith (2002). *Reductionism and the development of knowledge* (pp. 3–26). Mahwah, NJ: Erlbaum.

Cherniak, C. (1986). *Minimal rationality*. Cambridge, MA: MIT Press.

Clark, M. (2002). *Paradoxes from A to Z*. London: Routledge.

Cohen, L. J. (1986). *The dialogue of reason*. Oxford: Oxford University Press.

Cook, P. (1987). Postscript. In A. Bennett, P. Cook, J. Miller, & D. Moore (Eds.), *The complete Beyond the Fringe*. London: Methuen.

Demetriou, A., & Kazi, S. (2001). *Unity and modularity in the mind and the self: studies on the relationships between self-awareness, personality, and intellectual development from childhood to adolescence*. London: Routledge.

Eccles, J. S., & Wigfield, A. (2002). Motivational beliefs, values, and goals. *Annual Review of Psychology*, *53*, 109–132.

Flavell, J., Miller, P., & Miller, S. (1993). *Cognitive development* (3rd ed.). Englewood Cliffs, NJ: Prentice-Hall.

Fodor, J. (1983). *Modularity of mind: An essay on faculty psychology*. Cambridge, MA: MIT Press.

Fodor, J. (2000). *The mind doesn't work that way*. Cambridge, MA: MIT Press.

Gigerenzer, G., & Selten, R. (2001). Rethinking rationality. In G. Gigerenzer & R. Selten (Eds.), *Bounded rationality: The adaptive toolbox*. Cambridge, MA: MIT Press.

Goswami, U. (2002). Inductive and deductive reasoning. In U. Goswami (Ed.), *Blackwell handbook of childhood cognitive development*. Oxford: Blackwell.

Graham, S., & Weiner, B. (1996). Theories and principles of motivation. In D. Berliner & R. Calfee (Eds.), *Handbook of educational psychology*. New York: Macmillan.

Hillary, Sir E. (1999). *View from the summit*. London: Doubleday.

Hookway, C. (2000). Regulating inquiry: virtue, doubt, and sentiment. In G. Axtell (Ed.), *Knowledge, belief, and character: Readings in virtue epistemology*. Lanham, MD: Rowman and Littlefield.

Humphrey, G. (1963). *Thinking*. New York: Wiley.

Kant, I. (1933). *Critique of pure reason* (2nd ed.). London: Macmillan.

Kant, I. (1972). *Introduction to logic*. Westport, CT: Greenwood.

Kant, I. (1997). Lectures on ethics. In *Collected works*. Cambridge: Cambridge University Press.

Kitcher, P. (1983). *The nature of mathematical knowledge*. New York: Oxford University Press.

Longuenesse, B. (1998) *Kant and the capacity to judge*. Princeton, NJ: Princeton University Press

Macnamara, J. (1994). *The logical foundations of cognition*. New York: Oxford University Press.

Mele, A. (1995). *Autonomous agents: From self-control to autonomy*. New York: Oxford University Press.

Millgram, E. (2001). The current state of play. In E. Millgam (Ed.), *Varieties of practical reasoning*. Cambridge, MA: MIT Press

Mischel, T. (1971). Piaget: Cognitive conflict and the motivation of thinking. In T. Mischel (Ed.), *Cognitive development and epistemology*. New York: Academic Press.

Moravcsik, J. (1992). Learning as recollection. In J. M. Day (Ed.), *Plato's Meno in focus*. London: Routledge.

Piaget, J. (1918). *Recherche*. Lausanne: La Concorde.

Piaget, J. (1981). *Intelligence and affectivity: Their relationship during child development*. Palo Alto, CA: Annual Reviews.

Piaget, J. (1995). *Sociological studies*. London: Routledge.

Rousseau, J. J. (1974). *Emile*, London: Dent.

Searle, J. (2001). *Rationality in action*. Cambridge, MA: MIT Press.

Shayer, M., & Adey, P. (2002). *Learning intelligence: Cognitive acceleration across the curriculum from 5 to 15 years*. Buckingham: Open University Press.

Shuell, T. (1996). Teaching and learning in a classroom context. In D. Berliner & R. Calfee (Eds.), *Handbook of educational psychology*. New York: Macmillan.

Sloman, S. (1996). The empirical case for two systems of reasoning. *Psychological Bulletin*, *119*, 3–22.

Smith, L. (1993). *Necessary knowledge*. Hove: Erlbaum.

Smith, L. (2002). *Reasoning by mathematical induction in children's arithmetic*. Oxford: Pergamon.

Szeminska, A. (1976). Commentary. In B. Inhelder, B., Garcia, R., & Vonèche, J. (Eds.), *Epistémologie génétique et équilibration*. (pp. 119–122) Neuchâtel: Delachaux and Niestlé.

von Wright, G. H. (1983). *Practical reason*. Oxford: Blackwell.

Vygotsky, L. (1994). *The Vygotsky reader*. Oxford: Blackwell.

Weiner, B. (1992). *Human motivation: Metaphors, theories, and research*. Newbury Park, CA: Sage.

Williams, B. (2001). Internal and external reasons, with Postscript. In E. Millgram (Ed.), *Varieties of practical reasoning*. Cambridge, MA: MIT Press.

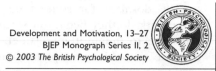

Development and Motivation, 13–27
BJEP Monograph Series II, 2
© 2003 The British Psychological Society

www.bps.org.uk

Ability conceptions, motivation and development

Carol S. Dweck*
Columbia University, USA

In this article, I use the literature on the development of ability conceptions to emphasize several points about motivation and development: (1) that development does not always proceed toward one correct or mature concept; (2) that analogous concepts or conceptual frameworks can arise at different points in development; and (3) that there is a critical difference between when a concept is formed and when it has motivational impact. Here I will show that only when ability conceptions coalesce into a coherent framework (a 'meaning system') do they begin to exert a consistent and systematic influence on children's motivation. I also suggest that within their constructed meaning systems, children may follow qualitatively different developmental trajectories.

The literature on the development of ability conceptions is a complex one. However, careful consideration of this literature can be extremely rewarding, adding a great deal to our understanding of both motivation and development.

In the present paper, I will use the literature on ability conceptions to make three developmental points:

(1) *Development does not necessarily proceed toward one correct/mature concept.* In contrast to much of what has been written, we will see that there is more than one correct, mature concept of ability, with strikingly different motivational consequences.

(2) *Analogous concepts (and even conceptual frameworks) can arise at very different times in different domains.* Here, we will see that years before children have built a motivational framework around ability conceptions, they have built a strikingly similar framework around a different aspect of the self: goodness. This has important implications for the conclusions we draw about children's self-conceptions and their cognitive-representational abilities.

(3) *There is a critical distinction between when a concept is formed and when it has*

Requests for reprints should be addressed to Carol S. Dweck, 402A Schermerhorn Hall, Columbia University, 1190 Amsterdam Avenue, Mail Code 5501, New York City, NY 10027, USA (e-mail: dweck@psych.columbia.edu).

motivational impact. Here, we will see that children may develop many conceptions that are potentially relevant to their motivation but these conceptions can lie dormant for some time. Only when they coalesce into a coherent framework do they begin to exert systematic influence on children's motivation. This leads to an important distinction between the development of a concept and the role that this concept may later play in children's motivation through its participation in a coherent conceptual framework.

I examine these points one at a time, using research findings to illustrate each, and ending with a consideration of the developmental mysteries that remain before us.

Is there one correct/mature conception of ability?

For many years, the literature on the development of motivation assumed that all roads led children to the idea of intelligence as a stable capacity that is separate from effort, and that is inversely related to it. Specifically, it was believed that at about the age of 10-12 years, children attained and converged on this one mature conception of ability or intelligence (Dweck & Elliott, 1983; Nicholls, 1984; Stipek & Daniels, 1988).

However, intelligence is a social construction (Carugati, 1990; Cornelius, Kenny, & Caspi, 1989; Rosenholz & Simpson, 1984; Wagner & Sternberg, 1984). It is something we invented to capture the psychological functions involved in intellectual activity, and therefore more than one legitimate construction is possible. That is, different people may legitimately differ in what they think the contents, properties, or workings of intelligence are. For example, people may differ in whether they think intelligence is an underlying capacity or a repertoire of intellectual skills (see Dweck, 1999), whether they think it is stable or expandable (see Dweck, 1999; Howe, 1990; Perkins & Grotzer, 1997) and whether they think it is separate from effort or that motivational factors are a key part of it (see Yang & Sternberg, 1997).

When children form conceptions about the physical world, they often get clear feedback about the correctness of their theories. They may try to fly unassisted, or to place objects on surfaces that provide insufficient support or to fit objects into containers that are too small. With the feedback they receive, they can readily correct their theories about the nature of objects and the way the physical world works (Baillargeon, 1995).

Similarly, with language, children are typically presented with a standard against which they can match what they produce and toward which they can strive. Although language acquisition is much more than simple matching and correction, there exists a standard of native proficiency which is widely shared and to which children are exposed (see Gleitman & Newport, 1995).

However, theories about psychological entities are different. Outcomes and events typically speak far less clearly to the adequacy of a particular belief: Does an intellectual failure mean that the idea of stable capacity is correct or incorrect? Does it mean that effort is separate from, or part of, ability? There is typically no concrete external feedback about the correctness of any specific belief. Indeed, as will be seen, outcomes and events are often interpreted *within* the conceptions that children have, rather than leading them to refine or jettison their theory.

Why did people think that all roads led to the conception of ability as a stable entity? Researchers had found that at about 10-12 years of age, children become *able* to think of intelligence in new ways, and in ways that implied that intelligence was a stable quality inversely related to effort (Nicholls, 1978, 1984). For example, when given the information that two children who worked equally hard achieved different outcomes, they can now agree that one child has more ability than the other. Or, if given information that two children put in different amounts of effort and achieved the same outcome, children can now agree that one child has more ability than the other.

What does this mean? The change in responding at this age probably does signal an advance in thinking. It may in fact mean that children are now capable of *understanding* the idea of a stable entity that is inversely related to another variable. And indeed this may be part of a more general cognitive change in abstract thinking that is often found to take place at around this time. In a related vein, this is also the time that children may be beginning to learn algebraic concepts, and these research tasks are tapping into emerging algebraic skills. They are giving children the values of two variables in an algebra equation (effort, performance) and asking them to solve for a third (ability).

However, the fact that children are now *able* to reason about ability or intelligence as a stable capacity that is inversely related to effort does not mean that this is the conception of intelligence they adopt as their own (Karabenick & Heller, 1976; Kun, 1977; Schuster, Ruble, & Weinert, 1999; Surber, 1980). In fact, in our work, we have shown that only some children (and usually only some older individuals) adopt this as their theory of intelligence and build their motivational framework around it. An equal number adopt a very different theory of intelligence, one that portrays intelligence as an expandable quality that can be developed through effort and learning (Dweck, 1999; Dweck & Leggett, 1988; see also Dweck, Chiu, & Hong, 1995). In this latter system, effort is not seen as inversely related to ability at all, but rather as something that allows people to turn on and use their abilities to maximal advantage, as well as to cultivate their abilities over time. Further, in this system, effort may not even be seen as always distinct from intelligence, but as something that is part and parcel of the functioning intellectual system—its energy or motor, or even part of the repertoire of self-regulatory skills that go into intelligent behaviour (Dweck, 1999; Yang & Sternberg, 1997).

Theories of intelligence are linked to different meaning systems

Which theory of intelligence a student chooses is of more than intellectual interest, for starting at about 10–12 years of age, children's theories of intelligence appear to spawn a whole motivational framework that I have called a 'meaning system'. What I mean by meaning system is a network of beliefs and goals—built around a core theory—that systematically guides behaviour.

Let us look at the two meaning systems that are built around the two different theories of intelligence. Drawing on our work (Blackwell, Dweck, & Trzesniewski, 2002; Henderson & Dweck, 1990; Hong, Chiu, Dweck, Lin, & Wan, 1999; Mueller & Dweck, 1998), I will show that the students who view their intelligence as a fixed trait (who hold an 'entity theory' of intelligence) build a meaning system that revolves around measuring and validating their level of fixed intelligence, whereas those who view their intelligence as an expandable quality (an 'incremental theory') build a meaning system that revolves around 'process', e.g. around effort, strategies and learning (see also Bickert, 2003; Krapp, 2003).

In two large studies, we tracked hundreds of students (of about 13 years old), making the transition to 7th grade, the first year of junior high school (Blackwell *et al.*, 2002; Henderson & Dweck, 1990). This is a very challenging transition for students. At this time, the academic work becomes substantially more difficult (especially in mathematics), the grading becomes much more stringent, and the environment becomes far more impersonal and unsupportive (Eccles & Midgley, 1989). Typically, students' grades drop as they enter junior high and continue to do so.

Since this is the time at which students' intelligence-related meaning systems are becoming coherent and influential, we expected the challenge of junior high school to exert a powerful motivational impact but a different impact on students who held an entity vs. an incremental theory of intelligence. For those with an entity theory, who are concerned about their level of fixed intelligence, this should be a very threatening time, since failure looms large. In contrast, for those with the incremental theory of intelligence, the new challenge of junior high school should be seen more as an opportunity for increasing their intellectual skills and should spur them on to greater effort. These different views of intelligence would not predict a great deal about students' motivation and achievement in less challenging situations. Only when the work is quite difficult, and failure is a real possibility should the differences between the students with two views really emerge.

In these studies (Blackwell *et al.*, 2002; Henderson & Dweck, 1990) we assessed students' theories of intelligence as they entered 7th grade, along with their other achievement-relevant beliefs and goals. (Students' theories of intelligence were assessed by asking them to agree or disagree with a series of statements depicting the theories of intelligence. For example, a statement representing the entity view was: 'Your intelligence is something very basic about you that you can't really change'.

We then followed them across the next year (in the Henderson & Dweck study) and the next 2 years of junior high (in the Blackwell *et al.* study), monitoring their maths grades. Although students with the incremental vs. entity theory of intelligence had entered junior high with similar maths achievement test scores, we saw marked differences in their motivation as they coped with the new, more challenging academic environment, and we saw their grades steadily diverge.

First, the students adhering to the incremental vs. entity theory of intelligence held different achievement goals (Blackwell *et al.*, 2002; cf. Robins & Pals, 2002). Those with the incremental view that intelligence can be expanded endorsed 'learning goals'— goals that put the premium on learning challenging new things as opposed to just trying to look smart—significantly more than did those with the entity view that intelligence is fixed (see Pintrich, 2003).

Next, those with the incremental view, far more than their entity-oriented peers, held positive effort beliefs (Blackwell *et al.*, 2002; cf. Dweck & Leggett, 1988). They believed that effort empowers and makes the most of your ability, can compensate for a lack of ability, and can increase your ability over time. Those with the entity view of intelligence were more likely to endorse the negative effort beliefs—that effort implies a lack of ability. Interestingly, even when students were told nothing about the difficulty of a task or about another person's performance on a task, these students believed that the need for effort in itself signalled an ability deficit. Moreover, they believed that once a person lacked ability, no amount of effort would help.

Third, the two groups interpreted setbacks in different ways (Blackwell *et al.*, 2002; Henderson & Dweck, 1990; cf. Grant-Pillow & Dweck, 2002). Just as those with the entity view saw effort as measuring and implying a lack of intelligence, so did they also see setbacks as implying a lack of intelligence or a lack of ability in the area. Even an initial setback in a subject they had liked led them, far more often than their incremental counterparts, to conclude that they had no aptitude for the subject matter (see also Hong *et al.*, 1999; Mueller & Dweck, 1998).

In the face of these differing beliefs, it is not surprising that they endorsed different strategies for dealing with setbacks in a course (Blackwell *et al.*, 2002; cf. Grant-Pillow & Dweck, 2002; Robins & Pals, 2002; see also Boekarts, 2003). Those with the entity view more strongly endorsed such 'helpless' strategies as: 'I would try never to take that course again', 'I would study *less* for the next test' and 'I would try to cheat on the next test'. From these responses, it is clear that the entity meaning system, with its emphasis on judging ability, gives no recipe for success following a setback. If one lacks ability and effort cannot compensate, then the student might easily think: 'Why bother studying more? It won't help and will only make me look even more inept'.

In another dramatic demonstration of the helpless strategies that are induced within this meaning system, Hong *et al.* (1999) found that college students who held an entity theory of intelligence showed little interest in a remedial course that could remove a skill deficit and alter the course of their academic careers. They were either unwilling to admit to the deficit or did not think that the deficit could be overcome. In either case, their theory gave them no recipe for promoting future success in the face of challenge. In a similar vein, Rhodewalt (1994) found that students holding an entity theory were more likely to report using self-handicapping strategies. These are strategies like procrastinating on an assignment or partying the night before a test—strategies that provide ability-saving alibis for failure, but that jeopardize students' chances for success.

To return to our students making the transition to junior high school, those holding the incremental view endorsed 'mastery-oriented' strategies more strongly than their peers did (Blackwell *et al.*, 2002; cf. Grant-Pillow & Dweck, 2002; Robins & Pals, 2002). Their strategies for confronting obstacles included studying more for the next test and trying different study strategies. Again, this meaning system puts the emphasis on effort, strategies and learning and, by doing so, gives students a clear recipe for dealing with setbacks and turning them into successes.

Finally, as noted earlier, students' theories of intelligence predicted their subsequent grades over and above their past achievement (Blackwell *et al.*, 2002; Henderson & Dweck, 1990) In fact, in one study (Blackwell *et al.*, 2002), students' theories of intelligence—and not past grades—predicted change in grade over time, with the entity theory predicting steadily decreasing grades and the incremental theory predicting steadily increasing grades.

In summary, students' conceptions of intelligence form the core of motivational meaning systems that appear to produce significantly different educational outcomes for students who begin with more or less equivalent ability.

Are the meaning systems fixed or malleable?

Are students' theories of intelligence and their allied meaning systems like deep-seated personality traits, or are they more like dynamic and malleable knowledge structures? They look very much like the latter. Although students' theories of intelligence can be rather stable if left to themselves (Robins & Pals, 2002), they seem quite amenable to change with intervention. Sometimes this intervention takes place within an experimental session, where students are asked to read a compelling science passage that illustrates an entity view or an incremental view. In such studies (see Dweck & Leggett, 1988; Hong *et al.*, 1999; cf. Levy & Dweck, 1999), we have found that those who are led to (temporarily) adopt one theory or the other then act in accordance with that theory. For example, those who are led to adopt an incremental vs. entity theory then adopt more learning goals (Dweck & Leggett, 1988), are more likely to take the remedial action to overcome their deficiencies (Hong *et al.*, 1999) and are more likely to adopt positive effort beliefs (Hong *et al.*, 1999).

We have also found in our experiments that certain types of feedback can instill a more incremental theory or a more entity theory. For example, in a series of studies, Mueller and Dweck (1998) showed that praising students' intelligence after they performed well on a task sent them more toward an entity theory than did praising their effort. Praising intelligence appeared to imply that a fixed intelligence that dwelt within them was being judged from their performance. In line with their heightened entity theory, these students became less learning-oriented and less able to cope with subsequent setbacks than the students who had received effort praise. In short, although intelligence praise is often thought to be an excellent way to build students' self-esteem and create eager and hardy learners, it instead, by fostering an entity theory, created greater vulnerability.

In contrast to these short-term experiments, sometimes the intervention is a longer-term one, designed to teach an incremental theory of intelligence and to assess the effects of this teaching on academic motivation and achievement. In a study with college students, Aronson, Fried, and Good (2001) taught a group of African-American and Caucasian students an incremental theory by means of a film and discussion and by having them tutor younger students in this theory. They then compared the students in this group to students in the control conditions who were similar in initial achievement and motivation. Those in the incremental intervention group, when examined later in the semester, now placed a greater value on their academic studies and reported more enjoyment of academic activities (such as studying and doing assignments) than did their peers in the other groups. Moreover, they earned higher grades. All of these results were especially strong for the African-American students, who presumably were able to use the incremental theory to combat stereotype threat. That is, the idea that your intellectual skills can be cultivated over time can make a stereotype message of lower ability far less threatening.

We, too, have recently completed an incremental intervention, with minority junior high school students. In this study (Blackwell *et al.*, Study 2), students were randomly assigned to the experimental or control groups. Over eight sessions, both groups experienced study skills training, anti-stereotype messages, discussions of academic issues, and information about brain functions. However, whereas the control group learned about memory and the brain, the experimental group learned the incremental theory. They learned that the brain grows new connections every time you learn something new and that the brain is a dynamic organ that continues to form connections throughout life, depending upon your input.

At the end of the semester, maths teachers (who did not know which treatment each student had received) singled out three times as many students in the experimental group as showing marked changes in their classroom motivation. What is more, students in the incremental group showed significantly higher maths grades for the semester than those in the control group, whose grades continued to decline.

Thus, even though the control condition was an excellent one and in fact fully as excellent as many interventions, the addition of the incremental message appeared to spur a change in motivation that led to enhanced achievement.

In summary, conceptions of intelligence and the meaning systems that form around them can be relatively stable and predictive of students' achievement. Yet, they are also dynamic and malleable knowledge structures that can be affected by interventions, and when they are, motivation and achievement appear to follow suit.

Before mature conceptions of ability: Young children's meaning systems

Because there was consensus among researchers that younger children (before the age of 10–12 years) did not have well-formed conceptions of intelligence or ability, there was a widespread belief that they were protected from motivational vulnerability (Dweck & Elliott, 1983; Nicholls, 1984; Stipek & Daniels, 1988). In other words, if children did not understand the idea of fixed ability, failures should not reflect badly on them and send them into a helpless reaction.

This agreement on the part of researchers was based on the assumption that only ability conceptions could rule motivation. It was not recognized that although young children may not have well-formed ability conceptions, they may have analogous conceptions and meaning systems in another domain. Indeed, another domain is earlier and more basic. As Erikson (1959) pointed out some years ago, children face a series of self-related issues before they confront the issue of competence in the school years, and most of these issues revolve around goodness.

When we socialize children in the early years, what do we focus on? The answer is that we focus a great deal on their conduct—the degree to which they follow rules and instructions or the degree to which they self-regulate appropriately (wait, share, etc.). We are shaping them to be good members of the household, of their peer group, and of society later on, and toward this end, we give them a steady stream of feedback about whether their behaviour was right, good or suitable to the occasion.

It should therefore come as no surprise that young children's motivation seems to be organized around issues of goodness and badness (Frey & Ruble, 1985; Paley, 1988; Smetana, 1985; Stipek & Daniels, 1990; Stipek & Tannatt, 1984; see also Dweck, 1998; Ruble & Dweck, 1995). Moreover, when one looks closely, one can find in young children the same kinds of theories and allied meaning systems that one finds in older children—but in terms of goodness–badness rather than in terms of intelligence. Specifically, young children (5 or 6 years old, or even younger) may have a view of goodness–badness as a stable or malleable quality of a person (Heyman, Dweck, & Cain, 1992). Those who have the stable view, like older children who hold an entity theory of intelligence, measure themselves from their outcomes and judge themselves to be bad following failure or criticism (Heyman *et al.*, 1992; see also Hebert & Dweck, 1985; Kamins & Dweck, 1999). Also like their older counterparts with the fixed view, they do not focus on formulating strategies for future success, but instead sink into helpless or ineffective patterns of behaviour (Heyman *et al.*, 1992; Heyman & Dweck, 1998; Kamins & Dweck, 1999; see also Smiley & Dweck, 1994).

In contrast, those with the more dynamic, malleable view remain mastery-oriented (Heyman *et al.*, 1992; see also Hebert & Dweck, 1985; Kamins & Dweck, 1999; Smiley & Dweck, 1994). Like their older counterparts, they see effort and strategies as the key to turning the problem into a success, and some of them even spontaneously deliver quite sophisticated speeches on the topic.

Interestingly, when we have young children talking aloud or role playing with dolls during the experimental session, we find that both the entity and the incremental children are obsessed with goodness (Heyman *et al.*, 1992; see also Hebert & Dweck, 1985; Kamins & Dweck, 1999; Smiley & Dweck, 1994). (No child ever mentioned anything about ability even in the face of failures on a puzzle or a number task.) Both entity and incremental children mention goodness frequently and appear to be giving serious thought to what makes children good or bad and whether, having done wrong, they can vindicate themselves. It is simply that the entity and incremental theorists are coming to different conclusions about these issues.

We saw that in older children, praising intelligence or effort could evoke the different theories of intelligence with their attendant meaning systems (Mueller & Dweck, 1998). So, too, with younger children, can praise for goodness vs. praise for effort/strategies evoke the different theories of goodness and their allied meaning systems. Specifically in a study by Kamins and Dweck (1999), children who were given goodness praise after a job well done, formed a more fixed view of goodness and then drew highly negative conclusions about the self when they later encountered a setback or a criticism. In line with this, they failed to come up with appropriate strategies for rectifying the situation. In contrast, those who received the effort or strategy praise, formed a more incremental view of goodness, remained optimistic despite setbacks, and were able to generate effective strategies for reaching success. Thus praise for goodness vs. praise for effort/strategies functioned very much in the same way that praise for intelligence vs. effort had functioned—orienting children toward different theories and fostering different reactions to setbacks.

In summary, we have good evidence that although children's ability conceptions may not reach full flower until around adolescence, this does not mean that children are not forming motivational frameworks earlier or that they are not vulnerable to debilitation. Rather, it appears that children are busy trying to figure out what the self consists of and how it all works—but in a different domain, the domain that is of greatest importance to them at these younger ages.

The emergence of ability conceptions: Isolated beliefs in search of a unifying framework

Soon after children enter school, researchers see a great upsurge in their interest in ability. For example, Ruble and her colleagues have noted a dramatic increase in children's social comparison for purposes of assessing their performance relative to other children (Frey & Ruble, 1985; Ruble, Boggiano, Feldman, & Loebl, 1980). Triggered by this interest in ability, children, over the grade school years, begin to accumulate more and more information about ability and develop more and more beliefs about ability. For instance, they begin to demarcate the domain of intellectual ability more clearly, separating it from the domain of goodness and conduct and from other types of skills (Droege & Stipek, 1993; Frey & Ruble, 1985; Heyman *et al.*, 1992; Stipek & Daniels, 1990; Stipek & Tannatt, 1984; Yussen & Kane, 1985). In addition, they begin to understand the idea of ability as an internal quality that can have predictive value (Droege & Stipek, 1993; Rholes & Ruble, 1984; Rotenberg, 1982; Stipek & Daniels, 1990).

Yet for some time, these seem to remain isolated pieces of knowledge that are not linked to each other or integrated into a coherent system. For example, even in the earlier school years, children can articulate a theory of intelligence, but it does not typically predict their other beliefs about ability or their behaviours in the face of academic setbacks as it does in older children (Bempechat, London, & Dweck, 1991; Cain & Dweck, 1995). In other words, these ideas have not formed themselves into a meaning system or acquired motivational value.

As another example, in the early school years, as children begin to tune into academic outcomes and begin to understand the idea of ability, they can understand when they have not done well and when they might be demonstrating lower ability than their peers (Benenson & Dweck, 1986; Butler, 1990; 1999; Ruble *et al.*, 1980). However, when this happens, it does not seem to lead them to lose interest in the material or to want to avoid it in the future—as it begins to do with many older children (Butler, 1990, 1999; Stipek & Gralinski, 1991; Wigfield *et al.*, 1997). Again, these emerging ideas about ability are not yet hooked into a meaning system and have not yet gained consistent motivational value. Even though these same outcomes viewed within the goodness domain may have had marked effects on children's motivation and behaviour, viewed within the ability domain, they do not yet seem to have the same impact.

These findings underscore the important distinction between when ideas are formed and when they begin to have motivational value. As I noted above, children appear able to articulate their theories of intelligence some time before these theories appear to be motivationally meaningful (Bempechat *et al.*, 1991; Cain & Dweck, 1995). It is important for developmental psychologists—cognitive and social developmentalists alike—to take note of the critical difference between understanding an idea intellectually and having it play a role in the 'hotter' motivational system that guides children's behaviour.

Ability conceptions gain coherence and impact

It is only when children reach the age of 10–12 years that their assorted ideas about ability coalesce and begin to exert systematic impact on their motivation (Bempechat *et al.*, 1991; Cain & Dweck, 1995; Nicholls & Miller, 1984; Rholes, Blackwell, Jordan, & Walters, 1980).

First, the beliefs themselves appear to become organized into the coherent meaning systems I described in detail at the outset (Blackwell *et al.*, 2002; see Dweck, 1999). The theories of intelligence now begin reliably predicting students' goals, their effort beliefs, and their attributions for setbacks, with the entity meaning system organized around judging intelligence and the incremental meaning system organized around the processes that develop intellectual skills.

Further, the beliefs now begin to exert their impact on academic behaviour and academic achievement (Blackwell *et al.*, 2002; Henderson & Dweck, 1990; see also Pomerantz & Ruble, 1997). For example, within the entity system, setbacks now seem to sap motivation, leading to decreasing effort and poorer performance, whereas within the incremental system, setbacks seem to inspire heightened effort and strategizing, often leading to improved performance.

That these ability meaning systems coalesce at around adolescence raises the idea that the different meaning systems may foster different developmental pathways through adolescence. It is this idea that I take up in the next section.

Meaning systems can define developmental pathways

One major implication of the foregoing discussion is that as children grapple with the issues that confront them at each point in development, they may form a network of beliefs (a meaning system) that they use to understand the domain and to cope with issues in that domain. However, the fact that children can form different meaning systems—be they about goodness, ability or relationships—suggests that different children may be inhabiting different psychological worlds as they negotiate developmental transitions and work their way through developmental periods.

If we accept Erikson's (1959) age-old idea that students enter adolescence asking themselves 'Who am I?', we can see that students who adopt different theories of intelligence may mean entirely different things by this question. Entity theorists may mean: 'Am I smart or dumb? Am I a winner or a loser?' The adolescent transition then becomes a very tense time of proving one's ability and avoiding situations that can undermine one's sense of ability—or performing tasks in a defensive or low-effort way that does not put one's ability to the test.

In contrast, to incremental theorists 'Who am I?' may mean: 'What am I interested in? What skills do I want to develop? What do I want to become?' Viewed in this way, adolescence can turn into a more exciting time of exploration and self-development. Moreover, their learning goals may give incremental theorists the leeway to stumble, have false starts, and simply go back to the drawing board without doubting the worthiness of their basic traits.

Often, developmental psychologists view children as going along the same pathways, with some just going more quickly, or more smoothly, or farther. The present view, however, depicts children as constructing important parts of their psychological worlds and then moving through these worlds in *qualitatively* different ways.

In summary, the meaning systems that children construct can define the tasks of adolescence (or other developmental periods) for them in very different ways. Understanding these kinds of meaning systems and the different motivational tasks they set forth for children is an important future goal for developmental psychologists.

Remaining developmental questions and mysteries

I have argued that close consideration of the literature on the development of ability conceptions can yield a host of interesting insights about motivation and about development. Yet many questions remain.

First, I have described a powerful motivational system in older children and its analogous system in younger children, but what happens in between? I have shown that in between those times, ability beliefs are developing but have limited motivational value. Does the earlier, goodness-based system continue to be in play in those in-between years (see Heyman & Dweck, 1998), or is it indeed a protected period in the sense that no powerful motivational framework is creating heightened vulnerability to negative outcomes?

What is the relation between the earlier good/bad-driven motivational system and the later intelligence/ability-driven system? Does the latter grow out of the former, for example, with the ability system being differentiated from a more amorphous good–bad self? Or is the ability-related meaning system created anew on the basis of experiences in that domain. The answer could well be a combination of the two, with the early good–bad system biasing children's perceptions of the new ability domain (see Heyman & Dweck, 1998), but with the experiences in the new domain also playing a role (see Butler & Baumer, 2001).

After the ability meaning system is formulated, what happens to the early good–bad system? Does it continue to exist, guiding behaviour in other domains? Does it lurk in the background in the form of contingent or non-contingent global self-worth, with the entity theorists continuing to doubt the self when things go wrong (see Burhans & Dweck, 1995)?

What about other domains, like peer relationships? There is evidence that meaning systems are forming in these other domains along with ability beliefs (see Benenson & Dweck, 1986; Erdley, Cain, Loomis, Dumas-Hines, & Dweck 1997; Levy & Dweck, 1999). It would be fascinating to map the motivational changes that take place in a variety of domains as the relevant meaning system emerged.

Summary and conclusion

In this article, I have highlighted three points. First, in much of motivation (and perhaps in much of social development), development does not proceed toward one correct/ mature concept. Unlike much of cognitive development and language development, where clear endpoints are available to the child, and incorrect hypotheses receive salient disconfirmation, in the realm of self-conceptions (or relationship conceptions), alternative ways of constructing the world are possible. Indeed, toward the end of his life, Piaget (Piaget, Garcia, Davidson, & Easley, 1991) admitted that the world views children developed might be as important to them in structuring their worlds as the logical concepts he studied for much of his life.

Second, analogous motivational/conceptual frameworks (meaning systems) can arise at very different times in different domains. These arising meaning systems may be linked to the issues that are focal at that time in the child's life.

Third, there is an important distinction between when a concept is formed and when it has motivational impact. As I demonstrated, knowledge and beliefs about ability are arising over the early school years, but it is not until later on that these ideas are organized into a coherent system and begin to exert strong or consistent motivational value. Often researchers attempt to assess the impact of a belief on motivation without regard to the age of the child. According to the present view, one would not expect a link between beliefs and motivation in a domain before those beliefs are organized enough to shape the child's goals and to guide the child's behaviour in a systematic way.

Finally, I argued that the meaning systems that children develop can lead them along qualitatively different developmental pathways. Adolescents believing in fixed traits of the self and adolescents believing in personal qualities that can be cultivated may move through adolescence asking different questions (Am I smart or dumb? Am I a winner or a loser? vs. What am I interested in? What skills and knowledge do I want to cultivate?) and therefore setting different life tasks for themselves during this important developmental period.

In conclusion, the literature on the development of ability conceptions is of interest in its own right, but it has also allowed us to raise key issues about motivation and about development in general. As a field, the study of motivation straddles different areas within developmental psychology. The development of beliefs and knowledge are typically issues of cognitive development, often with little consideration of how beliefs affect behaviour or adjustment. The topic of adaptive patterns of achievement and social relationships is typically treated within social development, but often with little consideration of the emerging belief systems that may underlie these patterns. As such, the field of motivation may have a unique role to play in forging a stronger link between cognitive and social development, asking questions both about the children's emerging understanding of themselves and their world and about the role that this understanding plays in their adaptive functioning.

References

Aronson, J., Fried, C., & Good, C. (2002). Reducing the effects of stereotype threat on African American college students by shaping theories of intelligence. *Journal of Experimental Social Psychology, 38*, 113–125.

Baillargeon, R. (1995). Physical reasoning in infancy. In M. S. Gazzaniga (Ed.), *The cognitive neurosciences* (pp. 181–204). Cambridge, MA: MIT Press.

Bempechat, J., London, P., & Dweck, C. S. (1991). Children's conceptions of ability in major domains: An interview and experimental study. *Child Study Journal, 21*, 11–36.

Benenson, J., & Dweck, C. S. (1986) The development of trait explanations and self-evaluations in the academic and social domains. *Child Development, 57*, 1179–1189.

Bickhard, M. H. (2003). An integration of motivation and cognition. *British Journal of Educational Psychology Monograph Series II, Part 2* (Development and Motivation), 41–56.

Blackwell, L. S. Dweck, C. S., & Trzesniewski, K. (2002). *Theories of intelligence and the adolescent transition: A longitudinal study and an intervention.* Manuscript submitted for publication.

Boekaerts, M. (2003). Towards a model that integrates motivation, affect and learning. *British Journal of Educational Psychology Monograph Series II, Part 2* (Development and Motivation), 173–189.

Burhans, K., & Dweck, C. S. (1995). Helplessness in early childhood: The role of contingent worth. *Child Development, 66*, 1719–1738.

Butler, R. (1990). The effects of mastery and competitive conditions on self-assessment at different ages. *Child Development, 61*, 201–210.

Butler, R. (1999). Information seeking and achievement motivation in middle childhood and adolescence: The role of conceptions of ability. *Developmental Psychology, 35*, 146–163.

Butler, R., & Baumer, S. (2001). *The role of context and development in children's constructions of motivational purposes and self-regulation.* Paper presented at the Meeting of the Society for Research in Child Development. Minneapolis, MN, April.

Cain, K., & Dweck, C. S. (1995). The development of children's achievement motivation patterns and conceptions of intelligence. *Merrill-Palmer Quarterly, 41*, 25–52.

Carugati, F. (1990). From social cognition to social representations in the study of intelligence. In G. Duveen & B. Lloyd (Eds.), *Social representations and the development of knowledge* (pp. 126–143). Cambridge: Cambridge University Press.

Cornelius, S. W., Kenny, S., & Caspi, A. (1989). Academic and everyday intelligence in adulthood: Conceptions of self and ability tests. In J. D. Sinnott (Ed.), *Everyday problem solving: Theory and applications* (pp. 191–210). New York: Praeger.

Droege, K. L., & Stipek, D. J. (1993). Children's use of dispositions to predict classmates' behavior. *Developmental Psychology, 29*, 646–654.

Dweck, C. S. (1998). The development of early self-conceptions: Their relevance for motivational processes. In J. Heckhausen & C. S. Dweck (Eds.), *Motivation and self-regulation across the life span* (pp. 257–280). Cambridge: Cambridge University Press.

Dweck, C. S. (1999). *Self-theories: Their role in motivation, personality and development.* Philadelphia: Taylor & Francis/Psychology Press.

Dweck, C. S., Chiu, C., & Hong, Y. (1995). Implicit theories and their role in judgments and reactions: A world from two perspectives. *Psychological Inquiry, 6,* 267–285.

Dweck, C. S., & Elliott, E. S. (1983). Achievement motivation. In P. Mussen & E. M. Hetherington (Eds.), *Handbook of child psychology.* New York: Wiley.

Dweck, C. S., & Leggett, E. L. (1988). A social-cognitive approach to personality and motivation. *Psychological Review, 95,* 256–273.

Eccles, J., & Midgley, C. (1989). Stage-environment fit: Developmentally appropriate classrooms for young adolescents. In C. Ames & R. Ames (Eds.), *Research on motivation in education* (Vol. 3, pp. 139–186). New York: Academic Press.

Erdley, C., Cain, K., Loomis, C., Dumas-Hines, F., & Dweck, C. S. (1997). The relations among children's social goals, implicit personality theories and response to social failure. *Developmental Psychology, 33,* 263–272.

Erikson, E. H. (1959). *Identity and the life cycle.* New York: International University Press.

Frey, K. S., & Ruble, D. N. (1985). What children say when the teacher is not around: Conflicting goals in social comparison and performance assessment in the classroom. *Journal of Personality and Social Psychology, 48,* 550–562.

Gleitman, L. R., & Newport, E. L.(1995). The invention of language by children: Environmental and biological influences on the acquisition of language. In Gleitman, L. R., & Liberman, M. (Eds.), *Language: An invitation to cognitive science* (Vol. 1. pp. 1–24). Cambridge, MA: The MIT Press.

Grant-Pillow, H., & Dweck, C. S. (in press). Clarifying achievement goals and their impact. Journal of Personality and Social Psychology.

Hebert, C., & Dweck, C. S. (1985). *Mediators of persistence in preschoolers.* Unpublished manuscript, Harvard University.

Henderson, V., & Dweck, C. S. (1990). Achievement and motivation in adolescence: A new model and data. In S. Feldman & G. Elliott (Eds.), *At the threshold: The developing adolescent.* Cambridge, MA: Harvard University Press.

Heyman, G. D., & Dweck, C. S. (1998). Children's thinking about traits: Implications for judgments of the self and others. *Child Development, 64,* 391–403.

Heyman, G. D., Dweck, C. S., & Cain, K. (1992) Young children's vulnerability to self-blame and helplessness. *Child Development, 63,* 401–415.

Hong, Y. Y., Chiu, C., Dweck, C. S., Lin, D., & Wan, W. (1999) Implicit theories, attributions, and coping: A meaning system approach. *Journal of Personality and Social Psychology, 77,* 588–599.

Howe, M. J. (1990). Children's gifts, talents, and natural abilities: An explanatory mythology? *Educational and Child Psychology, 7,* 52–54.

Kamins, M., & Dweck, C. S. (1999). Person vs. process praise and criticism: Implications for contingent self-worth and coping. *Developmental Psychology, 35,* 835–847.

Karabenick, J. D., & Heller, K. A. (1976). A developmental study of effort and ability attributions. *Developmental Psychology, 12,* 559–560.

Krapp, A. (2003). Interest and human development: An educational-psychological perspective. *British Journal of Educational Psychology Monograph Series II, Part 2* (Development and Motivation), 57–84.

Kun, A. (1977). Development of the magnitude-covariation principle and compensation schemata in ability and effort attributions of performance. *Child Development, 48,* 862–873.

Levy, S. R., & Dweck, C. S. (1999). Children's static vs. dynamic person conceptions as predictors of their stereotype formation. *Child Development, 70,* 1163–1180.

Mueller, C. M., & Dweck, C. S. (1998). Intelligence praise can undermine motivation and performance. *Journal of Personality and Social Psychology, 75,* 33–52.

Nicholls, J. G. (1978). The development of the concepts of effort and ability, perceptions of academic attainments, and the understanding that difficult tasks require more ability. *Child Development, 49*, 800–814.

Nicholls, J. G. (1984). Achievement motivation: Conceptions of ability, subjective experience, task choice, and performance. *Psychological Review, 91*, 328–346.

Nicholls, J. G., & Miller, A. (1984). Conceptions of ability and achievement motivation. In R. Ames & C. Ames (Eds.). *Research on motivation in education* (Vol. 1, pp. 39–73). New York: Academic Press.

Paley, V. G. (1988). *Bad guys don't have birthdays*. Chicago: University of Chicago Press.

Perkins, D. N., & Grotzer, T. A. (1997). Teaching intelligence. *American Psychologist, 52*, 1125–1133.

Piaget, J., Garcia, R., Davidson, P., & Easley, J. (1991). *Toward a logic of meanings*. Hillsdale, NJ: Erlbaum.

Pintrich, P. R. (2003). Multiple goals and multiple pathways in the development of motivation and self-regulated learning. *British Journal of Educational Psychology Monograph Series II, Part 2* (Development and Motivation), 137–153.

Pomerantz, E. M., & Ruble, D. N. (1997). Distinguishing multiple dimensions of conceptions of ability: Implications for self-evaluation. *Child Development, 68*, 1165–1180.

Rhodewalt, F. (1994). Conceptions of ability, achievement goals, and individual differences in self-handicapping behavior: On the application of implicit theories. *Journal of Personality, 62*, 67–85.

Rholes, W. S., Blackwell, J., Jordan, C., & Walters, C. (1980). A developmental study of learned helplessness. *Developmental Psychology, 16*, 616–624.

Rholes, W. S., & Ruble, D. N. (1984). Children's understanding of dispositional characteristics of others. *Child Development, 55*, 550–560.

Robins, R. W., & Pals, J. (2002). Implicit self-theories of ability in the academic domain: A test of Dweck's model. *Self and Identity, 1*, 313–336.

Rosenholtz, S., & Simpson, C. (1984). The formation of ability conceptions: Developmental trend or social construction? *Review of Educational Research, 54*, 31–63.

Rotenberg, K. (1982). Development of character constancy of self and others. *Child Development, 53*, 505–515.

Ruble, D. N., Boggiano, A. K., Feldman, N. S., & Loebl, J. H. (1980). Developmental analysis of the role of social comparison in self-evaluation. *Developmental Psychology, 16*, 105–115.

Ruble, D. N., & Dweck, C. S. (1995). The development of self-conceptions and person conceptions. In N. Eisenberg (Ed.), *Review of personality and social psychology. Vol. 15: Social development*. Thousand Oaks, CA: Sage.

Schuster, B., Ruble, D. N., & Weinert, F. E. (1999). Causal inferences and the positivity bias in young children: The role of the covariation principle. *Child Development, 69*, 1577–1596.

Smetana, J. (1985). Children's impressions in of moral and conventional transgressions. *Developmental Psychology, 21*, 715–724.

Smiley, P. A., & Dweck, C. S. (1994). Individual differences in achievement goals among young children. *Child Development, 65*, 1723–1743.

Stipek, D. J., & Daniels, D. (1988). Declining perceptions of competence: A consequence of changes in the child or the educational environment? *Journal of Educational Psychology, 80*, 352–356.

Stipek, D. J., & Daniels, D. H. (1990). Children' use of dispositional attributions in predicting the performance and behavior of classmates. *Journal of Applied Developmental Psychology, 11*, 13–28.

Stipek, D. J., & Gralinski, J. H. (1991). Gender differences in children's achievement-related beliefs and emotional responses to success and failure in mathematics. *Journal of Educational Psychology, 83*, 362–371.

Stipek, D. J., & Tannatt, L. (1984). Children's judgments of their own and peers' academic competence. *Journal of Educational Psychology, 76*, 75–84.

Surber, C. F. (1980). The development of reversible operations in judgments of ability, effort, and performance. *Child Development, 51*, 1018-1029.

Wagner, R. K., & Sternberg, R. J. (1984). Alternative conceptions of intelligence and their implications for education. *Review of Educational Research, 54*, 179-223.

Wigfield, A., Eccles, J. S., Yoon, K. S., Harold, R. D., Arbreton, A., Freedman-Doan, K., & Blumenfeld, P. C. (1997). Changes in children's competence beliefs and subjective task values across the elementary school years. *Journal of Educational Psychology, 89*, 451-469.

Yang, S., & Sternberg, R. J. (1997). Taiwanese Chinese people's conceptions of intelligence. *Intelligence, 25*, 21-36.

Yussen, S., & Kane, P. (1985). Children's conceptions of intelligence. In S. R. Yussen (Ed.), *The growth of reflection in children* (pp. 207-241). New York: Academic Press.

Development and Motivation, 29–40
BJEP Monograph Series II, 2
© 2003 The British Psychological Society

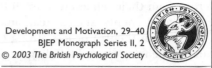

www.bps.org.uk

Morals, motives and actions

Elliot Turiel*

University of California, Berkeley, USA

The main issues addressed in this article bear on the questions of whether and how moral judgments are related to actions in the process of development. The issue of motivation has traditionally been linked to moral development and, especially, to moral behaviours. The reasons for concerns with moral motivation are readily comprehensible. How people act is particularly important in the moral realm. Regardless of how worthy the values people hold or the judgments they make may be, they are not of much value if people fail to act on them. In spite of this concern with how motives influence moral actions, there has been little research and more theoretical discussion on the topic in recent years. In my view, there has been little progress even within the context of theoretical discussions in formulating an adequate conception of motivation in moral development and in the connections between moral thought and action. Often it is theorized that motivational features distinguish between those who do and do not consistently act on their moral judgments. I present an alternative view: that moral judgments are intrinsic motives and that actions must be understood through specification of contexts that often entail the application of different domains of social judgments. I maintain that invoking motivational constructs to explain connections between moral judgments and actions is premature in light of our inadequate understanding of the issue. I propose that distinctions need to be made between realms in which people's judgments are intrinsically motivating and those in which mediating motivational constructs are applicable. Furthermore, morality is a realm in which judgments are intrinsically motivating in ways that lead people even to oppose certain cultural practices and systems of social organization.

Moral identity and moral action

A little history regarding psychological theory and research on moral development provides a context for this discussion. For much of the 20th century, morality was usually regarded as primarily a matter of motivation. In behaviouristic (Skinner, 1971),

*Requests for reprints should be addressed to Elliot Turiel, Graduate School of Education, University of California, Berkeley, 4533 Tolman Hall, Berkeley, CA 94720, USA (e-mail: turiel@uclinle4.berkeley.edu).

social learning (Aronfreed, 1968), and psychoanalytic (Freud, 1930) explanations, morality was seen as a function of whether people acquired the motives to act in ways different from their self-interest. In all these perspectives, social actions require strong affective components, such as fear, anxiety, shame and guilt, to offset the very strong (as in Freudian theory) or less strong (as in behaviouristic and socialization theories) natural tendencies toward fulfilling one's needs, desires and interests. In some of these perspectives (especially Freudian and socialization views), internal dispositions were posited as serving to motivate the control of behaviour. The proposed internal dispositions included a number of traits of character, conscience, and internal mechanisms of control and self-regulation. Internal mechanisms of conscience or character, including the abilities to resist temptation and defer gratification, were seen as central to actions serving moral and social functions.

However, there were pockets of resistance to these emotivist–motivational perspectives—especially from Piaget (1932) and later from Kohlberg (1963, 1969, 1971). Eventually, the research of Piaget, Kohlberg and others had substantial influence, revealing that evaluations, judgments and reasoning were important in psychological explanations of morality. Piaget (1932) regarded actions to be closely intertwined with judgments in that the development of children's moral judgments stems from their practices. In his research, he distinguished between the consciousness of rules and the practice of rules in children's development. However, consciousness and practice are interconnected, since the development of moral judgments stems from action and, once formed, judgments influence actions.

Kohlberg, too, proposed that judgments and actions are intertwined. His formulation of six stages of the development of moral judgments was influential in shifting the motivational question to one squarely directed to relations between thought and action. Many, however, went on to pose the question not in terms of interconnections between thought and action, but in terms of whether and how judgments lead to actions. If people do make moral judgments, the question 'Do their judgments affect their actions?' was asked. Some then proposed that mediating motivational variables can bridge a gap between judgment and action. Empirically, these issues have been framed in a search for levels of consistency between assessments of evaluations, beliefs or judgments and assessments of behaviours. The classic research conducted by Hartshorne and May (1928–1930) over 70 years ago has been an empirical impetus to pursue the question of why moral evaluations and attitudes are not closely linked to behaviour. Assessing children's attitudes towards honesty, along with behaviours in many situations, they found low correlations between children's endorsement of the value of honesty and behavioural measures of honesty in games and academic tests. Hartshorne and May also found much inconsistency in children's behaviours from one situation to the next. Most children cheated some of the time, but not most of the time. Other studies (e.g. Grinder, 1964) have obtained similar findings on children's cheating behaviours.

Subsequently, researchers have drawn comparisons between a general assessment of stage of moral judgments (most often based on Kohlberg's formulations) and actions of various kinds. In one key respect, the findings from those studies paralleled those of Hartshorne and May, since varying levels of consistency between moral judgments and actions were obtained (see Blasi, 1980). These findings have led to a search for characteristics, in addition to moral judgments, to explain the links—and missing links—between thought and action. The line of reasoning is that characteristics different from judgments account for the lack of a consistent correspondence between thought and action. The most frequent explanations involve attempts to account for personal characteristics that serve to motivate action. Through the years, a number of characteristics have been proposed, including strength of character, courage, willpower, commitment, and identity or self definition (Blasi, 1993; Colby & Damon, 1992; Kohlberg, 1971).

These formulations have converged on the idea that personal or moral identity motivates people to act on their moral beliefs and judgments. Several assumptions are at work here. One is that children undergo transformations in the organization of their moral thought that constitute a developmental sequence, and that moral judgments do influence actions. A second is that moral judgments can often be discrepant with actions. A third is that people with similar moral beliefs or judgments may act differently from each other. A fourth is that some people do usually (or frequently enough) act on their moral judgments and that many more people frequently fail to act on their moral judgments. A fifth is that people with similar moral judgments may differ in their identification with their own moral judgments and that it is the element of personal identity or self definition that accounts for differences in the ways in which people act on their moral judgments.

In these views, therefore, people differ in the extent to which their morality is a part of their identities. In so far as people's identities are closely determined by morality, they are motivated to act in accord with their moral judgments. Those for whom morality is less central to identity are less likely to act on their moral judgments. The core motivational feature in this regard is self-consistency. The need or desire that one's actions be consistent with one's self definition is the major impetus to action. As put by Blasi (1993, p. 99), 'self-consistency is the motivational spring of moral action'. It is important to note that it is a particular type of consistency that is central. The striving is for a consistency between action and moral identity and not necessarily for consistency between judgments and actions. If identity is defined by one's moral judgments, then we do get consistency. If identity is defined more by factors other than morality, than we get inconsistency. A developmental component in these individual differences formulations is in the hypothesis that a sense of moral identity comes about with age. Children develop moral judgments, but they do not define themselves through morality. The individual differences component is that people develop a sense moral identity to different degrees. Those who do form a strong moral identity can be distinguished from others by their moral acts.

This general paradigm underlies the studies, reported by Colby and Damon (1992), that involved case studies of a number of individuals, designated as moral exemplars, who had demonstrated lifelong commitments to helping others or to moral causes. These people were moral exemplars by virtue of the exemplary ways that their identities were defined by morality—and hence a commitment to action. By contrast, according to this argument, many do not maintain such personal identities—and hence less commitment to action.

Alternative considerations and propositions

An alternative position is that, for the most part, we cannot distinguish among people by the extent to which their identities are morally defined or by the connections of identity to actions. I propose that morality is not a domain in which judgments and goals are generally central for some and peripheral for others. Morality is central for most people. However, morality stands alongside other social judgments of importance. In order to understand relations between thought and action, it is necessary to consider how moral judgments and other domains of judgment are applied in particular contexts. Much of the research yielding inconsistencies between judgment and action has relied on one general type of assessment of moral judgment and has failed to account for social judgments other than moral. Global assessments do not provide sufficient specificity regarding the moral judgments that correspond to actions in particular contexts and do not allow for analyses of how non-moral judgments are coordinated with moral judgments. Morality is only one component of judgment—albeit an important component—that is involved in decisions leading to particular courses of action.

In asserting that morality is central for most people, I do not mean to imply that everyone agrees about morally relevant decisions. Indeed, moral issues are often highly disputed and may be sources of conflict. Differences between individuals, however, are not due to differences in the centrality of morality in identity. The many sources of moral disputes and conflicts is an issue I cannot address here (see Turiel, 2002, 2003a). However, it is in the context of similar moral concepts they hold that people may come to differing conclusions about priorities—moral and non-moral—in given contexts.

I would propose, therefore, that most people act on their moral judgments some of the time and that most of the same people do not act on their moral judgments some of the time. In elaborating on this proposition, I put forth two arguments. One is that it is premature to invoke motivational concepts such as personal identity or a need for self-consistency to explain relations between moral thought and action. It is premature because we still need to improve the way we conceptualize the interplay of thought and action before bringing in other kinds of motivational constructs. It is necessary to frame the question of relations between judgment and action differently so as to account for how people coordinate different domains of judgment in the decision-making process.

The second argument, which is likely to be more controversial, is that motivational variables of the sort discussed thus far are not applicable to the moral realm. For most people (for whom morality is central) moral evaluations and judgments are intrinsically motivating. Motivation may be regarded as intrinsic in the moral realm, but not as involving distinct psychological or personal characteristics such as character, will or identity. This is not to say that motivation is unimportant in development or that there are no individual differences in motivational characteristics in other realms. Just as we can draw domain distinctions in social judgments, we need to draw distinctions between realms in which separate motivational dispositions are more and less involved.

It might appear that there is a contradiction in, first, claiming that it is premature to invoke these motivational concepts for morality and then putting forth propositions about motivation in the moral realm. However, my aim is very limited in putting forth these propositions regarding motivation. It is to state a hypothesis and to demonstrate that it is a viable one using evidence showing that multiple moral, social and personal judgments are involved in decision-making within particular social contexts. Furthermore, I will try to show that cultural practices and societal arrangement are great motivators for action. This is not in the usual sense of actions that are in accord with societal norms, but as motivators for social opposition, subversion and change. I propose that social opposition and subversion are everyday activities among children, adolescents and adults—and are not restricted to organized movements, public protests or the activities of the exemplary or the highly developed. In childhood, adolescence and adulthood, there is a coexistence of sociability, social acceptance, opposition and conflict. This coexistence is part of the dynamics of social relationships and the ways that cultural practices can evoke opposition due to moral judgments. These coexisting orientations are linked to the distinct domains of moral, social and personal judgments, that children develop.

Domains of judgment and action

I have proposed that morality is one component of the judgments that can go into social decisions. This assertion is based on many studies, in several cultural settings, which have shown that the judgments of children, adolescents and adults entail distinctions among domains that are not captured by some of the global classifications of levels or stages of moral judgments (as in Kohlbcrg, 1969; Piaget, 1932). By the ages of 4–6 years, children begin to make moral judgments that are distinct from their judgments about social conventions. Children's moral judgments are based, at first, on understandings of harm or welfare, and later on understandings of justice and rights as well. Judgments about moral issues (e.g. physical and psychological harm, theft and inequitable distribution) are not based on the existence of rules, or the directives of people in positions of authority; and they are not based on commonly accepted practices.

Children develop different types of concepts about the conventions of social systems—such as conventions in the organization of a classroom or school (or conventions pertaining to such matters as forms of dress or modes of address). Conventions are judged to be contingent on rules and authority, and as particular to groups and institutional contexts. Morality and convention are also distinguished from what may be referred to as the personal domain. The personal domain reflects concerns with persons as autonomous and with areas legitimately deemed as within the purview of personal prerogative and jurisdiction.

Many studies have demonstrated that judgments about morality and social convention constitute distinct domains (for extensive reviews, see Turiel, 1983, 1998, 2002). Most of the studies on domains assessed judgments in non-behavioural contexts, involving the presentation of situations stated in hypothetical terms. A number of studies, however, have shown that children's social interactions differ in accord with the moral, conventional and personal domains (e.g. Nucci & Nucci, 1982a, 1982b; Nucci & Turiel, 1978; Nucci & Weber, 1995). In a still unpublished study (Turiel, 2003b), I have extensively examined actions around moral and conventional events, as well as judgments about those naturally occurring events. The study was designed around observations of events in elementary and junior high schools with children from the first, third, fifth and seventh grades (ages of about 6–12 years). The events observed were reliably classified as moral, conventional, or as those that included a mixture of moral and conventional components. The moral events often involved transgressions on the part of children, including inflicting physical or psychological harm, taking the property of others and unequal distribution of resources (some events involved positive acts). The conventional events involved transgressions of classroom rules, disobedience of authority and violations of other school procedures. In some cases, events included both types of components (e.g. rules, practices or authority dictates that entailed unfair treatment).

A large number of the three types of events were observed, with recordings of participants' reactions to transgressions and communications among the participants.

Not long after an event occurred (always on the same day), several of the children involved were interviewed about the event in order to assess a set of judgments. Assessments were made of evaluations of the acts and rules, as well as judgments as to whether the acts would be acceptable if no rule existed and if the teacher said it was acceptable. Assessments were also made of participants' reasons or justifications for the evaluations and judgments.

The results of the study showed that on key dimensions relevant to the domain distinctions, moral events were judged differently from the conventional events. The majority of the children evaluated both types of transgressions negatively, thought that there were rules in place governing each type of act and positively evaluated those rules. Two of the questions posed are central definitional dimensions of the domains: rule contingency and authority expectations. It was found that judgments on these two dimensions differed by domain. Moral transgressions were judged negatively by most, even in the absence of rules (65% of the participants) or when accepted by the person in authority (70%), whereas conventional transgressions were judged negatively by only a minority (28 and 22%). Under those circumstances, clear-cut differences between the two types of events were also obtained in the justifications given for evaluations and judgments. The reasons given for the evaluations and judgments about the moral events focused mainly on issues of welfare, justice and rights. In contrast, evaluations and judgments about the conventional events were based on considerations bearing on traditions, authority and social organization.

Furthermore, these distinct judgments were applied even in situations that included a combination of the domains (the events I have referred to as mixed). The children distinguished the moral and conventional components and attempted to coordinate them. Typically, greater importance was given to the moral over the conventional considerations. In that context, justifications also differed for the two components.

In this study, we also assessed participants' judgments and justifications about comparable hypothetical situations. The hypothetical situations were presented about 1 month after the events and original interview had taken place. An additional group of children, who had not been interviewed about the actual events, were administered the interview about the hypothetical events. The findings were comparable with findings about the actual events. This was also the case for mixed events and for justifications. However, the distinctions were more clear-cut with regard to domains in judgments about hypothetical events than for the actual events, with even larger majorities responding in the expected ways. This difference is due to three factors. One is that a larger variety of specific content was represented in actual events. For the hypothetical situations, two events of each type were presented, whereas the naturally occurring ones were more numerous in content differences. A second is that some positive moral actions were represented in the actual events and evaluated differently from the negative moral events. The third factor is that the particular parameters presented in the hypothetical events could be specified with more precision than for the actual events.

Nevertheless, the patterns of findings on judgments and justifications were similar for actual and hypothetical events. These findings, along with analyses of social interactions and communications within the observed actual events, indicate that actions are connected to thinking within the domains. The observations revealed that participants' reactions and communications also differed by domain of the events (and components within the mixed events). In the moral events, communications were about injury, loss, people's feelings and issues of fairness. In the conventional events, communications revolved around rules, commands, sanctions and social order.

For the most part, the focus of this research was on dimensions that previous research had indicated are not age-related. The data on domain distinctions did not show any age differences. There were some indications, however, that justifications within domains were age-related. For instance, it was found that older children conceptualized rules and social organizations in more abstract ways than younger children. There were also age differences in some of the contexts for the events. As an example, the younger children rarely engaged in moral or conventional transgressions in classrooms, whereas older children (especially the seventh graders) did so. This does not mean that younger children did not engage in transgressions. They did so in other school contexts—especially in the playground and in lunch-time settings.

Contextual variations in judgments and actions

In my estimation, the information derived from this study regarding moral thought and action is both far-reaching and modest. The findings are far-reaching in that they demonstrate that in certain important respects, there are close connections between thought and action. The findings show there are reciprocal interactions between thought and action and that different types of judgments are applied to different types of actions. The findings show that in order to understand relations between social/ moral judgments and actions, it is necessary to specify the types of judgments involved in particular situations. Since this has not been done in much of the previous research, it calls into question some commonly held conclusions from that research. A significant source of the inconsistencies found in previous studies is the lack of specificity in assessments of types of judgments and types of actions. This could well mean that inconsistencies between, say, moral judgments and actions may be due to the ways that other types of social judgments are coordinated with moral judgments. If that were the case, then it would not be a matter of a discrepancy between thought and action. In that case, it would not follow that personality characteristics, like identity, account for a possible gap between moral judgments and actions.

The findings of the study can also be seen as modest, since they do not directly provide answers to the question, how it is that people do and do not act on their moral judgments. Moreover, the findings do not reveal the nature of contextual variations in actions beyond what is accounted for by domain differences. It is consistently found that there are contextual variations in people's judgments and in their actions, which suggests that we cannot divide people on the dimensions of consistencies or inconsistencies in their moral commitments. We know from some of the classic social psychological experiments that contextual variations occur in social behaviours. Studies of conformity (Asch, 1952), bystander intervention (Latané & Darley, 1970) and obedience to authority (Milgram, 1974) have shown that behaviours vary by contexts. For example, it has been found that people conform with (erroneous) perceptual judgments by the group in some experimental situations but not in others. Similarly, people intervene to help others in distress under some social circumstances and fail to do so in other social circumstances. In turn, people obey an authority who instructs them to inflict pain on another in some experimental situations but defy an authority in other experimental situations. Moreover, in all the experimental conditions in the research on obedience to authority, most participants were quite conflicted about the two courses of action. In my view, the most plausible interpretation of those findings is that people were struggling with two types of considerations. On the one hand, they were dealing with moral considerations having to do with inflicting pain. On the other hand, they were dealing with social-organizational and conventional considerations having to do with the role of authority.

The general point to be stressed is that behavioural variations are systematic and can involve the application of more than one type of judgment in a situation. As systematic variations, based on the coordination of domains of thought, the primary issues are neither levels of consistency between one kind of judgment and behaviour nor individual differences as to whether there is any consistency between moral judgments and actions. This, in turn, means that it is premature to invoke personality notions of a motivational kind to explain action.

However, matters are even more complex, because one of the major premises underlying the quest for consistencies or inconsistencies between judgment and action is contradicted by the evidence. I am referring to the premise that action, and not judgment, is the source of inconsistencies. It turns out that seeming contextual variations are also evident in judgments in non-behavioural contexts. Consider, as an example, research on honesty and deception. The Hartshorne and May studies of the 1920s (Hartshorne & May, 1928–1930) and later studies showed, as already noted, that children's attitudes toward honesty are not consistent with their behaviours. Whereas children say that they value honesty, they act dishonestly in many situations. However, judgments about honesty or deception are not themselves uniform—as demonstrated by several studies.

An informative example is a study of the judgments of adult physicians about deception in the context of medical practices (Freeman, Rathore, Weinfurt, Schulman, & Sulmasy, 1999). A sample group of physicians were presented with six stories depicting doctors who consider deceiving a third-party payer (a health maintenance organization or an insurance company) in order to obtain treatment or a diagnostic procedure for a patient. Each story depicted a patient who could not afford to pay for the procedure and would not receive it without the insurance payment, and it is known that the insurance company would not change its policy. The stories depicted medical conditions of different degrees of severity. The most severe were two life-threatening conditions, one requiring coronary bypass surgery and the other a bypass grafting of an artery. The least severe depicted a patient's desire for surgical alteration of nasal bones for cosmetic purposes. In between were conditions that required intravenous pain medication and nutrition for a cancer patient, a psychiatric referral for depression, and a mammography.

The physicians were asked whether the doctor in each story should deceive the third-party payer. The percentages of physicians who judged that a doctor was justified in engaging in the deception were high and low. In the two most severe conditions, 58 and 56% of the physicians in the study thought that a doctor was justified in engaging in deception. Only 3% thought that deception was legitimate for cosmetic surgery (the percentages were in between for the other conditions: 48% for pain medication, 32% for psychiatric referral, and 35% for mammography). It is likely that these physicians would generally judge dishonesty to be wrong, but in specific situations, they sometimes judge it wrong and sometimes judge it to be justified. Other research has documented that physicians do typically engage in deception in some situations in order to promote the well-being of their patients, and sometimes in order to spare patients distress or anguish (Wynia, Cummins, VanGeest, & Wilson, 2000). Children, too, judge deception in varying ways. Whereas they evaluate lying for personal gain as wrong (Kahn & Turiel, 1988; Peterson, Peterson, & Seeto, 1983), they accept the legitimacy of some lies aimed at sparing the feelings of others or protecting them from harm (Bussey, 1999; De Paulo, Epstein, & Wyer, 1993).

These types of situational variations are by no means limited to honesty. It has been well documented, for instance, that judgments about rights vary by the situation (Helwig, 1995; McCloskey & Brill, 1983; Turiel & Wainryb, 1998). Contextual variations are also evident in judgments about inflicting harm. In one study (Astor, 1994), assessments were made of the judgments of a group of children who had been identified with a history of violent activities and a group with no such history. Two types of hypothetical situations were presented to the children: one type depicted unprovoked acts of hitting, and the second depicted hitting in response to a provocation (e.g. teasing, name-calling). Both groups of children judged hitting to be wrong in the unprovoked situations. However, the group of children with histories of violence judged as acceptable the acts of hitting in provoked situations, whereas the other children judged those acts as wrong. Considering the children's background, it might appear from the results on the situations depicting unprovoked acts that some children's judgments are discrepant with their actions. The results from the situations depicting provoked acts suggest, instead, that judgments about particular types of situations correspond with actions in like situations.

The message of all these findings is that correlational analyses entailing general assessments of moral judgments and of actions tell us little as to whether and how thought and action are related. This is because (1) assessments of choices in non-behavioural contexts do not reveal consistencies; (2) embedded in many situations are multiple considerations, and therefore more than one type of judgment may be implicated; (3) many situations involve conflicts between different moral considerations or conflicts between moral and non-moral considerations; and (4) whether consistencies or inconsistencies emerge depends on the particular judgments and actions examined. Moreover, the variability in choices in non-behavioural and behavioural contexts is neither random nor solely due to the situation. Rather, the interactions of the individual and the situation entail systematic applications of judgments.

Action and cultural practices

It is, at best, still unclear that we can speak of individual differences in moral commitments that would explain a greater consistency between moral thought and action on the part of some. My hypothesis, based on the proposition that morality is intrinsic for most, is that people struggle with priorities and conflicts in a complex social world. The study with the physicians is a good illustrative example. They were attempting to make priorities regarding the value of honesty and the value of preserving the health and welfare of patients. The study also shows that people are sometimes willing to go against the system and social norms to achieve what they consider to be a greater good. Part of the general hypothesis is that moral actions are motivated by perceived injustices, especially in societal arrangements and cultural practices. In this regard, too, action is not restricted to exemplary people with unusual characteristics of courage, commitment or moral identity.

Social and political movements are at times led by individuals who seem exemplary in their moral vision. In the USA, Martin Luther King Jr. provided such leadership and vision during the Civil Rights movement of the 1960s. However, leadership in social movements does not necessarily stem from moral identity. The dynamics of moral leadership in social movements are not well understood. In the case of Martin Luther King Jr., it is evident that he possessed unusually clear moral conceptions and a keen ability to communicate to large numbers of people. In King's own view, the conditions for effective social movements rest on people's ongoing judgments about freedoms, rights and justice. As he put it (King, 1963), 'Oppressed people cannot remain oppressed forever. The urge for freedom will eventually come. This is what happened to the American Negro'.

Concerns with freedoms, rights and justice are connected to actions in opposition to the prevailing norms and practices that are part of the everyday lives of children, adolescents and adults. The process of social development combines sociability and opposition, social harmony and conflict. A number of studies have demonstrated this combination in children's development (see Turiel, 1998). Oppositions, from a moral perspective, are also evident among adults who hold positions of lesser power or subordination in social hierarchies. And it is in this respect that cultural practices can be great motivators to action. Anthropological and psychological research clearly suggests that opposition, often through deceptive activities aimed at subverting societal arrangements, is part of everyday life.

Studies conducted in the USA (Turiel, 2002), India (Neff, 2001), and among Druze Arabs residing in Israel (Turiel & Wainryb, 1998; Wainryb & Turiel, 1994) demonstrate that girls, women, and sometimes men, are critical of the unfairness of societal arrangements that grant power and privileges to males at the expense of females. Anthropologists studying Bedouin women in Egypt (Abu-Lughod, 1993) and the poor in Cairo (Wikan, 1996) have shown that people continually act to counter what they consider to be unfair restrictions and denial of their rights. As an example, Abu-Lughod has documented that Bedouin women typically use a variety of strategies to counter traditional social practices and to get around the control imposed by men. There is opposition to arranged marriages, polygamy and many of the restrictions on daily lives—including educational and work opportunities.

The research findings are consistent with many journalistic accounts of life in patriarchal non-Western cultures (as discussed in Turiel, 2002). In many nations, women act to resist the power and control exerted by men—power and control institutionalized in the organization and practices of cultures. Men, too, engage in acts of resistance when they perceive governmental and religious authorities to unjustly restrict freedoms and rights. In recent years, many examples have been reported from Iran and Afghanistan. In Iran, for example, people frequently engage in hidden activities that constitute violations of laws and religious prohibitions—including ways of dressing, listening to music, using alcohol and contact between males and females. These activities occurred even though the authorities made intense efforts to detect the offenders. In Afghanistan, before and following the fall of the Taliban in 2001, there were reports of many examples of similar phenomena. These examples have included secret schools for girls (who were banned from schooling), devious means for male doctors to provide health care for women, burying banned televisions in backyards for future use, hiding music, birds and kites (all also banned), and camouflage of prohibited art works.

The journalistic accounts, along with supporting research findings, have implications for characterizations of cultures and their relations to individuals or groups of individuals. Specifically, the evidence indicates that moral action is not a realm to be explained through exemplary individuals with a heightened sense of moral identity, or those who have the courage of their convictions, or those who strive for a consistency of their action with their identity. Social circumstances motivate most people to action because moral judgments are central to their thought. Such actions are not mediated by motivational variables. Individuals engage in social interactions, by which social contexts are processed through a heterogeneous set of judgments. Understanding the heterogeneity of social judgments has required the formulation of domain categories. Analogously, distinctions can be made regarding motivation. We can distinguish those realms predominantly entailing intrinsic motivation from realms in which mediating motivational constructs arc applicable.

References

Abu-Lughod, L. (1993). *Writing women's worlds: Bedouin stories*. Berkeley, CA: University of California Press.

Aronfreed, J. (1968). *Conduct and conscience: The socialization of internalized control over behavior*. New York: Academic Press.

Asch, S. E. (1952). *Social psychology*. Englewood Cliffs, NJ: Prentice-Hall.

Astor, R. (1994). Children's moral reasoning about family and peer violence: The role of provocation and retribution. *Child Development*, 65, 1054–1067.

Blasi, A. (1980). Bridging moral cognition and moral action: A critical review of the literature. *Psychological Bulletin*, 88, 1–45.

Blasi, A. (1993). The development of identity: Some implications for moral functioning. In G. Noam & T. Wren (Eds.), *The moral self* (pp. 99–122). Cambridge, MA: MIT Press.

Bussey, K. (1999). Children's categorization and evaluation of different types of lies and truths. *Child Development*, 70, 1338–1347.

Colby, A., & Damon, W. (1992). *Some do care: Contemporary lives of moral commitment*. New York: Free Press.

De Paulo, B. M., Epstein, J. A., & Wyer, M. M. (1993). Sex differences in lying: How women and men deal with the dilemma of deceit. In M. Lewis & C. Saarni (Eds.), *Lying and deception in everyday life* (pp. 126–147). New York: Guilford.

Freeman, V. G., Rathore, S. S., Weinfurt, K. P., Schulman, K. A., & Sulmasy, D. P. (1999). Lying for patients: Physician deception of third-party payers. *Archives of Internal Medicine*, 159, 2263–2270.

Freud, S. (1930). *Civilization and its discontents*. New York: Norton.

Grinder, R. E. (1964). Relations between behavioral and cognitive dimensions of conscience in middle childhood. *Child Development*, 35, 881–891.

Hartshorne, H., & May, M. A. (1928–1930). *Studies in the nature of character. Volume I: Studies in deceit. Volume II: Studies in self-control. Volume III: Studies in the organization of character*. New York: MacMillan.

Helwig, C. C. (1995). Adolescents' and young adults' conceptions of civil liberties: Freedom of speech and religion. *Child Development*, 66, 152–166.

Kahn, P. H., & Turiel, E. (1988). Children's conceptions of trust in the context of social expectations. *Merrill-Palmer Quarterly*, 34, 403–419.

King, M. L., Jr. (1963, April). *Letter from Birmingham city jail*. Nyack, NY: Fellowship Reconciliation.

Kohlberg, L. (1963). The development of children's orientations toward a moral order: 1. Sequence in the development of moral thought. *Vita Humana*, 6, 11–33.

Kohlberg, L. (1969). Stage and sequence: The cognitive-developmental approach to socialization. In D. Goslin (Ed.), *Handbook of socialization theory and research* (pp. 347-480). Chicago: Rand McNally.

Kohlberg, L. (1971). From is to ought: How to commit the naturalistic fallacy and get away with it in the study of moral development. In T. Mischel (Ed.), *Cognitive development and epistemology* (pp. 151-235). New York: Academic Press.

Latané, B., & Darley, J. M. (1970). *The unresponsive bystander: Why doesn't he help?* New York: Appleton-Crofts.

McClosky, M., & Brill, A. (1983). *Dimensions of tolerance: What Americans believe about civil liberties*. New York: Russell Sage.

Milgram, S. (1974). *Obedience to authority*. New York: Harper & Row.

Neff, K. D. (2001). Judgments of personal autonomy and interpersonal responsibility in the context of Indian spousal relationships: An examination of young people's reasoning in Mysore, India. *British Journal of Developmental Psychology. 19*, 233-257.

Nucci, L. P., & Nucci, M. S. (1982a). Children's reponses to moral and social conventional transgressions in free-play settings. *Child Development, 53*, 1337-1342.

Nucci, L. P., & Nucci, M. S. (1982b). Children's social interactions in the context of moral and conventional transgressions. *Child Development, 53*, 403-412.

Nucci, L. P., & Turiel, E. (1978). Social interactions and the development of social concepts in preschool children. *Child Development, 49*, 400-407.

Nucci, L. P., & Weber, E. (1995). Social interactions in the home and the development of young children's conceptions of the personal. *Child Development, 66*, 1438-1452.

Peterson, C. C., Peterson, J. L., & Seeto, D. (1983). Developmental changes in the ideas about lying. *Child Development, 54*, 1529-1535.

Piaget, J. (1932). *The moral judgment of the child*. London: Routledge and Kegan Paul.

Skinner, B. F. (1971). *Beyond freedom and dignity*. New York: Knopf.

Turiel, E. (1983). *The development of social knowledge: Morality and convention*. Cambridge: Cambridge University Press.

Turiel, E. (1998). The development of morality. In W. Damon (Ed.), *Handbook of child psychology, 5th ed., Vol. 3:* N. Eisenberg (Ed.), *Social, emotional, and personality development* (pp. 863-932). New York: Wiley.

Turiel, E. (2002). *The culture of morality: Social development, context, and conflict*. Cambridge: Cambridge University Press.

Turiel, E. (2003a). Resistance and subversion in everyday life. *Journal of Moral Education, 32*, 115-130.

Turiel, E. (2003b). *Thought and action in social domains: Morality, social interactions, and social behaviours*. Unpublished manuscript. University of California, Berkeley.

Turiel, E., & Wainryb, C. (1998). Concepts of freedoms and rights in a traditional hierarchically organized society. *British Journal of Developmental Psychology. 16*, 375-395.

Wainryb, C., & Turiel, E. (1994). Dominance, subordination, and concepts of personal entitlements in cultural contexts. *Child Development, 65*, 1701-1722.

Wikan, U. (1996). *Tomorrow, God willing: Self-made destinies in Cairo*. Chicago: University of Chicago Press.

Wynia, M. K., Cummins, D. S., VanGeest, J. B., & Wilson, I. B. (2000). Physician manipulation of reimbursement rules for patients: Between a rock and a hard place. *Journal of the American Medical Association, 283*, 1858-1865.

Development and Motivation, 41–56
BJEP Monograph Series II, 2
© 2003 The British Psychological Society

www.bps.org.uk

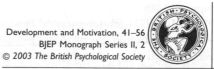

An integration of motivation and cognition

Mark H. Bickhard*

Lehigh University, Bethlehem, USA

Motivation and cognition are commonly modelled as distinct processes: motivation as some form of initiating and directing—pushing and pulling—behaviour, and cognition as the manipulation of encoded representations in memory. This produces grave difficulties in understanding the interrelationships between them, and their interactions in behaviour and development. I argue for a model of representation and motivation in which they emerge as different aspects of one underlying organization of interactive process. This natural integration yields an equally natural model of the joint development of higher-order motivation and cognition, as interactions with learning and emotional processes are taken into account.

Models of motivation and cognition often have little intrinsic relationship with each other. If, for example, cognition consists of manipulating encoded symbols (such as in the standard information processing paradigm), while motivation is concerned with energizing and directing an action system (such as in the Freudian paradigm), the interface between them is likely to be relatively *ad hoc*. Furthermore, such a fragmented model of mental phenomena is almost certainly false: motivation and cognition have evolved together and develop together and, consequently, must be more strongly integrated in order for their co-evolution and co-development to remain coordinated. If so, such models necessarily misrepresent the nature and interrelationships of motivation and cognition, and provide flawed guidance for developmental and educational policies and interventions.

I will argue, in fact, that such models of cognition and motivation are false in themselves, independent of any issues regarding their interrelationships. The encoding paradigm, for example, including both its symbolic and its connectionist incarnations, faces a multitude of fatal problems, including the fundamental fact that it cannot account for representational content and, thus, cannot account for representation at all. The energizing conception of motivation, in turn, is incompatible with the basic fact

*Requests for reprints should be addressed to Mark H. Bickhard, Cognitive Science, 17 Memorial Drive East, Lehigh University, Bethlehem, PA 18015, USA (e-mail: mark.bickhard@lehigh.edu).

that motivated action only occurs in systems that are, of ontological necessity, open and in ongoing interaction with their environment. Inertness that must be 'energized' is not an option.

Nevertheless, such fragmented models of mind are not only common, but are forced by dominant theoretical approaches and their presuppositions. I outline an alternative model in which motivation and cognition are tightly—ontologically, not merely ontogenetically—integrated, and will illustrate some of its consequences. The alternative model, however, requires changes in theoretical presuppositions, not just their contents.

Metaphysics: Substance and process

The presuppositions of a theoretical approach—even to the level of metaphysical presuppositions—can strongly constrain the kinds of theories that are possible within that approach. In particular, they may well preclude theories of the kind that ultimately prove to be correct. For example, as long as models of fire were presumed to be models of some kind of substance, the phlogiston theory seemed like a good theory, albeit with empirical refinements yet to be worked out (Kuhn, 1970).

The phlogiston example illustrates what I argue is a fundamental metaphysical issue in studies of the mind: substance metaphysics versus process metaphysics. Every science has gone through a historical phase in which it assumed that its basic phenomena were phenomena of some special sort of substance. Fire was thought to be the release of phlogiston; heat was a fluidic substance called caloric; magnetism was a substance; life was constituted in vital fluid; and so on. Every science has moved on from such substance approaches to a recognition that its basic phenomena are phenomena of process: fire is combustion; heat is random kinetic energy; magnetism is a field process; life is a particular kind of far-from-thermodynamic-equilibrium complex system; and so on.

But there is one major exception to this historical generalization: most studies of the mind and mental phenomena still routinely presuppose that they are phenomena of some particular kinds of substances or structures. Genuine process models are difficult to find; most—such as Piaget's—have emerged in one way or another out of the action framework of pragmatism (Bickhard & Campbell, 1989; Joas, 1993).

The historical trend mentioned above already creates a strong presumption in favour of process models, but the case is in fact much stronger. This is not the place to examine the problems and problematics of substance and structure models in detail, but some illustrative ones include the following:

(1)   Modern physics shows that there are no substances and no particles (Brown & Harré, 1988; Cao, 1999; Huggett, 2000; Weinberg, 1977, 1995, 1996, 2000). Instead, there are quantized fields, in which the quantization of field processes superficially appears as a particle count. However, the number of oscillatory waves in a guitar string is also restricted to discrete possibilities, and there are no guitar sound particles. The world is composed of quantized field processes at all scales, large and small (Bickhard, 2000a).

One consequence of a shift from a particle or substance framework to a process framework is that explanatory defaults reverse: stability is the default for substances and structures, and change must be explained; while change is the default for processes, and stability must be explained. This has critical implications for phenomena such as motivation or psychopathology: the fundamental nature of what is taken as problematic and as requiring explanation is reversed (Bickhard, 2000b; Bickhard & Christopher, 1994; Christopher & Bickhard, 1994).

(2)   Substance and particle models make genuine causally efficacious emergence impossible. All causality is located at the level of the fundamental particles (or substances), and all higher-level phenomena are just the working out of the causal dance of the particles at the basic level.

   In particular, higher-level phenomena, such as mental phenomena, are causally epiphenomenal (Bickhard, 2000a; Kim, 1993). Such a position forces a micro-physicalism, at the lowest level of particles, as the only causally efficacious level of reality and precludes any genuine naturalism (Bickhard, 2003). It faces serious problems with prima facie causal efficacies of higher-level phenomena, such as atoms, chemical properties and interactions, biological phenomena, and psychological and social processes. To construe these entire realms as epiphenomenal illusion, akin to the illusion of motion in a movie, as is forced by such a micro-physicalism, is a prima facie refutation of the substance presuppositions that compel such a stance.

(3)   A corollary of the second point is that no genuinely new kinds of phenomena can emerge; new kinds of substance or particle cannot emerge, instead, the original ones can blend or structure themselves in differing ways. But most of what the sciences are interested in, including mental phenomena, did not exist at the time of the Big Bang, and does exist now. So it has to have emerged. Any model that makes such emergence impossible is thereby refuted (Bickhard, 2000a).

   This problem is especially acute for normative phenomena, such as representation, rationality, learning and so on: normativity is not generally accepted as endemic in the physical world so, if emergence, and thus the emergence of normative phenomena, is impossible, then virtually all mental phenomena are impossible. More to the current point, *working within* a substance metaphysics makes *accounting for* such normative phenomena impossible.[1]

   There are numerous additional problems with substance and particle approaches (Bickhard, 2000, 2003), but these points suffice to indicate that they face serious difficulties. A process metaphysics is correspondingly recommended, although not necessarily easily honoured: substance and structure presuppositions can be quite subtle and unnoticed.

Representation and fragmentation

One aspect of psychological phenomena that is still caught in substance presuppositions is that of cognition, especially with respect to representation. Substance models of representation are at least as old as Plato's and Aristotle's signet rings pressing their

---

[1] *So long as such conceptual possibilities as dualism or idealism are eschewed. So, the point is that a naturalistic account of normative phenomena is precluded (Bickhard, 2003).*

forms into wax.[2] Such an impressing-into-wax creates a *correspondence* between the impression in the wax and the form that it is supposed to represent. This is the basic kind of substance model of representation that has been pursued ever since.[3] Locke's blank sheet of paper is just a slightly technologically advanced version of something to receive correspondences, whether singular or structural, and contemporary talk of 'transduction' or 'sensory encoding' is a suitably updated version of the same basic model (Bickhard, 1993; Carlson, 2000; Fodor, 1975, 1991).

Unfortunately, correspondence approaches to the nature of representation are fatally flawed as models of representation, and they yield equally flawed models of interrelated mental phenomena as well.

Encoding models of representation

There is a large family of problems with correspondence models of representation, some very old and some being discovered recently. Furthermore, there are multiple subordinate families of problems, one for each of the many particular forms of such correspondence models (Bickhard, 1993, in press; Bickhard & Terveen, 1995). One way in which correspondence models differ, for example, is in terms of what kind of correspondence is taken to be the special representation-constituting kind of correspondence—these can posit causal correspondences, informational correspondences, nomological correspondences, trained or learned correspondences, and so on. I will not attempt an exhaustive survey of such variants and their general and particular problems but, as for substance metaphysics more broadly, will attempt to demonstrate via a few examples that such models are in serious difficulty.

Encodings

There is, in fact, a class of correspondences that *are* representational: encoding correspondences. Correspondence models of representation in effect, and sometimes explicitly, assume that all representation has the nature of encodings. In Morse code, for example, '...' encodes 's'. The encoding correspondence is a representational correspondence, but it generates a circularity if encoding is used to account for representation in general: an encoding functions as such only if an interpreting agent knows both ends of the encoding relationship, and knows the encoding relationship itself. '...' encodes 's' only if '...' and 's' and the encoding relationship between them are known. But this kind of knowledge is representational knowledge; it is precisely what we seek to model. Artificial codes of this sort are useful because they change the form of the representation, and a new form can have properties that the original form does not. '...', for example, can be sent over telegraph wires, while 's' cannot. They are not generators of new representations in themselves; codes borrow representational

---

[2] *Neither Plato nor Aristotle was a pure substance philosopher. The involvement of forms and of the soul or psyche, in differing ways in the two frameworks, transcends some of the restrictions of substance presuppositions. Nevertheless, there does tend to be a continuation of the intuition of 'like represents like' carried over into the more sophisticated kinds of representation and cognition (Bickhard, 2003; Gill, 1989)*

[3] *A second theme of representational models is also to be found in the 'ring in wax' analogy: a representation being similar to that which it represents. Similarity models, however, suffer from immediate special problems, especially having to do with generality and abstraction. For example, is the representation of a triangle similar to an isosceles or to a scalene triangle, or how can you model a representation of truth or beauty? Similarity models and correspondence models are at root deeply related: a similarity, or, in more modern form, an iso- or homo-morphism, is a correspondence of structure – of relations among points – as well as a correspondence of points to points. There are some interesting issues here, but they are not germane to the topics that I want to pursue in the text.*

powers from what is encoded: '...' borrows its representational character from 's'. It does not generate any new representation and, therefore, cannot account for the grounding representation for any such encoding.

Circularity

The general point, furthermore, does not depend on the social arbitrariness of something like Morse code. We might find the claim that neutrino counts encode properties of fusion in the interior of the sun. This is a natural correspondence, not a conventional one. However, it is in itself only an informational correspondence (and also a causal and nomological correspondence). It functions as an encoding, or representational, correspondence only for someone who knows about fusion process and neutrino counting and the relationships between them. Again, as an account of the fundamental nature of mental representation, this generates a circularity.[4]

A differing perspective on this circularity can be found in Piaget's argument that our mental representations of the world cannot be copies of the world, because, if they were, we would have to already know the world in order to construct our copies of it (Piaget, 1970). Still another perspective is the radical sceptical argument that we cannot ever check whether our representations are accurate because, in order to do so, we would have to have some epistemic access to the relevant parts of the world that is independent of our representations in order to make the comparison. We do not have any such independent epistemic access, so any such check is circular.

Over-extension

This basic circularity is just one of a family of fatal flaws in correspondence, or encoding, models of representation. Consider that all of the proposed forms of correspondence—informational, lawful, causal and so on—are ubiquitous throughout the universe. Every instance of every causal law, for example, is an instance of a causal correspondence, an informational correspondence, and a nomological correspondence, and causality is not the only class that yields such proliferations. Informational correspondences, for example, do not even require causal connection. Furthermore, almost none of these are representational. At best, these enormous classes of correspondences require drastic pruning down to the representational correspondences.

It might appear that structural correspondences are more particular than causal, informational or nomological correspondences and, therefore, not as subject to the charge of massive over-extension beyond anything that is representational. This appearance, however, evaporates once it is recognized that the point-to-point correspondences, the relation-to-relation correspondences and even what counts as a point at all are all logically arbitrary and subject to unbounded variation in how they are defined and which ones 'count'. Every aspect of a purported structural correspondence is unboundedly arbitrary and, therefore, can be defined everywhere.

Further, all such correspondences iterate and proliferate in time. Any activity in my occipital lobe that is in correspondence (of whatever kind—causal, perhaps) with a table in front of me is also in correspondence (of that kind) with activities in my retina, with the patterning of light in front of me, with the quantum processes in the surface of that table, with the table a second ago, with the table yesterday, with the construction

---

[4] *That the only genuine representational correspondences are encodings has led me to dub correspondence models of representation in terms of their presupposition that all representations are encodings: encodingism.*

of the table, with the growth of the trees from which the table was made, with the creation of the sun that helps those trees grow, and so on all the way back to the Big Bang. Which one of this proliferation of correspondences is the representational correspondence? Again, at best, drastic principled pruning of some sort is required.

Normativity: The possibility of error

Correspondence models of representation are massively over-extended, and they are circular. Another perspective on them focuses on the fact that they cannot account for the normative aspects of representation. They cannot account for the simple possibility of representation being in error. In such a model, if the favoured special kind of correspondence exists, then the representation exists, and it is correct. If the correspondence does not exist, then the representation does not exist. But the correspondence either exists or does not exist. Those are the only two modelling possibilities. The modelling task, however, requires three cases to be modelled: the representation exists and is correct, the representation exists and is incorrect, and the representation does not exist. Three cases cannot be modelled in a model that has only two categories. This inability to model representational error has generated a small industry of attempts in the last decades, but without success (Bickhard, 1993, in press; Cummins, 1996; Dretske, 1988; Fodor, 1990, 1991, 1998; Levine & Bickhard, 1999; Millikan, 1984, 1993).

System detectable error

An even stronger desideratum for models of mental representation is that they not only account for the possibility of representational error, but account for the possibility of system or organism detectable representational error. Not all organisms are capable of such detection, but certainly some of them are some of the time. So any model that makes such detection impossible is thereby refuted. If organism-detectable representational error is not possible, then error-guided behaviour and error-guided learning are not possible.[5] No model in the literature, other than that to be outlined below, even attempts to account for system detectable error.[6,7]

Substance approaches to representation have grave difficulties. These difficulties might be taken as refutations if there seemed to be any alternative, but there has not appeared to be any alternative prior to the advent of pragmatism a little over a century ago.

Models of fragmented minds

Encoding models of representation not only encounter fatal difficulties as models of representation, but must fit into models of mental phenomena more broadly, and they (and their underlying substance presuppositions) wreak foundational damage with respect to this broader range of considerations as well. In particular, they induce

---

[5] Note that the strong sceptical argument mentioned above is an argument that such organism error detection is not possible.
[6] Connectionism, for all its differences with the symbolic and information-processing frameworks, does not differ in these fundamental respects with regard to the assumed nature of representation. A symbolic system has transduced encodings; a connectionist system has trained encodings. Neither can solve or avoid the problems of encoding or correspondence models of representation (Bickhard & Terveen, 1995).
[7] For more extensive discussions of problems with encoding models in general, and with specific models of representation available in the literature, see Bickhard (1993, in press) and Bickhard and Terveen (1995).

models of fragmented minds, in which various aspects of mental process are reified into distinct subsystems and modules.

A bank of encoded representations is inert. What is required for its formation and use is a perceptual process to generate them and a cognitive process to manipulate them, not to mention a language process to re-encode them and transmit them into the world. In itself, such a cognitive system would not act and has no need for any action system. In particular, under these modelling assumptions, there is no need for action in order for the system to be a cognitive system, with genuine representations.

We know, however, that animals do act, so we need some sort of action module. Such a subsystem needs to access, and be guided by, the representational information in the encoding bank; it needs to be energized into activity at appropriate times and in appropriate circumstances, and in some sense to seek appropriate outcomes of its interactions. We might also want to account for memory, consciousness, values and so on, and each one of these can also have its own dedicated subsystem.

The basic split here is between representation and action: correspondence models of representation do not need action, so any interface between cognition and action, including issues of motivation, is theoretically *ad hoc* (Bickhard, 1997a). There is little intrinsic constraint in the relationships between cognition and action, at least in such models. Moreover, the underlying substance and structure assumptions can permeate further, to generate a proliferation of modules and submodules, systems and subsystems. As discussed earlier, such an architecture is highly unlikely, and thus counts against substance models in general, and encoding models of representation in particular, from an even broader perspective.

The problem of action selection

Substance and structure presuppositions, then, are not acceptable as a metaphysical framework, and, when they do frame explorations of cognition, they yield correspondence models of representation, which are fatally flawed both as models of representation *per se* and as accounts of the representational aspect of mental phenomena more broadly.[8] A shift to a process metaphysics is required, but how is that to be undertaken? In particular, what would a process model of representation look like (Bickhard, 1993, in press; Bickhard & Terveen, 1995)? I approach this question via a prior issue regarding how organisms solve the problem of selecting their actions and interactions.

Complex organisms will generally have numerous actions that are possible at a given moment. Somehow these possibilities must be available for the organism to select among, and somehow that selection must take place. I will focus on just a few aspects of this overall problem.

Some simple cells, perhaps sulphur-consuming bacteria, do only one thing, and do it continuously. Slightly more complex would be bacteria that can swim if they find themselves swimming up a sugar gradient but tumble if they find themselves swimming down a sugar gradient; they can do two things, and can switch between them more or less appropriately. A frog, however, can in general do any of a number of things at a

---

[8] Piaget's 'structures' are more akin to formal structures, as in mathematics, than to substantial structures. I argue elsewhere, nevertheless, that they involve serious problems, including vestiges of correspondence models (Bickhard, 1992a; Bickhard & Campbell, 1989; Campbell & Bickhard, 1986).

given moment, so the simple triggering of the sugar-seeking bacterium will not suffice. Furthermore, what it would be appropriate for the frog to do will shift from time to time: flicking its tongue at a fly is inappropriate if there are no indications that such tongue-flicking might have a positive outcome.

The frog, or some more complex organism, then, must have some way of indicating what actions and interactions are available to it at a given time, and must select among them based on further considerations, such as their potential utility for achieving goals. They will be of potential relevance to goals in so far as their anticipated outcomes or their anticipated future courses of interaction satisfy heuristic criteria for instrumental movement towards those goals. Indications of currently possible interactions, then, must also include indications of anticipated courses or outcomes of those interactions.[9]

Interactive representation

This brief sketch of a model of action selection is already sufficient to ground a model of at least primitive representation. In fact, primitive representation is already an aspect of the model outlined: no further model-building is required for this basic point, only the pointing out of properties already involved in the model. That is, representation in this primitive sense is not a distinct component or system but instead is a differentiable aspect of any complex system by which an organism selects actions. Representation is an intrinsic aspect of the evolutionary solution to the action selection problem.

The key is to note that the anticipations of future courses of interaction, or of their outcomes, involve presuppositions about the environment.[10] In some environments, an action will fulfil the anticipations, in others not. In some environments, the frog flicking its tongue is likely to succeed in producing eating, while in others it will not. These dynamic presuppositions involved in action anticipations are presuppositions about the environment, and they can be true or false about that environment. This, I claim, is the fundamental emergence of representational truth value.

The dynamic presuppositions of an indicated interaction are the conditions under which the interaction would in fact satisfy those anticipations, in which the interaction would have the indicated outcomes or follow the anticipated course. Implicitly, they

---

[9] *If those indicated future courses or outcomes must themselves be 'represented', then the account being adumbrated will be circular, in that a model of representation will be based on a notion of representation. But those future courses and outcomes need be represented only if they are external to the organism. If they are internal flows of interaction or internal outcome states, then they need only be indicated, and indication can be a strictly functional notion: in a computer architecture, indication can be accomplished with simple pointers. There are good reasons to avoid simple computer models, and good reason to think that they are radically inadequate for understanding human mentality, but the example does make the point that there is nothing mysterious about the function of indication. Of course, once the possibility of representation is granted, there is nothing to prevent the organism from using represented external outcomes as part of its process for action selection.*

A similar problem of potential foundational circularity occurs with respect to the role of goals in this model. If goal conditions must be represented, then circularity appears in a similar manner as with indications of future outcomes. But goals, at least in the most primitive sense, need only be functional set points for conditions, internal conditions perhaps, such as 'above threshold level of blood sugar', that are detected or not, and appropriate control theoretic switching can follow from such detection or failure of such detection. However, detection is not representation, and does not require representation, though, again, representation can be used if otherwise available, so the threatened circularity does not exist (see Bickhard, 1993, in press; Bickhard & Terveen, 1995).

[10] *The notion of dynamic presupposition is a normative one: an interaction dynamically presupposes those conditions under which that interaction would succeed. The normative notion of success, in turn, is relative to contributing toward goal attainment, or, more generally, contributing toward the well-being of – being functionally useful for – the overall organism. Such issues of functional normativity are interesting, important and complex, but are not addressed here: see Bickhard (1993, 2000c, 2003, in press; Christensen & Bickhard, 2002).*

are predications about the environment: this environment is of the type that will satisfy the anticipations involved in this interaction. For interaction **P**, this environment is a **P**-type environment. And such (implicit) predication will have a truth value.

More sophisticated representations

These simple indications of interactive potentiality may suffice for worms, but perhaps frogs and certainly mammals are capable of much more complex representations, such as of objects and abstractions like numbers. How can an interactive model handle those?

The first step in addressing this question is to elaborate some of the relevant resources available in the model. One of them, in fact, has already been mentioned: indications of interactive potentiality can involve indications of multiple potentialities at one time. That is, such indications can branch.

Recognition of a second resource begins with the recognition that indications of interactive potentiality are necessarily conditional. The bacterium swims if it detects that it is swimming up a sugar gradient. The frog flicks its tongue if it detects something like a moving black dot in an appropriate range of its vision.

How do such detections occur? The simple answer is: via the course and outcomes of previous interactions. That is, if a (or the) previous interaction has in fact ended in one of its anticipated outcomes, then (depending perhaps on precisely which outcome state) a flick of the tongue in such-and-such a manner and direction should yield an opportunity for eating. More generally, the course of an interaction will depend in part on the organization of the subsystem engaging in the interaction, and in part on the environment being interacted with. In some environments, the interaction may end with internal outcome **A**, while in others it may end in **B**. Such an interaction can then differentiate **A**-type environments from **B**-type environments, though the detection *per se* neither obtains nor creates any available information about what properties characterize **A** or **B** types of environments. Nevertheless, the differentiation can be quite useful if the organism learns, or has hard-wired, that in **A**-type environments such-and-such a tongue-flicking with eating as an outcome is possible, while in **B**-type environments, it is not. That is, such a differentiation can be useful if the organism has available a conditionalized indication of the possibility of tongue-flicking followed by the possibility of eating in **A**-type environments.[11]

Such conditionalized indications of potentiality are available in the organism even if not being activated at some given time. The frog 'knows' about the relationship between **A**-type environments and tongue-flicking and eating even when it is underwater and not engaged in the right kind of interactions (visual scans of some sort presumably) to yield the outcome **A** at all. Furthermore, the iterated conditional of tongue-flicking yielding eating is also similarly available. More generally, interactive indications not only branch but also iterate, with the outcomes of one serving as the differentiating outcomes for further indications of the next potentialities.

Such branched and iterated (and continuous) organizations of indications of interactive potentiality can form vast and complex webs. It is these webs that provide the answer to the question of how something like objects could be represented.

---

[11] *This is all worded in discrete terms for ease of discussion. More realistically, sets of possible outcome states and their indicative relationships to further potentialities will be more complex, perhaps even continuous in nature.*

In particular, some subwebs of such an overall web will have two special properties. Every point in it will be reachable from every point. This is illustrated by a child's toy block in which every visual scan is reachable from every other via some intermediary manipulations. And such an internally reachable subweb may be invariant under some special class of possible interactions, such as manipulations and transportations. The child's block affords manipulations and visual scans in a fully reachable manner, and this organization of interactive potentialities is itself invariant under many kinds of transportations, locomotions, chewings, and so on—although not invariant under burning or crushing. An internally reachable web of interactive potentialities that has such an invariance *is* (epistemologically) a manipulable object.

Clearly, this is just a translation into the language of the general interactive model of Piaget's model of object representation (Piaget, 1954). It is possible to borrow Piaget's model in this way because both are based on action and interaction as the foundational framework within which representation is modelled. There is not the space to develop it here, but I would offer a similarly Piagetian answer to the question of how an interactive model of representation could model the representation of abstractions, such as of numbers (Campbell & Bickhard, 1986).

While still focused on representation, let me note that the detections upon which indications of interactive potentialities are based are, in most models, taken to be or to generate the paradigm cases of correspondence representation. A simple form of interaction is one in which there are no outputs from the system—a passive processing of inputs. Such passive input processing is the standard model of sensory encoding, as in the visual system (Bickhard & Richie, 1983). Such a detection process does set up informational, perhaps causal and nomological, relationships with whatever the properties (perhaps objects) are that characterize the detected environments, but standard models assume that the input process thereby yields a representation of those properties, with all of the fatal consequences outlined earlier. The interactive model, in contrast, makes use of the environmental differentiations involved but without reifying a detection or differentiation into a representation.[12]

Motivation

Representation, then, is an aspect of processes of action selection: the aspect of environmental dynamic presuppositions. What about motivation (Bickhard, 2000b)? As for representation, the model is already in place; what is required is to bring out the aspect of it that is motivational in nature.

A critical step in arriving at a motivational focus is to clarify what the problem of motivation is. Classically, and in fragmented models in general, the system is inherently passive or inert, and the question that defines motivation is 'What makes the system do something rather than nothing?' The answer has to be in terms of some sort of directional energizers, pushes or pulls or both, that mobilize the action system into real action.

Living beings, however, are far-from-equilibrium systems that must always be in interaction with their environment in order to maintain their far-from-equilibrium

---

[12] *Furthermore, the representations, the interactive anticipations, that are evoked by a particular differentiation will change from time to time with learning and over time with development, if the organism is capable of such. So, if an infant is in fact seeing an object, there is no temptation to assume that 'an object' is necessarily what is being represented for that infant (Bickhard, 1997b, 2001).*

conditions. The bacterium must swim and tumble under appropriate conditions, or die. The frog must flick its tongue under appropriate conditions, or die. Absence of action is not an option. It is ongoing, continuously. So the relevant question cannot be 'What makes the system do something rather than nothing?' Nothing is not an option; the system will always be doing something so long as it is alive. The relevant question for motivation is 'What makes the system do one thing rather than another?' That is, the problem of motivation is the problem of action selection, not of action instigation (Mook, 1996).

Action selection is the framework within which the representational model has been developed. The overall system is one of functional interaction with the organism's environment, with action selection one of the basic problems involved, and representation at the centre of solutions to the problem of action selection. In other words, representation evolved in the service of motivational problems—selection problems—encountered in interacting so as to keep the organism alive.[13]

Both representation and motivation are aspects of a more fundamental form of process in certain far-from-equilibrium systems. They are not, foundationally, distinct subsystems. I introduce the caveat of 'foundationally' because, having originated in evolution as aspects in this manner, there is nothing to preclude the further differentiation and specialization of subsystems that may be relatively devoted to these functional aspects, similar to the sense in which there is massive differentiation and specialization of subsystems for interaction in the central nervous system that are devoted to the function of detection rather than of manipulation in the environment. We call them sensory systems.

Thus, there will be higher order and more sophisticated versions of both representation and motivation. In the representational case, one example would be that of representations of abstractions, which I address elsewhere (in a generally Piagetian manner). In the case of motivation, I wish to focus on one more sophisticated motivational emergence—roughly, intrinsic motivation—but at least rough character-izations of some properties of learning and emotions are needed to do so.

Some properties of learning, development and emotions

Only a few basic properties of learning and emotions are essential here (Bickhard, 2000b). For learning, the central point is that learning is initiated by error, by failure of the anticipations involved in representations. The organization of system processes in which such anticipations are embedded is destabilized by learning, thereby creating a new trial, a new anticipation, the next time that the same condition is encountered. Conversely, successful anticipations—successful interactive 'knowing' of the object of interaction—will stabilize, and yield the stability of the representations constituted in those anticipations. Such a dynamic suffices for a minimal trial-and-error learning process: success stabilizes, failure destabilizes. Much more is required in order to account for heuristic trials, for the learning of heuristics *per se*, for the development of rationality and logic, and so on, but this minimalist model will suffice for current purposes.

---

[13] A more careful analysis of the relationships among far-from-thermodynamic-equilibrium processes and an organism's activities in the service of maintaining those far-from-equilibrium conditions can be found elsewhere (Bickhard, 1993, 2000c, 2003; Christensen & Bickhard, 2002).

Learning and development

Learning, then, is a constructive process—a variation and selection, evolutionary epistemology constructive process (Campbell, 1974). There is little incentive in an action-based model to suppose that the world can impress itself into a passive mind: successful interaction systems cannot be pressed into the mind by the world. They must be constructed, and—so long as those constructions are non-prescient—this will be a variation-and-selection kind of constructive process. If such constructions are each totally independent of others (as might perhaps be the case in simple organisms), then each new construction will start from the same basis and in the same functional context, so there will be no relevant historicity in the overall constructive history of the organism.

If, however, new constructions can make use of, and are in the functional context of, already available successful previous constructions—if the constructive process is recursive—then the process becomes inherently historical, with previous learning framing, constraining and making possible further constructions. Particular domains of construction, for example, may develop that have rich resources for further development, while some other domain may have early constructions, early learning, that make further development difficult or distorted in some way. Furthermore, with such historicity involved, multiple additional sources of constraint on historical trajectories of constructions can come into play. Developmental psychology focuses on such historistic constraints and possibilities regarding constructive trajectories.

Developmental constraints might involve, for example, intrinsic relationships among domains of learning, such as the fact that you cannot learn calculus without having learned algebra first. Or constraints might emerge that depend on what sorts of new constructions are easy to construct given the constructive processes and currently available resources. Constructions, and thus kinds of learning and development, that are too difficult with a particular framework of resources are not likely to occur without appropriate scaffolding (Bickhard, 1992b). I argue that one major intrinsic constraint on constructive trajectories is one that emerges from levels of reflective knowing (Campbell & Bickhard, 1986, 1992). If some sort of knowledge, such as the invariance of number in a set of objects so long as none are added or removed, requires reflection on prior knowledge, such as how to differentiate units and distinguish and keep track of sets, then the dependent form of knowledge cannot be constructed prior to the depended upon form; they must be constructed in sequence. Such levels of knowing impose a major sequential hierarchy on the possibilities of child development.

Emotions

The case of emotions involves an additional complication: there is no consensus on even basic characterizations of the nature of emotion (e.g. Ekman & Davidson, 1994; Frijda, 1986; Griffiths, 1997; Lazarus, 1991; Oatley, 1992). The model that I propose has the notion of interactive anticipation at its core. In particular, anticipations of future interactive processing may involve occasions in which the anticipations break down. This occurs when the situation is novel or difficult. For whatever reason, full anticipations for interactive flow have not been learned. In such a case, the anticipations of interactive processing may anticipate interactive failure, or uncertainty about how to proceed. If a signal of such interactive uncertainty could be fed back into the system as an input to be interacted with, then the system could interact with its own conditions of interactive uncertainty.

This would be useful, among other reasons, because it would allow the organism to develop general strategies for dealing with various kinds of uncertainties, rather than having to wait for actual interactive failure and then engaging learning processes. The first time you encounter a tiger on jungle trail, it would be good to have a general response already available, rather than cycling through various learning trials.

In particular, I propose that emotions are interactions with such internal conditions of interactive uncertainty.[14] Negative emotions emerge when the further anticipations involve anticipations of failure to resolve the uncertainty, and differing kinds of negative emotion involve differing strategies for trying to handle such failures. Positive emotions involve anticipations of success in resolving interactive uncertainty. This can range from the immediate resolution of walking in on your own surprise birthday party to the anticipation of solving a complex problem of a kind that you feel competent to tackle.

An emergent motivation

One of the attractive characteristics of this model is that it accounts for the natural emergence of new kinds of motivational processes, the emergence of new forms of action selection. This holds both for phylogeny and for ontogeny. I illustrate this with an example of the emergence of something like curiosity and aesthetic motivation.[15]

There will be multiple influences on the activities of the central nervous system, but it also has endogenous tendencies that will be manifested over time and may be paramount in their influence at particular times when other modulatory influences, such as hunger, are quiescent. Consider, for example, the joint outcome of (1) system processes do not cease, (2) learning stabilizes successful forms of interaction, and (3) anticipations of uncertainty resolution are successful emotional interactions. Over time, this will tend to produce tendencies, when other influences are not dominant, to engage in activities of sorts that involve anticipations of successful emotional interactions. But what are those?

Successful emotional interactions are those that encounter uncertainty—novelty, complexity—with an anticipation of being able to resolve that uncertainty. So, a kind of activity that anticipates such uncertainty with resolution will engage something that is of sufficient novelty or complexity to elicit uncertainty, but of a sort for which the organism has learned it can generally anticipate successful resolution. Encountering such uncertainty and then resolving it, however, generally involves learning how to resolve it, at least in this instance.

Thus the joint effect of the three principles is that the organism will seek kinds of interactions that it has not mastered but that it has learned that it has a reasonable expectation of being able to master. Various manifestations of this motivational tendency are called curiosity, mastery motivation, competence motivation, or aesthetic motivation. Finally, such intrinsic motivations—intrinsic to the activity of exploring the object or phenomenon—can be centrally involved in discovering or creating new approaches and new solutions, that is, in creativity itself (Collins & Amabile, 1999).[16]

---

[14] The model, then, is consistent, for example, with the dynamic and developmental perspective of Griffiths (1999).

[15] The caveat is because such specific motivations, like motivation itself, do not have well-defined characters. So what I am proposing is in part a specification of what these notions mean, as well as an explication of their prior meaning.

[16] Note that extrinsic motivation emerges directly in this model in the action-selection properties of hierarchies of goals and, perhaps even more interesting, in hierarchies of goals about goals – in which the aboutness requires a move up the hierarchy of knowing levels (Bickhard & Christopher, 1994; Campbell & Bickhard, 1986; Christopher & Bickhard, 1994).

In this model, such motivations emerge in the interrelationships between activity, learning and emotions; there is no need to posit separate motivational systems or drives. This point is in addition to the more general one that motivation is an aspect of the activity of an interactive system, not a component of it.

Conclusion

Cognition and motivation do not constitute distinct subsystems of psychological processes. Instead, they are aspects of one underlying ontology of interactive systems. Such a model carries forward the basic process commitments that are urged on psychological studies by both historical and metaphysical considerations, accommodates the interactive-process model of the nature of representation and cognition, and accounts for higher-order motivation as emergents of the interactions between processes of knowing, learning and emotions.

References

Bickhard, M. H. (1992a). Piaget on variation and selection Models: Structuralism, logical necessity, and interactivism. In L. Smith (Ed.), *Jean Piaget: Critical assessments* (pp. 388–434). London: Routledge.

Bickhard, M. H. (1992b). Scaffolding and self scaffolding: Central aspects of development. In L. T. Winegar, & J. Valsiner (Eds.), *Children's development within social contexts: Research and methodology* (pp. 33–52). Hillsdale, NJ: Erlbaum.

Bickhard, M. H. (1993). Representational content in humans and machines. *Journal of Experimental and Theoretical Artificial Intelligence*, *5*, 285–333.

Bickhard, M. H. (1997a). Is cognition an autonomous subsystem? In S. O'Nuallain, P. McKevitt, & E. MacAogain (Eds.), *Two sciences of mind* (pp. 115–131). Amsterdam: John Benjamins.

Bickhard, M. H. (1997b). Piaget and active cognition. *Human Development*, *40*, 238–244.

Bickhard, M. H. (2000a). Emergence. In P. B. Andersen, C. Emmeche, N. O. Finnemann, & P. V. Christiansen (Eds.), *Downward causation* (pp. 322–348). Aarhus, Denmark: University of Aarhus Press.

Bickhard, M. H. (2000b). Motivation and emotion: An interactive process model. In R. D. Ellis, & N. Newton (Eds.), *The caldron of consciousness* (pp. 161–178). Amsterdam: John. Benjamins.

Bickhard, M. H. (2000c). Autonomy, function, and representation. *Communication and Cognition—Artificial Intelligence*, *17*(3–4), 111–131.

Bickhard, M. H. (2001). Why children don't have to solve the frame problems: cognitive representations are not encodings. *Developmental Review*, *21*, 224–262.

Bickhard, M. H. (2003). *The whole person: Toward a naturalism of persons—Contributions to an ontological psychology*. Manuscript in preparation.

Bickhard, M. H. (in press). The dynamic emergence of representation. In H. Clapin, P. Staines, & P. Slezak (Eds.), *Representation in mind: New approaches to mental representation*. Westport, CT: Praeger.

Bickhard, M. H., & Campbell, R. L. (1989). Interactivism and genetic epistemology. *Archives de Psychologie*, *57*(221), 99–121.

Bickhard, M. H., & Christopher, J. C. (1994). The influence of early experience on personality development. *New Ideas in Psychology*, *12*(3), 229–252.

Bickhard, M. H., & Richie, D. M. (1983). *On the nature of representation: A case study of James Gibson's theory of perception*. New York: Praeger.

Bickhard, M. H., & Terveen, L. (1995). *Foundational issues in artificial intelligence and cognitive science: Impasse and solution*. Amsterdam: Elsevier Scientific.

Brown, H. R., & Harré, R. (1988). *Philosophical foundations of quantum field theory*. Oxford: Oxford University Press.

Campbell, D. T. (1974). Evolutionary epistemology. In P. A. Schilpp (Ed.), *The philosophy of Karl Popper* (pp. 413–463). La Salle, IL: Open Court.

Campbell, R. L., & Bickhard, M. H. (1986). *Knowing levels and developmental stages: Contributions to human development*. Basel, Switzerland: Karger.

Campbell, R. L., & Bickhard, M. H. (1992). Types of constraints on development: An interactivist approach. *Developmental Review, 12*(3), 311–338.

Cao, T. Y. (1999). *Conceptual foundations of quantum field theory*. Cambridge: University of Cambridge Press.

Carlson, N. R. (2000). *Physiology of Behavior* (7th ed.). Boston: Allyn & Bacon.

Christensen, W. D., & Bickhard, M. H. (2002). The process dynamics of normative function. *Monist, 85*(1), 3–28.

Christopher, J. C., & Bickhard, M. H. (1994). The persistence of basic mistakes: Re-exploring psychopathology in individual psychology. *Journal of Individual Psychology, 50*, 223–231.

Collins, M. A., & Amabile, T. (1999). Motivation and creativity. In R. J. Sternberg (Ed.), *Handbook of creativity* (pp. 297–312). New York: Cambridge University Press.

Cummins, R. (1996). *Representations, targets, and attitudes*. Cambridge, MA: MIT Press.

Dretske, F. I. (1988). *Explaining behavior*. Cambridge, MA: MIT Press.

Ekman, P., & Davidson, R. J. (1994). *The nature of emotion*. Oxford: Oxford University Press.

Fodor, J. A. (1975). *The language of thought*. New York: Crowell.

Fodor, J. A. (1990). *A theory of content*. Cambridge, MA: MIT Press.

Fodor, J. A. (1991). Replies. In B. Loewer & G. Rey (Eds.), *Meaning in mind: Fodor and his critics* (pp. 255–319). Oxford: Blackwell.

Fodor, J. A. (1998). *Concepts: Where cognitive science went wrong*. Oxford: Oxford University Press.

Frijda, N. H. (1986). *The emotions*. Cambridge: Cambridge University Press.

Gill, M. L. (1989). *Aristotle on substance: The paradox of unity*. Princeton, NJ: Princeton University Press.

Griffiths, P. (1997). *What emotions really are: the problem of psychological categories*. Chicago: University of Chicago Press.

Griffiths, P. (1999). Author's response. *Metascience, 8*(1), 49–62.

Huggett, N. (2000). Philosophical foundations of quantum field theory. *British Journal for the Philosophy of Science, 51*(Supp.), 617–637.

Joas, H. (1993). American pragmatism and German thought: A history of misunderstandings. In H. Joas (Ed.), *Pragmatism and social theory* (pp. 94–121). Chicago: University of Chicago Press.

Kim, J. (1993). *Supervenience and mind*. Cambridge: Cambridge University Press.

Kuhn, T. (1970). *The structure of scientific revolutions* (2nd ed.). Chicago: University of Chicago Press.

Lazarus, R. S. (1991). *Emotion and adaptation*. Oxford: Oxford University Press.

Levine, A., & Bickhard, M. H. (1999). Concepts: Where Fodor went wrong. *Philosophical Psychology, 12*(1), 5–23.

Millikan, R. G. (1984). *Language, thought, and other biological categories*. Cambridge, MA: MIT Press.

Millikan, R. G. (1993). *White Queen psychology and other essays for Alice*. Cambridge, MA: MIT Press.

Mook, D. G. (1996). *Motivation: The organization of action* (2nd ed.). New York: W. W. Norton.

Oatley, K. (1992). *Best laid schemes: The psychology of emotions*. Cambridge: Cambridge University Press.

Piaget, J. (1954). *The construction of reality in the child*. New York: Basic Books.

Piaget, J. (1970). *Genetic epistemology*. New York: Columbia.

Weinberg, S. (1977). The Search for unity: Notes for a history of quantum field theory. *Daedalus*, *106*(4), 17–35.

Weinberg, S. (1995). *The quantum theory of fields. Vol. I. Foundations*. Cambridge: Cambridge University Press.

Weinberg, S. (1996). *The quantum theory of fields. Vol. II. Modern applications*. Cambridge: Cambridge University Press.

Weinberg, S. (2000). *The quantum theory of fields. Vol. III. Supersymmetry*. Cambridge: Cambridge University Press.

Development and Motivation, 57–84
BJEP Monograph Series II, 2
© 2003 The British Psychological Society

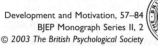

www.bps.org.uk

Interest and human development: An educational-psychological perspective

Andreas Krapp*

Universität Bundeswehr München (University of the Federal Armed Forces Munich), Neubiberg, Germany

Hardly any other research field in the domain of educational psychology has received so much attention in the past few years than motivation and its role in academic learning (Boekaerts, Pintrich, & Zeidner, 2000; Efklides, Kuhl, & Sorrentino, 2001; Sansone & Harackiewicz, 2000; Volet & Järvelä, 2001; Wigfield & Eccles, 2002). Similar to other fast-growing research fields, many new concepts and ideas have been developed that dominate the actual scientific discussion. However, it is questionable whether or not these new concepts have a significant impact on the educational discourse in everyday practice. By contrast, the traditional concept of interest holds a central position in educational thinking and acting. Educational laymen (e.g. parents) as well as professional educators (e.g. teachers, trainers) often use arguments with interest topics when they think about the motivational prerequisites for teaching and learning or about students' more or less successful development processes. Furthermore, educators agree that the differentiation and stabilization of interests relevant to learning are an important goal of education (H. Schiefele, 1978, 1981).

In view of the extraordinary importance of interest related argument patterns within the educational context, it is to be expected that the interest construct and theories about the development of interests and how they work is an important field of educational psychology. At the beginning of empirical scientific psychology in the late 19th century this was actually the case. Famous psychologists advocated that interests were the most important motivational factors in learning and development (Claparède, 1905; Dewey, 1913; Thorndike, 1935; for a summary, see Arnold, 1906; Berlyne, 1949; Prenzel, 1998). Later the interest concept was pushed into the background as first behaviourism, and later the shift towards cognitive approaches in psychology brought forth numerous new concepts related to motivated learning (H. Heckhausen, 1991;

*Requests for reprints should be addressed to Prof. Dr. Andreas Krapp, Universität der Bundeswehr München, Fakultät Sozialwissenschaften, Werner-Heisenberg-Weg 39, D-85577 Neubiberg, Germany (e-mail: andreas.krapp@unibw-muenchen.de).

Prenzel, 1988). As a result, the inclusive theories on interest have been excluded from scientific discussion in the field of educational-psychological research on learning and development.

It was only in the late 1970s that there was a re-awaking of interest research, when the realization prevailed in various areas of research that important aspects of learning motivation which are circumscribed in traditional thinking about interest cannot adequately be reconstructed with the theoretical concepts that have been most popular in modern (cognitive) motivation research. Without going into detail about the background and the course of scientific debates (see Krapp, 2000, 2002a; Prenzel, 1988), I would like to point out that researchers from psychology as well as educational science were involved in this development, and there was fruitful exchange from the beginning (Hoffmann, Krapp, Renninger, & Baumert, 1998; Lehrke, Hoffmann, & Gardner, 1985; Renninger, Hidi, & Krapp, 1992).

In the meantime, it may be asserted that interest research has become considerably more influential within educational psychology. Today the interest construct represents successfully applied theoretical concept in many areas of research (see Hidi, 1990; Hoffmann *et al.*, 1998; Krapp & Prenzel, 1992; Renninger *et al.*, 1992; Schiefele & Wild, 2000, for an overview). Recent educational psychology interest research has admittedly concentrated on studying the relationship between interest, learning and achievement (Baumert & Köller, 1998; Krapp, Hidi, & Renninger, 1992; Krapp & Prenzel, 1992; Prenzel, 1998, Renninger, 1998; Schiefele, 1999, 2001; Schiefele, Krapp, & Winteler, 1992). Developmental studies have been concerned with the description of the development of interests in the early years (elementary school, pre-school, e.g. Fink, 1991; Renninger, 1989, 1990) or the exploration of general developmental trends in certain student population with respect to certain school subjects or learning contents. Just as in other areas of motivation research, interest research has only touched on the reciprocal relationships of motivation and personality development from a life-span perspective. In psychological motivation research, there appears to be a kind of reversal of the trend (see Heckhausen, 2000). From my point of view, educational psychology should also be called upon to pay more attention to this field (e.g. Wigfield & Eccles, 2002).

The ideas presented here are in the tradition of a theoretical approach developed by Hans Schiefele and associates for an 'educational theory of interest' (H. Schiefele, Krapp, Prenzel, Heiland, & Kasten, 1983). It was supplemented and partially revised in certain subareas (see Krapp, 1992; Prenzel, 1988, 1992; U. Schiefele, 1991, 1996). Using the keywords *'person object theory'* I have attempted to summarize the current state of theory development and to specify statements derived from this theoretical conception (see Krapp, 1999a, 2000, 2002a).

In the following I first give an outline of the interest construct, from the perspective of a person object theory of interest (POI). The main part deals with the question of how interests develop. Here, both descriptive and explanatory aspects will be discussed. In the final section, I also present some considerations and hypothetical statements about the interrelations between interest and personality development.

The person–object approach to interest

Most researchers interpret interest as a more or less enduring specific relationship between a person and an object of his or her 'life-space' (Lewin, 1936). Interests are always directed towards a certain object. Content specificity is, thus, a main criterion of this concept. In this respect it differs considerably from the concept of *attitude* or the numerous concepts that operate under the term *motivational orientation*. There is, however, conceptual overlapping, as theories about motivational goals or self-efficacy now also recognize the idea of domain specificity (Bandura, 1997, 2001; Pintrich, 2000, 2003).

In conceptions of personality theory, a person's individual interests have the status of more or less lasting motivational dispositions, whereby the main interests especially reflect the components of the constantly changing 'self-system'. This at least is the view of the interest conception described below. An individual's actual pattern of interests is closely related to what in other theories are called *personal goals* (Sheldon & Elliot, 1998, see also Boekaerts, 2003), *personal strivings* (Emmons, 1991), content-specific *task-value beliefs* (Pintrich & Schunk, 1996), or motivational aspects of a person's *meaning system* (Dweck, 2003). Interests can be activated in specific teaching/learning situations and have then—in addition to other factors and personality structures important for motivation—an influence on the intensity and quality of the current learning motivation. It is not possible to delimit all of the variations of the interest concept that are currently to be found in scientific discussions completely from other motivational concepts. A sufficiently clear differentiation can be made only on the basis of an explicit theoretical model. In the 'person–object conception of interest' (POI) described here, an attempt was made to develop an interest theory which was explicitly oriented to the demands of educational practice and in this connection also offered a chance to reconstruct what happens motivationally from a development theory perspective.

Superordinate goals and theoretical statements

POI includes metatheoretical considerations about the domain of theoretical explanation and about an appropriate theoretical framework[1] that rightly deals with the general (theoretical and/or practical) goals of the theory. POI does not claim to be able to make a statement about all the facts that can be circumscribed by the everyday concept of interest. Its universe of discourse is limited to those phenomena that are directly or indirectly connected to learning and development. An important aspect is its usefulness for—or at least the compatibility with—the central problems discussed in the field of educational theory and practice.

A further aspect is *object specificity*. Since education is normative, an educator or teacher has to take into account which contents or objects are chosen for teaching and learning and what the long-term goals of development are to be. A theory of interest which takes educational demands into consideration should, thus, state how contextual preferences develop and what the conditions are for a learner to have a more or less lasting interest in certain subjects or contents and to be ambivalent about others or even develop an aversion. It is also important that the theory is open to this kind of question and offers psychological explanations for the processes and developments connected with it.

---

[1] *In POI, the terms 'framework' and 'frame conception' are used in a somewhat different way than in the context of certain metatheoretical discussions (e.g. Fodor, 1983, 2000). Although a theoretical framework or frame-conception is understood as the ensemble of overarching and more general statements of the theory, such as the ultimate theoretical and practical goals, it does not necessarily imply that every theoretical statement must be in congruence with the statements in the frame concept.*

Theoretical frame conception

Every theory is based on a commitment to a certain research paradigm and a theoretical frame conception corresponding to this paradigm. The practice of researchers is such that these decisions are very seldom made explicitly. Often the followers of a certain theory do not think about it because they simply attach themselves to it without metatheoretical reflection of a currently generally accepted way of thinking or theory. Since the so-called cognitive shift in psychology, concepts and theories predominate in educational-psychological motivation research that are based on a cognitive oriented action-theoretical frame, mostly concretized in some form (or aspect) of the general expectancy-value model. (see Eccles, 1983; Pintrich & Schunk, 1996). Theories derived from cognitive models have shortcomings with respect to their educational use, and these shortcomings are an even more important problem when describing and explaining the role of motivational factors in the course of human development during the life span. For example, action-theoretical approaches do not provide adequate concepts and models for describing the dynamic structure of personality or important developmental aspects, such as identity formation and the related ongoing changes in the self-system of the growing personality. Furthermore, they have to struggle with the problem of how to take emotional experiences into account, or how to consider processes that appear to have an effect mainly at a subconscious level of action control. We have, therefore, chosen a theoretical frame which tries to reconstruct motivational structures and processes from a more general system-oriented ('systemic') perspective. Referring to early conceptions of motivation and interest from Dewey (1913), Kerschensteiner (1922), and others, who emphasized that interest should be interpreted not only as a characteristic of a person, but as a specific 'relationship' between the person and the object of his or her interest, our approach is also theoretically based on a person–object conception. The special quality of the relationship between person and object should be made at the beginning of the theoretical explication of the interest construct. Thus, at the first definition level, an interest can be characterized as a specific *'person–object relationship'* (PO relationship).

In accordance with the ideas of Lewin (1936), Nuttin (1984), Deci and Ryan (1985, 1991) and many others, it is postulated that the individual, as a potential source of action, and the environment as the object of action, are constituted by a bipolar relation.[2] Consequently, the interest construct is conceptualized as a relational concept: an interest represents a more or less enduring specific relationship between a person and an object in his or her 'life-space' (Lewin, 1936).

Objects of interest

As a result of the ongoing interactions between person and environment, it is assumed that the person builds up a representation system that consists of cognitive and non-cognitive entities or components. It is further assumed that an individual experiences and represents his or her environment in a meaningful structure. The cognitively represented environment consists of units that are separated from one another to a greater or lesser extent. POI refers to these units as 'objects'. Under certain conditions, which will be spoken of later, every cognitively represented area of the environment can become the object of interest. It is important to point out that the POI uses a

---

[2] *Mark Bickhard (2003) provides a much more differentiated and rather rigorous theoretical position ('interactivism') that is in some respect also based on this core idea.*

relatively broad concept of object: an object of interest can refer to concrete things, a topic, subject matter, an abstract idea, or any other content of the cognitively represented 'life-space' (Lewin, 1936). Smith (2002a, 2002b) has pointed out that Piaget's epistemic model, especially his concept of developmental levels, provides an appropriate theoretical reconstruction of the sequence from actual to abstract objects. The advance from concrete to abstract is neither easy nor straightforward during the development of the child. It must be noted that the person himself or herself also represents an area of the real world, and thus able to refer an interest to facts which concern one's own person (e.g. expansion and critical reflection of self-perception in therapy).

The object of interest is represented in the person's mental system as a subjective construct. This, however, does not necessarily imply that the object of interest will be represented idiosyncratically. Perceptions of an object and object-related evaluations are influenced by the social context, i.e. by socially shared thoughts and norms (Valsiner, 1992). Thus, object-related knowledge is to some extent shared, exhibiting a certain degree of objectivity in the sense that an inter-subjective consensus can be found with regard to its meaning and can provide a basis for social communication about it.

In the course of development during a lifetime, the structure and the dynamics of interests change due to factors that will be studied more closely later. Furthermore, it must be realized that the functional property of a certain interest is determined not only by the specific qualities of the person–object relationship in question but also by how this interest is embedded in the entire spectrum of interests that are represented in specific structures of the memory system ('self-system'; see below).

Two levels of analysis

Conceptualizing interest as an interactive relation between an individual and certain aspects of his/her life-space makes it possible to study the conditions for or and effects of, interest from various research perspectives as well as from different analytic levels.

At the *first level*, research is concerned with the processes and states that are relevant during concrete interactions between a person and his or her object of interest. In this case, the analysis focuses on the description and explanation of interest-triggered actions. The realization of an interest requires a situation-specific interaction between the person and the object. The term *object engagement* is used to indicate such an interaction at the most general level (Prenzel, 1988, 1992). An interest-related motivational state or process has usually been characterized as intrinsic, and the experience of realizing a personal interest is often equated with intrinsic motivation (see, for example, the various chapters in Sansone and Harackiewicz, 2000 and Deci and Ryan, 2002).[3]

On a *second level*, interest refers to the dispositional (or 'habitual') structure of an individual. Here, interest is interpreted as a relatively stable tendency to occupy oneself with an object of interest. It is seen as a more or less lasting motivational characteristic of the person. In accordance with other interest researchers (e.g. Renninger, 1990, 1992, 2000) the concept '*individual interest*' is used to signify this level of conceptualization.

---

[3] *Nevertheless, the theoretical relation between these two concepts is far from being clear (see, for example, Hidi, 2000; Krapp, 1999b; Murphy & Alexander, 2000; Pintrich & Schunk, 1996; Renninger, 2000; Schiefele, 1996).*

I think it is very important to make a clear distinction between these two levels of analysis because they refer to rather different research paradigms, including different directions of research questions, methodological approaches and practical implications. At the first analytic level, research is concerned with processes and functional relationships that, in principle, hold true for every individual. This is the classical approach of general (experimental) psychology. The second analytic level interprets psychological phenomena such as motivation from the perspective of personality psychology. In this tradition of psychological theorizing, processes have become substances (see Bickhard, 2003) in the sense of more less stable personality structures such as 'traits' or 'orientations'. Research that is based on the paradigm of 'differential psychology' (Anastasi, 1958; Asendorpf, 1991) is first of all interested in measuring individual characteristics on the basis of existing (stable) differences between individuals and in describing and 'explaining' the emergence and effects of these differences including the prediction of future differences in practically relevant aspects of behaviour (e.g. academic achievement). Most research in this tradition is 'correlational', that is to say that empirical relations are explored by statistical techniques that allow for an estimation of 'explained' variance. Although there has been long-standing discussion about these 'two disciplines of scientific psychology' (Cronbach, 1957, 1975) and a shared belief among psychological researchers, many authors in our domain seem not to be aware of the metatheoretical and methodological problems that derive from this distinction. In reviews about the role of motivational factors (e.g. goal orientation; Elliott & Dweck, 1988; Pintrich, 2000) in teaching and learning, it is rather common to refer to both experimental and correlational findings. The only difference between the kind of information gained with these methods that is regularly mentioned is the problem of presumed ecological validity. In this respect, findings from correlational studies which are often (incorrectly) equated with 'field studies' are rated higher than results from experimental studies and therefore are interpreted as more relevant for educational practice. The much more severe and far-reaching problem—that the results eventually represent totally different information which cannot be directly compared—is hardly ever discussed.[4]

The attempt to draw a clear distinction between dispositional and situational (process-oriented) theories and research strategies in the field of motivation is certainly not new. It can be easily traced back to well-known theories of achievement motivation (Atkinson, 1964; Atkinson & Raynor, 1974, 1978; see also H. Heckhausen, 1991) but the core idea and the related scientific problems have already been discussed in the earliest psychological theories on personality and motivation (e.g. Allport, 1937; Dewey, 1913; Stern, 1918).

From a development theory perspective, both levels of analysis are important. At the first level, the processes primarily studied are those responsible for the dynamics of the developmental course, whereby it is attempted, for instance, to identify the formation of new interests or the changes in already existing ones. At the second level of analysis, interest research deals with the 'crystallized' results or effects of the developmental processes. Here it is a matter of analysing ontogenetic developmental processes by means of intra-individual or inter-individual comparative studies over time as well as the identification of influential factors responsible for these developmental processes.

---

[4] *A related problem refers to the question what kind of information we get in developmental research approaches that use measures of motivational dispositions and explore developmental trajectories on the basis of correlational techniques (Valsiner, 1986).*

Characteristics of an interest-specific person–object relationship

Interpreting interest as a content-specific concept fits well with modern theories on knowledge acquisition and instruction in so far as knowledge is always structured and acquired in particular domains. In addition, formal criteria have to be taken into consideration. They refer to cognitive aspects, emotional and value-related components of interest-based activities (see Krapp, 2002a, for a more detailed discussion).

It is assumed that an interest develops and the structural components change with respect to both cognitive and emotional representations. Thus, a well-developed interest differs from an interest at its earlier stages. There is ample empirical evidence for the assumption that a person's cognitive structure related to the knowledge domain of an established individual interest is highly differentiated and shows many connections to other cognitive domains (Krapp, 1992; Renninger, 1990, 2000). Furthermore, an interest is closely connected with cognitive processes of change. A person who is interested in a certain subject area is not content with his or her current level of knowledge or abilities in that interest domain. Rather, there is a high readiness to acquire new information, to assume new knowledge, and to enlarge the competencies related to this domain. But there is also a high readiness for activating (using) interest-related competencies in situations that do not require new learning. Based on Piaget's (1985) notion that interest is aimed both at expanding knowledge and skills (accommodation) and at applying existing knowledge and skills in new situations (assimilation), one could interpret an interest-based activity as a combination of two closely interrelated processes. One is primarily concerned with the acquirement of new interest-related knowledge and competencies (e.g. phases of deliberate intentional learning in school); the other is primarily concerned with the enrichment of the 'treasure trove' of interest-based experiences, for example when realizing an interest in well-known situations without an explicit intention to enlarge the existing pattern knowledge and competencies. Nevertheless, it is possible that the individual learns something new without being aware of the occurrence of cognitive growth.[5] In both cases, the person must have a metacognitive knowledge about things he or she does not know yet and situations that provide an opportunity to apply his or her actual interests. Thus, POI assumes that the knowledge structure concerning the object domain of an individual interest also contains more or less differentiated knowledge about future opportunities for learning and development (Prenzel, 1988). At the same time, the trend to further develop and improve the pattern of interest-related competencies is an essential indicator for the current dynamics and liveliness of a certain interest.

A central criterion of the interest construct is the close combination of value-oriented and emotional components. POI assumes that a person shows a high subjective esteem for the objects and actions in his or her areas of interest. These have the quality of *personal significance*. In accordance with earlier as well as more recent theories, POI assumes that the person's individual interests are closely related to his or her self-system (see Deci & Ryan, 1985; Fend, 1991, 1994; Hannover, 1997, 1998; Kuhl, 2000, 2001; Sheldon & Elliot, 1998). From such a theoretical perspective, positive evaluation results from the degree of identification with the object of interest. In POI, the value component of an interest is also referred to by using the concept of '*self-intentionality*' to make it clear that the goals and volitionally realized intentions related to the object

---

[5] *There is a growing body of research in different fields of psychology that is concerned with this kind of implicit learning (e.g. Lewicki, Hill & Czyzemska, 1992; Reber, 1989; Sun, 2002).*

area of an interest are compatible with the attitudes, expectations, values and other aspects of the self-system.

The global characterization that an interest-based action is accompanied by mostly positive *emotional experiences* has to be specified with respect to qualitative criteria. Considering models and empirical results from other fields of psychological research, it has been suggested that tension, in the sense of an optimal level of arousal and feelings of enjoyment, involvement and stimulation, is the most typical emotional aspect of an interest-based activity (Prenzel, 1988; U. Schiefele, 1991). Referring to 'Self-Determination Theory' (SDT; Deci & Ryan, 1985, 2002; Ryan, 1995), I have proposed considering emotional experiences that are related to the 'basic needs' for competence, autonomy and social relatedness in order to characterize interest-specific emotional experiences (Krapp, 1998, 1999a, 2002a). Under extremely congenial conditions, flow may be experienced (Csikszentmihalyi, 1990; Csikszentmihalyi & Csikszentmihalyi, 1988). In a person's cognitive-emotional representation system, experiences that precede, accompany or follow an interest-triggered activity are stored in their specific quality for a longer period of time and can to some degree be remembered as positive 'feeling-related valences' (U. Schiefele, 1992, 1996). But one has also take into account that important and rather influential components of these representation are not accessible to our conscious-cognitive information-processing system.

The assumption that an interest is characterized by optimal experiential modes with respect to personal involvement and emotional feedback during a sequence of interest-based activities is quite close to the concept of 'undivided interest' or 'serious play' which is used by Rathunde (1993, 1998) and Rathunde and Csikszentmihalyi (1993) to describe an optimal mode of task engagement. John Dewey (1913) had already used the notion of interest as an 'undivided activity' in which no contradiction is experienced between the assessment of personal importance of an action and positive emotional evaluations of the activity itself. There is no gap between what a person has to do in a specific situation, and what the person wants (or likes) to do.

Interest development from an ontogenetic perspective

An ontogenetic theory of interest development—like every other theory—has to be both *descriptive* and *explanatory*. On the one hand, it has to provide concepts, models and results that can be used to describe individual and/or general developmental changes with respect to both the whole pattern of individual interests and the course of development of a particular interest. On the other hand, it has to provide explanations, including theoretical statements about factors that can explain and predict inter- and intra-individual differences as well as statements about functional dependencies with regard to developmental processes.

Typical empirical results and theoretical models to describe ontogenetic aspects of interest development

At first glance, the description of ontogenetic changes is apparently easily made, and there are empirical approaches that attempt to master the scientific processing of these tasks with relatively simple means, e.g. by longitudinal survey studies. But from these findings, one cannot directly draw conclusions about psychological regularities and principles that characterize interest development at the level of intra-individual changes. This second type of question has been investigated much less.

Exploration of general developmental trends in populations

In cross-sectional and longitudinal studies with students at different grade levels, general developmental trends in a student population have been explored. Although there are some serious methodological problems (e.g. the changing content in a certain scholastic or academic subject area which does not allow exactly the same instruments to be used over many years) the empirical results from various research approaches provide a rather consistent and differentiated picture (Gardner, 1985, 1998). For example, the results clearly seem to show that the average interest in any subject tends to decrease—especially in secondary school (Baumert & Köller, 1998; Gardner, 1985, 1998; Prenzel, 1998; Todt & Schreiber, 1998). This is in accord with results in other areas of research, which also found that as children get older, their task-value beliefs or attitudes toward school in general and toward specific subject areas tend to deteriorate (Anderman & Maehr, 1994; Eccles & Wigfield, 1992; Hidi & Harackiewicz, 2001; Lepper & Henderlong, 2000).

Several studies have tried to differentiate the developmental trajectories according to gender, school type, a subject's topic areas or context conditions. Here, considerable differences and sometimes even contrary trends can be found. In a longitudinal study about the development of physics interest in 5th- to 10th-grade students (Hoffmann, Lehrke, & Todt, 1985; Hoffmann, Häusler, & Lehrke, 1998), various areas of physics (e.g. optics, mechanics or radioactivity) were taken into consideration, as well as contexts within which each of the physics themes were taught in class (e.g. in the context of scientific argumentation: proving the validity of a scientific hypothesis, or in the context of practically important problem solutions which require basic knowledge in physics). When analysing the general (global) developmental trajectories, again a continually negative trend can be found, especially with girls. However, very different development trends can be observed when the analysis is broken down into certain topic areas and/or contexts. In lessons where physics is primarily taught as a scientific endeavour (proving the validity of a general physical laws), neither girls nor boys judge the contents of this subject as being very attractive. However, both genders show a very strong interest when the contents of the lessons and the way physics is taught can be related to their own world of experience. Girls react especially sensitively to contextual integration. This type of differential effect can also be observed in other subjects, e.g. sociology/political science (Todt & Schreiber, 1998).

In scientific discussions of the theoretical and practical conclusions from these results, it is often forgotten that data gained from survey studies do not allow direct statements about intra-individual developmental trends. It is not justifiable, in principle, to draw conclusions from population data about 'general laws' that can be used to describe and explain developmental processes at the intra-individual level. Even the estimation of the likelihood for the occurrence of a certain phenomenon with respect to an individual case cannot be derived directly from population data. Even though this problem is generally known, neither educational nor developmental psychology plays consequential attention to it. For example, Valsiner (1986) has demonstrated that misinterpretations are not unusual—even in the leading journals in the area of developmental psychology.

Descriptive and explanatory analyses of interest development from an intra-individual perspective
The fact that group-related results allow no reliable conclusions about the direction and principles of interest development in the individual case can be demonstrated by research approaches that explore interest development in a certain field with the same group of subjects, both at the level of group-specific developmental trajectories and at the level of intra-individual changes. In a longitudinal study on the development of job-related interests during a 2-year vocational training of insurance salespeople, we used both of these methodological approaches in order to analyse the interest development of both analysis perspectives and compare them with each other (Krapp & Lewalter, 2001; Lewalter, Krapp, Schreyer, & Wild, 1998). In this research project, we studied the interest development process in two ways: first, by means of descriptive analyses of the average level of interest in the entire sample ($N = 117$) using questionnaire data; second, on the basis of individual reconstructions of specific job-related interests using data from retrospective interviews at the end of the first and of the second year of vocational training in a smaller group of randomly selected subjects from the entire sample ($N = 49$ in the first year; $N = 71$ in the second year). The descriptive analyses in the entire sample ended with the same negative picture found in other longitudinal studies: interest decreases especially clearly during the first year of training. The intra-individual analyses, however, deliver a rather different picture. Here we find a marked positive developmental trend: in both the first and the second year of apprenticeship, all subjects report—without exception—that they had discovered new areas of interest during the past year of vocational education. Thus, their profile of job-related interests showed a general increase.

It might be argued that these two different results are an artefact. But what I want to show here is that results from a 'differential' research approach based on group data give no correct answer or estimate about the likelihood of developmental trends at the level of intra-individual changes. The two differing statements about the direction of interest development during the time period of this project involve rather different aspects of interest development. In the first case, it is a matter of describing (and explaining) general developmental trajectories in populations, whereby the object of interest is defined by all of the contents, activities and events in vocational training. In the second case, the focus is on indicators for the emergence of new contents or topics in the structure of a subject's pattern of (training-related) interests that provide a basis for the description of intra-individual changes. Thus, without claiming sufficient validity of the results gained with retrospective interviews, this example can demonstrate that it is very problematic to compare and evaluate empirical results about developmental trajectories without ensuring that the different research approaches really measure the same concepts and refer to the same kind of theoretical questions.

Empirical approaches that explore conditions and effects of interest development at the level of detailed intra-individual processes are rare, since it takes a great amount of effort to gain valid data during concrete interest-related activities over a longer period of time. Several research groups in Germany in the field of physics education have attempted to analyse the continuous interrelations between student's situation-specific individual experiences, cognitive processes and the occurrence and stabilization of content-specific interests. Their research approach focuses on the learning processes of students during a longer period of time. The interactions in a small group are video-documented, and the ongoing learning process is being reconstructed on the basis of observations and thinking-aloud protocols using a fine-grained interpretation system. In a further step, the results of these process analyses are related to data from questionnaires measuring different aspects of motivation and learning outcome (e.g. Fischer & Horstendahl, 1997; Schick, 2000a; von Aufschnaiter, 1999; von Aufschnaiter, Schoster, & von Aufschnaiter, 1999). Among the studies that attempt to explore gender-related developmental processes over a longer period of the life span are those of Gisbert (1995, 2001). Using both quantitative data from an extensive longitudinal study on educational careers of German students and qualitative data (retrospective interviews with single cases), she tried to reconstruct women's individual courses of interest development from childhood to mid-adulthood and to identify those conditions and experiences that—from a subjective point of view—had an influence on the emergence and further development of the women's typical and 'atypical' interests (e.g. mathematics).

Interest development as structural change

When interest development is studied at the level of processes that refer to intra-individual changes over time, it is almost mandatory to take the structural texture of a person's spectrum of interest into consideration. Traditional methods of measuring interest on the basis of standardized interest-scales do not supply adequate information. The primary aim of these tests is to measure those aspects of behaviour that allow a reliable and valid differentiation between people and not so much to identify characteristics that allow a differentiation between the behaviour of a person in different situations or at different stages of development.

Only a few research approaches have tried to explore the course of interest development with respect to structural changes of an individual's pattern of interests over a longer period of time. Using POI as a theoretical background, Kasten and Krapp (1986) conducted a longitudinal study to explore early stages of interest development in pre-school and elementary-school children. A broad variety of data were collected continuously over a 5-year period from a small group of children ($N = 12$), starting with their entry in pre-school (e.g. observations, interviews with the children and their parents and kindergarten). A central aim of this study involving several case studies was to develop methodical tools and theoretical concepts for analysing structural changes from an intra-individual research perspective (see Fink, 1991, Krapp & Fink, 1992). Without going into the details of the procedure we used to reconstruct an individual's pattern of interests at a certain point of time, Fig. 1 demonstrates in a prototypical way the kind of information we gained from these structural analysis.

Figure 1 shows the result of our reconstructions for one child over four measuring points (t1–t4). The components of the central interest objects show that this child has a high preference for everything that has to do with animals, and she likes to be read to. In this case, as well as in most others, we found a rather high stability of the main components in a child's pattern of interests. The picture, however, changes when we go into detail and try to reconstruct the themes, activities and topics on a more concrete level. Here, we find a number of changes during the different stages indicated by the reconstructions at time points 1–4.

Reconstructions of the course of development found in particular cases of kindergarten children lead to the specification of *hypothetical developmental models* that offer an indication of how the occurrence and growth of an individual interest can be interpreted as specific kinds of structural changes in a person's already existing pattern of interest-related PO relationships. Fink (1991) has set out to differentiate between typical developmental models such as the growth model or the channelling

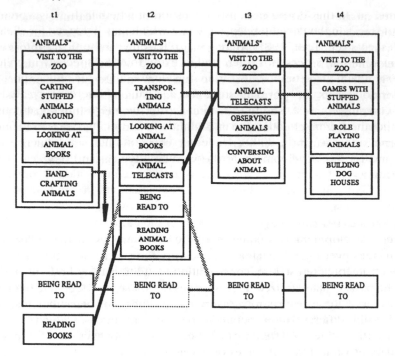

Figure I. Reconstruction of structural changes in an individual's pattern of interest over time (from Fink, 1991, p 194)

model (see also Krapp, 2002b). The '*growth model*' describes the way we tend to think about the normal pattern of interest development: the successive steps of structural reorganization of a certain PO relationship are directed towards increased differentiation. The '*channelling model*' represents a course of development that is usually found in individuals with a high degree of specialization: according to this model, the structural reorganization of a growing interest occurs through increased differentiation of one particular aspect of an already existing PO relationship. This component comes to assume central importance, while other parts are excluded. Channelling of interest may also occur with respect to a person's total pattern of interest. Interest development in adolescence quite often follows this pattern. In professional life, focusing on personal interests in a few fields is often an important prerequisite for acquiring superior skills and producing exceptional achievements in a certain field of work.

Although, the description of intra-individual courses of development in view of the changes of content-related and structural components is an important aspect of an ontogenetic theory of interest, it has found too little recognition in recent research.

Stages of interest development
Independently of whether one views the development of an individual topic-specific interest or the changes in a person's whole field of interests, one can ask whether it is possible (or theoretically appropriate) to describe the course of interest development on the basis of a concept that postulates typical stages of development. In the area of interest research, there are two lines of discussion for this question. In the first case, it is a question of the developmental sequence from the first occurrence of a situational interest, which is brought to the individual from the outside, to a longer-lasting

individual interest. In the second case, it is a question of whether there is a predictable succession of stages in the development of interest which may hold true for all children and/or adolescents (eg. Todt, 1985). Here I will refer only to the first approach.

In the course of life, a person is interested in many things. Especially in childhood, many interests which are often induced from outside are 'alive' for only a short period of time. In school, for example, it is assumed that a situational interest is created by the interesting 'composition' of a teaching situation and/or the interesting presentation of a lesson and that this interest will hold over the period of teaching this specific interest-related subject or topic (Hidi, 2000). Under certain conditions, a longer-lasting PO relationship which meets the criteria for a personal interest can grow out of such a situational interest. This process, however, is usually a multi-stage process which cannot be sufficiently described by the two concepts situational and individual interest. In fact, we must consider a developmental continuum between the very beginning of a situational interest, a state which might be close to the experience of curiosity, on the one hand, and a stabilized interest of an adult who has totally identified with the related object of interest, on the other hand.

Such a multi-stage model would have to differentiate at least among three kinds or levels of interest, which—from a ontogenetic perspective—represent three proto-typical stages of interest development (Krapp, 1998): (1) a situational interest awakened or triggered by external stimuli for the first time, (2) a 'stabilized situational interest' that lasts during a certain learning phase, and (3) an individual interest that represents a relatively enduring predisposition to engage a certain object-area of interest because the person has identified himself or herself with the object of interest. The first occurrence of a situational interest is primarily a matter of 'actual-genetic' processes.[6] From an ontogenetic perspective, the next two levels of interest development are of central importance. They include two qualitatively different *steps of interest development* (Krapp, 1998, 2002b): first, the shift from the transitional state of actual attraction or curiosity to a more stable motivational state which is a necessary condition for effective learning, and second, the shift from a rather stabilized situational interest to a more or less enduring individual interest (see also Renninger, 2000; Renninger & Hidi, 2002).

All three stages are important for educational action. At the first stage, it is important that the teacher succeeds in making as many students as possible curious and in creating a willingness to learn when working with new material. With respect to learning and teaching, the second level of interest development is the most important one, because—from a motivation point of view—(interest-based) learning will occur only when a sufficiently stable situational interest has been established. The third level is of central importance when we take the ultimate aims of education into account, namely to support an individual's course of personality development and identity formation. According to POI, this also depends on motivational factors, including the contents and the structure of an individual's personal interests. The development of one's own structure of interests according to one's own abilities, personal values and life-goals is a typical developmental task during adolescence and, thus, one of the most important general goals of education (H. Schiefele, 1978). And this problem remains to be solved at later stages of the life course as well.

---

[6] *In earlier theories of developmental and general psychology, the term 'actual genetic' was used to notify the situation-specific processes and changes of behaviour (including perception and problem-solving) which are not identical with ontogenetic processes but might be the starting point of an ontogenetic developmental process.*

Concepts and considerations for explaining educationally relevant aspects of interest development

In this section, I present some ideas about the kind of ontogenetically imported facts that an educational-psychological interest theory should inform about and how the theoretical concepts and models could be advanced by taking recent research approaches/theories from neighbouring areas of psychology into consideration. In doing so, I will discuss three questions in more detail:

(1)   Where are the ontogenetic sources of the development to be found?
(2)   How are new interests generated, and what kind of psychological mechanisms are responsible for stabilizing an interest?
(3)   What role do individual interests play in lifelong learning and in personality development?

The origins of interest development

Completely developed interests are possible only at a certain level of development as it sees the ability to plan action as a prerequisite. However, the origins of interest are probably laid much earlier. Concurring with many development and personality theories, I believe that humans by nature tend to deal proactively with their life space themselves and that the processes necessary for acquiring knowledge and for increasing competence are experienced most directly as enjoyable and subjectively satisfactory (see also research on curiosity and exploration). Just as in Self-Determination Theory (SDT), posited by Deci and Ryan (1985, 2002), it is assumed that human beings are active by nature, and this 'intrinsic proactivity' can be found from earliest childhood onwards. Children are curious, explore their surroundings, manipulate things, try to affect the objects in their social and physical environment, and through these activities elaborate their own sense of self (Krapp, 2002a).

In early childhood, children are almost only concerned about phenomena and objects they find 'interesting' at that moment. At the same time, clear preferences for certain kinds of stimuli and/or opportunities for activity are recognizable relatively early (for a related discussion, see Donaldson, 1992). According to Renninger (1990, 2000), stable preferences for playing certain games or interacting with certain objects have crystallized by kindergarten age at the latest.

An interesting psychological question, which—as far as I know—has hardly been a topic of educational-psychological motivation research, concerns the origins of, and the conditions for, the formation of these early preference structures. Taking psycho-biological research into account, it seems reasonable to assume that individuals differ rather early with respect to 'sensibilities' for certain classes of environmental stimulation in addition to environmental stimuli. On the whole, the conclusion appears to be justified that one has to anticipate the development of relatively stable individual preferences and idiosyncrasies at a very early stage of development. These are not consciously perceived for the most part and, therefore, exercise considerable influence on the later phases of interest development. One can, for example, imagine that a child with an increased sensibility for notes and acoustic stimuli develops quite early definite preferences which the environment interprets as 'musically talented' and more or less systematically encourages in voluntarily exercised person–environment confrontations. In such a case, it is most probable that a lasting interest in music will develop.

Yet one must avoid suggesting that interest development as a quasi-linear process manifest at the outset in the development of early childhood preferences for objects—

with corresponding stimulus and encouragement from the environment—must necessarily lead to a certain type of content in the interests. Completely different topic-related interests can result from the same basal preference structure. However, this model leaves unclear how a new interest, whose contents or object cannot be interpreted by differentiating or continuing an already existing preference or interest, comes to develop.

The ontogenetic transition from situational to individual interest
The previous section discussed interest development (intra-individual) being described in the form of a heuristic stage model which can lead from an externally induced situational interest to a more or less lasting individual interest. From an ontogenetic perspective, it must be clarified how an individual interest comes to develop. What kind of psychological conditions and processes are responsible for the shift from a situational to an individual interest? Fig. 2 shows the ontogenetic transition from situational to individual interest.

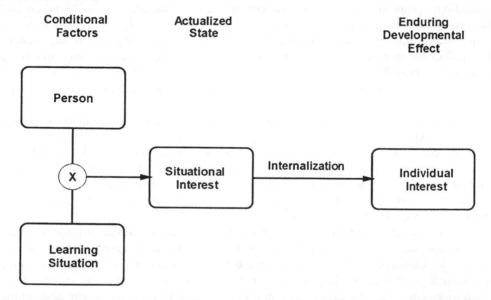

Figure 2. The ontogenetic transition from situational to individual interest (Krapp, 1998, p. 191).

In my opinion, the course of the formation of interest can be adequately explained psychologically only when one tries to understand the fundamental control process from a systemic viewpoint. It does not suffice to identify the conditional factors—that is, those factors which are intrinsic to that individual's mental system—with whose help inter-individual variance in characteristics can be statistically explained. In addition, one has to attempt to identify the functional processes in learning and development.

In POI, some theoretical considerations were developed which still need to be supplemented. On the one hand, they refer to the explanation for '*selective persistence*' (Prenzel, 1988, 1992) which is a prerequisite for continual interest action. On the other hand, it is a matter of the role of current and previous individual interests in a person's *self-system* and the influences on the development of personality that can possibly be derived from it.

An approach to explain how selective persistence comes about: The concept of a dual regulation system
The first approach concerns the problem of stabilizing an interest for a longer period, as this is an important prerequisite for maintaining a situational interest stimulated externally and the emergence of a genuine individual interest controlled from within. How can it be explained that the learner directs his or her actions selectively and steadily towards a certain object area and even holds on to it when difficulties and problems arise. Prenzel (1988, 1992) speaks of selective persistence in this connection. When an explanation is sought at the level of psychological functional principles, it seem necessary to postulate a rather complex control system which includes both conscious cognitive processes of intention formation and volitional intentional realization as well as emotional (affect-related) processes, which work partly on a preconscious or subconscious level.

With respect to the development of interests I have hypothesized that the maintenance of an existing PO relationship is directed by *two functional systems* which in principle act independently of each other (see Krapp, 2000, 2002a). According to this hypothesis, two kinds of determining factors have to be taken into account: first, cognitively represented factors, especially with respect to personal values, goals and volitionally derived intentions; second, feeling-related experiences during the ongoing actions which are connected to the object area of an individual's interest. POI postulates that longer-lasting interest development will occur only if both factors are experienced together in a positive way; more specifically, if a person experiences his or her actual engagements (e.g. a learning task) as personally relevant or 'meaningful' because they are related to personal goals, and if the emotion-related (affective) experiences during these engagements reach a certain qualitative level of positive feedback. The basic principle of this idea is not new. In the tradition of Dewey's conceptualization of the developing person, such a 'cognitive-affective' synthesis has been postulated repeatedly as a central condition of the emergence of a 'lasting' or 'abiding interest' (e.g. Dewey, 1913; Rathunde, 1998; Rathunde & Csikszentmihalyi, 1993).

I believe that traditional cognitive approaches to human motivation provide a variety of important and useful conceptual models that refer to the cognitive aspects within this dual regulation system. What is missing, however, are (empirically tested) concepts and models that refer to the emotional components. POI sets out to specify those emotional experiences that play a function in interest development, on the basis of the concept of *basic psychological needs*. According to Nuttin's (1984) relational theory of behavioural dynamics and the theory of self-determination (SDT; Deci, 1998, Deci & Ryan, 1985, 1991; Ryan, 1995), it is assumed that living organisms are naturally endowed with a system of primary, innate basic biological and psychological needs. During ontogenesis, these needs become more and more integrated into the increasingly complex systems of behaviour control.

Based on SDT (Deci 1998; Deci & Ryan, 1985, 1991, 2002), three qualitatively different needs can be distinguished within this system: competence, self-determination and social relatedness. Just as the fulfilment of basic biological needs is a natural necessity, sufficient fulfilment of the three psychological needs is a necessary requirement for optimal functioning of the psychological system (Deci & Ryan, 1985; Nuttin, 1984; Ryan, 1995).

The system of basic psychological needs has to be understood as a holistically working system that provides continual signals about the functional effectivity of the current person–environment interactions. With respect to interest development, the need-related qualities of experience are important because they provide permanent, emotional feedback on the micro-level of behaviour regulation, thus contributing to the emergence of object-related preferences or aversions. It is postulated that a person will engage continuously in a certain area of tasks or topic-related objects only if he or she assesses these engagements, on the basis of rational considerations, as sufficiently important, and if he or she experiences the course of interactions on the whole as positive and emotionally satisfactory (Krapp, 1999a, 2002a; see also Deci, 1992, 1998).

The assumption that human behaviour, and thus motivation, is directed by a complex system of influence factors which are found at various levels of consciousness and act in part independently from each other has been stated in many psychological theories. Freud was probably the most prominent representative of this belief. His psychodynamic theory, however, was too speculative, and behaviourists as well as cognitive researchers rejected his multi-level theory as being unscientific and vulnerable from different perspectives. Piaget (1978), for example, has criticized the often-drawn inference that cognition is a conscious process and therefore can be deliberately controlled by the individual (Ferrari, Pinard, & Runions, 2001). That the interrelation between cognition, consciousness and control is much more complicated has been a point of discussion ever since (see Perrig & Grob, 2000). In the mean time, the trend has changed direction partly due to the influence of new research findings, e.g. in neuropsychology (see LeDoux, 1995). A growing number of psychological theories and research programmes now refer to the idea of a multi-level steering system which can be concretized in more or less obvious dichotomies such as explicit vs. implicit learning (Anderson, 1993; Reber, 1989; Sun, 2002), rational vs. experiential conceptual system (Epstein, 1990) or conscious vs. unconscious procession (Jacoby, Toth, Yonelinas, & Deubner, 1994). Until recently, these discussions have hardly been recognized in the field of educational-psychological research, although a small group of researchers have proposed similar ideas with respect to motivation (e.g. Kuhl, 2000, 2001; McClelland, Koestner & Weinberger, 1989; Spangler & Zimmermann, 1999) and self-regulated learning (e.g. Boekaerts, 1999, 2001, 2003). The growing body of empirical results presented in these research approaches appears to confirm the idea that human experience and behaviour are directed by two regulation systems and that these systems are based on different psychological function principles.

This strengthens our belief that the theoretical idea of a *dual regulation system* should be followed up and investigated in empirical studies with respect not only to the development of interests but also to the development of other educationally relevant motivational categories. When speaking of how need-related emotional experiences function, there are a number of empirical results that corroborate the theoretical assumptions. Studies have been carried out, for example, with students and young adults in vocational settings (Krapp & Lewalter, 2001; Prenzel, Kramer, & Drechsel, 1998) and in the domain of physics education (e.g., Schick, 2000a, 2000b; von Aufschnaiter, 1999; von Aufschnaiter *et al.*, 1999). In our research group, we are currently studying the conditions and processes of interest development in the context of vocational education on the basis of longitudinal studies (Krapp & Lewalter, 2001; Lewalter *et al.*, 1998; Wild, Krapp, Schreyer, & Lewalter, 1998). Here, the mechanisms of need-related qualities of experience are studied by using both quantitative and qualitative methods. The quantitative analyses are based on data from questionnaires and the Experience Sampling Method. The qualitative analyses are based on retrospective interviews with a smaller number of randomly chosen subjects from the main study. Although the results from different research approaches differ in several aspects, they seem to support the overall hypothesis that the quality of emotional experiences has an influence on the emergence and stabilization of epistemic interests, induced in an educational setting.

There are still many unanswered questions which desperately require clarification. I am sure that basic research in different fields of modern psychology can supply valuable evidence for continuing and specifying specific explanatory hypothesis. For example, Kuhl (2000, 2001) recently developed a *'Theory of Personality Systems Interactions'* (PSI theory), where he formulated very precise hypotheses, which also appear most relevant when explaining interest development. This theory provides a rather differentiated model about the complex interrelations between action control, affect (emotional experiences during action) and long-term personality development. It includes—among other things—the assumption that the processes of activating or repressing the four basic macro-structures of personality are continuously controlled by emotional experiences (affects), and that both positive and negative affects are involved. Besides, it is not only a matter of the kind of 'emotional colouring' accompanying the action over a shorter or longer period of time; even more important are the experienced changes of positive and/or negative affects in dependence of the state of the whole psychological system at that moment.

Individual interests as components of the self-system
When one looks at interest development over a longer period of time, one realizes that some objects of interest can have a considerably higher subjective importance than others. In this respect, there are also shifts typical for a particular age group. A child or adolescent is interested in different things than an adult at the beginning of his or her career, or than an older person who has already reached the end of his or her professional life (see also J. Heckhausen, & Farruggia, 2003). Some of these ontogenetic changes can also be described and explained with the help of an action regulation system, e.g. the effects of changes in physical and mental skills dependent on age. They have a direct effect on experienced competence and influence (according to the dual-system regulation model), the probability of resumption, and of the kind and direction of future interest-related actions and strivings.

This explanatory approach does not suffice to understand all of the educationally important aspects of interest development during the entire life span. From everyday experience it is known, for example, that interests that were satisfactorily maintained for a long time are occasionally dropped for no apparent reason. However, interests are maintained even when their realization and continuation require relatively much effort. In developmental psychology, there are a number of concepts and results which supply plausible explanations for some of these phenomena, e.g. Havighurst's (1948) concept of *developmental tasks*, the concept of *critical life experiences* (e.g. Filipp, 1990) or the *'action-phase model of engagement and disengagement with developmental goals'* (J. Heckhausen, 2000, Heckhausen & Farruggia, 2003). These especially allow good reconstruction of the general trends of interest development, taking both biological factors and the cultural and societal frame conditions into consideration.

If, however, one wants to focus primarily on the intra-individual course of interest development and its relationship to personality development, one then needs theoretical conceptions going beyond these explanatory approaches. According to POI, a dynamic model of personality development is necessary to open up the possibility of describing and explaining motivational aspects of the developing person not only with respect to individual differences, but with respect to functional relations.

Besides other aspects, such a theory has to take into account that the person is aware of himself or herself, and that the 'object' of this awareness is some sort of representation of the individual's '*self*'. From the beginning, the hypothesis represented in POI was that there are close interrelations between a person's structure of individual interests and the development of his or her self and/or identity. In order to indicate that the self has to be understood as a dynamic entity representing structural and functional properties, I prefer to use the term *self-system*. It should be noted that concepts such as 'self', 'self-system' or 'identity' only make sense within a personality theory framework that attempts to reconstruct the functional relations and dynamic 'roots' during the ongoing process of human development. From this theoretical perspective, the self is interpreted as a central constituent in the dynamic structure of the growing personality. On the one hand, the self represents the crystallized result of past development; on the other hand, it is an agent of 'intentional development' that provides both ideas about the preferred direction of development and competencies for realizing developmental intentions (Brandtstädter, 1999; see also Heckhausen & Farruggia, 2003). This idea is rather similar to Dweck's concept of a 'meaning system' which is characterized 'as a network of beliefs and goals—built arround a core theory that systematically guides behaviour' (Dweck, 2003).[7]

In accordance with theoretical approaches that interpret the course of human development from the perspective of a dynamic theory of personality (Deci & Ryan, 1985; Epstein, 1973; Fend, 1994; Kuhl, 2000, 2001; Ryan, 1993), I assume that within the complex representational structure of personality, there are areas which are recognized as components of a self-system. An individual's self (or self-system) is manifest not only in the way the person perceives himself or herself (self-concept), but also in the way the person evaluates his or her capacities, goals and attitudes (self-esteem), and in the way he or she assesses the potential for coping with actual and forthcoming life tasks. In addition to cognitive representations, emotional and motivational aspects determine the structure of the self. Under normal circumstances, the different components of the self-system represent a unified structure: a mentally healthy person lives in relative harmony with his or her attitudes, goals, accumulated capacities and knowledge structures. Nevertheless, the self-system is subject to permanent change because the social and physical environments constantly require new adaptations and force the individual to set up new goals of action and development.

With respect to human development, I assume that the self is not simply a social construct or a reflection of social appraisals and a product of developmental processes; rather, I am convinced that the individual has a great influence on his or her own development from earliest childhood onwards. At a very young age, a person already tries to affect the 'objects' in the social and physical environment depending on his or her actual needs and personal goals. The ongoing developmental changes lead to a continuous differentiation of the individual's structure of self, and it is only because there is an inborn propensity towards integration that this process of differentiation and reorganization does not lead to a compartmentalization of the self. Thus, the person tries to create and maintain a coherent image, a 'good Gestalt' of his or her sense of self.

---

[7] *In cognitive approaches to motivation, these concepts are often regarded with suspicion. They seem not be necessary, and it is argued that they cannot really be measured at a satisfying level of reliability. The appropriateness of theoretical concepts, however, is not a matter of meeting certain measurement criteria but has primarily to do with the question about the ultimate aims of research and theory building in this domain (see Bickhard, 2003).*

As a consequence, he or she cannot identify completely with all thoughts, actions, tasks and strivings, even when they are experienced as being important for the individual's wishes and future goals at the moment.

Theoretical statements about the structure and functions of the self-system formulated earlier in the POI are mainly based on general theoretical reflections and postulates that were more closely founded in other theories (e.g. in the SDT; Deci & Ryan, 1985, 1991). In more recent literature on research about human memory (e.g. on brain regions that represent *autonoetic consciousness*; see Wheeler, Stuss, & Tulving, 1997) and the dynamics of human development, there are a growing number of empirical studies that seem to prove the 'real' existence of an 'implicit memory of self-representations' (Kuhl, 2000), which is possibly closely connected with the self-system postulated in the POI. For example, in Kuhl's PSI Theory, one of the four postulated main *macrosystems* of personality organization refers to the idea of an 'integrated self'. According to Kuhl (2000) the self-system is only partially open to reflective, cognitive access as it is mainly made up of implicit, verbally not complete, explicable knowledge. This assumption breaks with traditional views in modern psychology. Whereas approaches to the concept of self that can be found in current personality and social psychology relate to explicit beliefs about the self, 'PSI theory postulates an implicit or "intuitive" knowledge base that integrates an extended network of representations of one's own states, including personal preferences, needs, emotional states, options for actions in particular situations, and past experiences involving the self' (Kuhl, 2000, p. 131).

The self as a central aspect in theories on personality and human development is currently gaining new importance in various areas of psychology (see Greve, 2000) and, to a certain extent, in the narrower field of educational psychological motivation research as well (e.g. Hannover, 1997, 1998; see also Fend, 2000). Many of these approaches seem to support the basic idea about the central role of the self-system for describing and explaining the dynamics of human action and personality development.

Summary and conclusion: The role of interest in human development

At the beginning of this chapter, I pointed out that in everyday education, one is still quite oriented to the concept of interest when it is a matter of describing and explaining motivational problems in school. The students' individual interests are seen as being an important prerequisite for effective and longer-lasting self-determined learning. Beyond this, relationships to individual development are to be made with reference to the interest concept. Since Herbart (1806/1965), they have served to describe pedagogically desired goals in development and education. It is assumed that the interest structure in question has an important influence on how a person develops.

The conception of an educational psychology theory of interest described here and the research approaches referring to it also attempt to give scientifically based answers to both of the practically important questions that have to be increasingly differentiated in the course of further scientific development. One main concern of all educational psychology concepts of interests is the explicit consideration of the contents of learning and development motivation. They should explain why a relatively strong or weak willingness to learn can be observed in certain people and/or in certain situations. The question should also be why someone is interested in just this topic while others hardly pay any attention to it or even reject it (Lewalter & Schreyer, 2000).

From a great variety of empirical studies in many different fields of research, we know that interest-based learning has many advantages. Students with well-developed interests in a certain subject more often use deep-level learning strategies and achieve qualitatively better learning results (Baumert & Köller, 1998; Hidi, 1990, Krapp *et al.*, 1992; Renninger, 1998; Schiefele, 1996, 2001). Therefore, it seems reasonable to claim that teachers should, as much as possible, take care to use the already-existing interests of their students and/or to establish 'situational interest', even when this is held only for a short period of time (Hidi & Harackiewicz, 2001; Krapp, 1998).

POI assumes that interests also have a significant influence on human development. As stated above, the actual interests of a person can be seen—under certain conditions—as epistemic motivational dispositions that guide the direction and the quality of goal-oriented actions. They provide an orientation when the individual has to make decisions about the direction of future learning goals and the direction of the next step of intentional learning and development. Seen from this theoretical perspective, one could say that a person's actual pattern of interests represents the dynamic components on the way to their realization in the 'zone of proximal development' (Valsiner, 1986; Vygotsky, 1978) in the direction of a desirable 'possible self' (Fend, 1994; Markus & Nurius, 1986). Whereas Vygotsky maintains that the realization of the next steps in a person's development always requires the explicit help of another person, who is more advanced, Piaget's social model also covers the possibility of a self-determined autonomous creation of one's own development (Piaget, 1981, 1995; for commentary, see Brown, 1996, 2001; Smith, 1996, 2002b).

According to POI, a person's individual interests can become a more or less stable part of the personality structure. Thus, well-developed individual interests can be interpreted as components of the self or the self-system of a person (see above). Interests differ with regard to their ranking in the hierarchy of personal values and goals. There are some that are more on the periphery, experienced with less 'ego-involvement', and others that are much more central to the self-concept of a person; they are recognized from within and from without as characteristics of a person's actual and longer-lasting identity.

Depending on the kind of position occupied by a certain interest in a person's self-system, it has a greater or lesser influence on how the personality develops. On the one hand, the influence acts through conscious cognitive control processes, e.g. through interest-based intentions that are developed in principle according to an expectancy-value model. On the other hand, one has to take into account that there is an additional influence operating at the lower levels of conscience awareness, including even subconsciously operating factors. In the end, these pre- or subconsciously mediated influences can have the same effect in principle as the conscious-cognitive decision-making procedures: besides other effects, they ensure that certain chances for learning and development receive preferential treatment, while others are neglected.

The person's currently affective interests control how behaviour is organized at various levels. As well as other aspects, interests bring about both the self-intended acquisition of new knowledge and skills in a certain area and the application of already acquired knowledge and skills in new situations. As the accumulated knowledge, together with the representations of emotional experience, forms the basis of human development, the growth of personality is determined by individual interests to the extent that the individual has the chance and the ability to structure his or her own life and to act autonomously. In this respect, individual courses of human development show huge differences, from both an intra-individual and an inter-individual point of view.

In addition to the currently affective interests, the earlier ones that have been given up in the meantime may also have an important potential influence on a person's development. This hypothesis can be derived from PSI theory (Kuhl, 2000) and other theories which show that actions, events and experiences of personal importance are stored in a particular way in a self-related memory system. As interest-based activities, by definition, have personal importance, it may be concluded that knowledge structures, skills, pattern of activities and other aspects of interest realization are also permanently stored in a person's representational system in this particular way. And I would assume that there are considerable differences between these kinds of long-term effects when interest-based, and thus 'intrinsically' motivated, learning is compared with extrinsically motivated learning. In the long run, this can become very important for a person's life in many ways. For example, it may be assumed that knowledge, skills and patterns for action acquired on the basis of a personal interest in earlier stages of life will be much easier to reactivate at a later point in time when the opportunity or the necessity is there; for example, reviving previous interest-based activities in older age, when many people seem to have severe problems in using their time in a meaningful way.

Taken together, one could speculate that the direction and the experienced quality of an individual's course of development are dependent to a considerable degree on the contents, quality and structure of one's personal interests that have been developed, realized and dropped at various stages during the life span.

References

Allport, G. W. (1937). *Personality: A psychological interpretation*. New York: Holt.

Anastasi, A. (1958). *Differential psychology*. New York: MacMillan.

Anderman, E. M., & Maehr, M. L. (1994). Motivation and schooling in the middle grades. *Review of Educational Research*, *64*, 267–309.

Anderson, J. R. (1993). *Rules of mind*. Hillsdale, NJ: Erlbaum.

Arnold, F. (1906). The psychology of interest. I/II. *Psychological Review*, *13*, 221–238/291–315.

Asendorpf, J. (1991). *Die differentielle Sichtweise in der Psychologie*. Göttingen: Hogrefe.

Atkinson, J. W. (1964). *An introduction to motivation*. Princeton, NJ: von Nostrand.

Atkinson, J. W., & Raynor, J. O. (Eds.) (1974). *Motivation and achievement*. Washington, DC: Winston.

Atkinson, J. W., & Raynor, J. O. (Eds.) (1978). *Personallity, motivation and achievement*. Washington, DC: Hemisphere.

Aufschnaiter, C. von (1999). *Bedeutungsentwicklung, Interaktionen und situatives Erleben beim Bearbeiten physikalischer Aufgaben*. Berlin: Logos.

Aufschnaiter, C. von, Schoster, A., & Aufschnaiter, S. von (1999). The influence of students' individual experiences of physics learning environments on cognitive processes. In J. Leach & A. C. Paulsen (Eds.), Practical work in science education—recent research studies (pp. 281–296). Dortrecht: Kluwer.

Bandura, A. (1997). *Self-efficacy: The exercise of control*. New York: Freeman.

Bandura, A. (2001). Social cognitive theory. *Annual Review of Psychology*, *52*, S 1–26.

Baumert, J., & Köller, O. (1998). Interest research concerning secondary level I: An overview. In L. Hoffmann, A. Krapp, K. A. Renninger, & J. Baumert (Eds.), *Interest and learning: Proceedings of the Seeon-Conference on interest and gender* (pp. 241–256). Kiel: IPN.

Berlyne, D. E. (1949). Interest as a psychological concept. *British Journal of Psychology*, *39*, 184–195.

Bickhard, M. H. (2003). An Integration of motivation and cognition. *British Journal of Educational Psychology Monograph Series II, Part 2* (Development and Motivation), 41–56.

Boekaerts, M. (1999). Motivated learning: Studying student–situation transactional units. *European Journal of Psychology in Education, 14*, 41-55.

Boekaerts, M. (2001). Context sensitivity: activated motivational beliefs, current concerns and emotional arousal. In S. Volet & S. Järvelä (Eds.), *Motivation in learning contexts: Theoretical advances and methodological implications* (pp. 17-31). London: Elsevier.

Boekaerts, M. (2003). Towards a model that integrates motivation, affect and learning. *British Journal of Educational Psychology Monograph Series II, Part 2* (Development and Motivation), 173-189.

Boekaerts, M., Pintrich, P., & Zeidner, M. (2000). *Handbook of self-regulation.* London: Academic Press.

Brandtstädter, J. (1999). The self in action and development: Cultural, biosocial, and ontogenetic bases of intentional self-development. In J. Brandtstädter & R. M. Lerner (Eds.), *Action and self-development: Theory and research through the life span* (pp. 37-65). Thousand Oaks, CA: Sage.

Brown, T. (1996). Values, knowledge, and Piaget. In E. Reid, E. Turiel, & T. Brown (Eds.), *Values and knowledge*. Mahwah, NJ: Erlbaum

Brown, T. (2001). Bärbel Inhelder and the fall of Valhalla. In A. Tryphon & J. Vonèche (Eds.), *Working with Piaget: Essays in honour of Bärbel* (pp. 179-191). Hove: Psychology Press.

Claparède E. (1905). *Psychologie de l'enfant et pedagogie expérimentale.* Geneva: Kundig.

Cronbach, L. J. (1957). The two disciplines of scientific psychology. *American Psychologist, 12*, 671-684.

Cronbach, L. J. (1975). Beyond the two disciplines of scientific psychology. *American Psychologist, 30*, 116-127.

Csikszentmihalyi, M. (1990). *Flow.* New York: Harper & Row.

Csikszentmihalyi, M., & Csikszentmihalyi, I. S. (1988). *Optimal experience.* New York: Cambridge University Press.

Deci, E. L. (1992). The relation of interest to the motivation of behavior: A self-determination theory perspective. In K. A. Renninger, S. Hidi, & A. Krapp (Eds.), *The role of interest in learning and development* (pp. 43-47). Hillsdale, NJ: Erlbaum.

Deci, E. L. (1998). The relation of interest to motivation and human needs: The self-determination theory viewpoint. In L. Hoffmann, A. Krapp, K. A. Renninger, & J. Baumert (Eds.), *Interest and learning. Proceedings of the Seeon-Conference on interest and gender* (pp. 146-162). Kiel: IPN.

Deci, E. L., & Ryan, R. M. (1985). *Intrinsic motivation and self-determination in human behavior.* New York: Plenum.

Deci, E. L., & Ryan, R. M. (1991). A motivational approach to self: Integration in personality. In R. Dienstbier (Ed.), *Nebraska Symposium on motivation. Vol. 38: Perspectives on motivation* (pp. 237-288). Lincoln, NE: University of Nebraska Press.

Deci, E. L., & Ryan, R. M. (2002). *Handbook of self-determination research.* Rochester: University of Rochester Press.

Dewey, J. (1913). *Interest and effort in education.* Boston: Riverside.

Donaldson, M. (1992). *Human minds.* London: Allen Lane.

Dweck, C.S. (2003). Ability conceptions, motivation and development. *British Journal of Educational Psychology Monograph Series II, Part 2* (Development and Motivation), 13-27.

Eccles, J. S. (1983). Expectancies, values and academic behaviors. In J. T. Spence (Ed.), *Achievement and achievement motives: Psychological and sociological approaches* (pp. 75-146). San Francisco: Freeman.

Eccles, J. S., & Wigfield, A. (1992). The development of achievement-task values: A theoretical analysis. *Developmental Review, 12*, 256-273.

Efklides, A., Kuhl, J., & Sorrentino, R. M. (2001). *Trends and prospects in motivation research.* London: Kluwer.

Elliott, E. S., & Dweck, C. S. (1988). Goals: An approach to motivation and achievement. *Journal of Personality and Social Psychology, 54*, 5-12.

Emmons, R. A. (1991). Personal strivings, daily life events, and psychological and physical well being. *Journal of Personality, 59*, 453-427.

Epstein, S. (1973). The self-concept revisited or a theory of a theory. *American Psychologist, 28*, 404-416.

Epstein, S. (1990). Cognitive-experiential self theory: Implications for developmental psychology. In M. Gunnar & L. A. Sroufe (Eds.), *Minnesota symposia on child psychology: Self processes and development* (Vol. 23, pp. 79-123). Hilsdale, NJ: Erlbaum.

Fend, H. (1991). *Identitätsentwicklung in der Adoleszenz: Lebensentwürfe, Selbstfindung und Weltaneignung in beruflichen, familiären und politisch-weltanschaulichen Bereichen.* Bern: Huber.

Fend, H. (1994). *Die Entdeckung des Selbst und die Verarbeitung der Pubertät.* Bern: Huber.

Fend, H. (2000). Entwicklungspsychologie des Jugendalters. Opladen: Leske + Burich.

Ferrari, M., Pinard, A., & Runions, K. (2001). Piaget's framework for a scientific study of consciousness. *Human Development, 44*, 195-213.

Filipp, S. H. (Ed.) (1990). *Kritische Lebensereignisse.* Weinheim: Beltz-PVU.

Fink, B. (1991). Interest development as structural change in person–object relationships. In L. Oppenheimer & J. Valsiner (Eds.), *The origins of action: Interdisciplinary and international perspectives* (pp. 175-204). New York: Springer.

Fischer, H. E., & Horstendahl, M. (1997). Motivation and learning physics. *Research and Science Education, 27*, 411-424.

Fodor, J. (1983). *The modularity of mind.* Cambridge, MA: MIT Press.

Fodor, J. (2000). *The mind doesn't work that way.* Cambridge, MA: MIT Press.

Gardner, P. L. (1985). Students' interest in science and technology: An international overview. In M. Lehrke, L. Hoffmann, & P. L. Gardner (Eds.), *Interests in science and technology education* (pp. 15-34). Kiel: IPN.

Gardner, P. L. (1998). The development of males' and females' interest in science and technology. In L. Hoffmann, A. Krapp, K. A. Renninger, & J. Baumert (Eds.), *Interest and learning: Proceedings of the Seeon-Conference on interest and gender* (pp. 41-57). Kiel: IPN.

Gisbert, K. (1995). *Frauenuntypische Bildungsbiographien: Diplom-Mathematikerinnen.* Frankfurt: Lang.

Gisbert, K. (2001). *Geschlecht und Studienwahl. Biographische Analysen geschlechtstypischer und -untypischer Bildungswege.* Münster: Waxmann.

Greve, W. (2000). *Die Psychologie des Selbst.* Weinheim: Beltz-PVU.

Hannover, B. (1997). *Das dynamische Selbst.* Bern: Huber.

Hannover, B. (1998). The development of self-concept and interests. In L. Hoffmann, A. Krapp, K. A. Renninger, & J. Baumert (Eds.), *Interest and learning. Proceedings of the Seeon-Conference on interest and gender* (pp. 105-125). Kiel: IPN.

Havighurst, J. R. (1948). Research on the developmental-task concept. *School Review, 64*, 215-223.

Heckhausen, H. (1991). *Motivation and action.* Berlin: Springer.

Heckhausen, J. (Ed.). (2000). *Motivational psychology of human development.* London: Elsevier.

Heckhausen, J., & Farruggia, S. (2003). Developmental regulation across the life span: A control-theory approach and implications for secondary education. *BJEP Monograph Series, 2* (Development and Motivation), 85-102.

Herbart, J. F. (1965). Allgemeine Pädagogik, aus dem Zweck der Erziehung abgeleitet. In J. F. Herbart (Ed.), *Pädagogische Schriften* (Vol. 2, pp. 9-155). Düsseldorf: Küpper (Originally published 1806.)

Hidi, S. (1990). Interest and its contribution as a mental resource for learning. *Review of Educational Research, 60*, 549-571.

Hidi, S. (2000). An interest researcher's perspective on the effects of extrinsic and intrinsic factors on motivation. In C. Sansone & J. M. Harackiewicz (Eds.), *Intrinsic and extrinsic motivation.* New York: Academic Press.

Hidi, S., & Harackiewicz, J. M. (2001). Motivating the academically unmotivated: A critical issue for the 21st century. *Review of Educational Research, 70,* 151–179.

Hoffmann, L., Häussler, P., & Lehrke, M. (1998). *Die IPN-Interessenstudie Physik.* Kiel: IPN.

Hoffmann, L., Krapp, A., Renninger, A., & Baumert, J. (Eds) (1998). *Interest and learning: Proceedings of the Seeon-conference on interest and gender.* Kiel: IPN.

Hoffmann, L., Lehrke, M., & Todt, E. (1985). Development and change of pupils' interest in physics: Design of longitudinal study (grade 5 to 10). In M. Lehrke, L. Hoffmann, & P. L. Gardner (Eds.), *Interests in science and technology* (pp. 71–80). Kiel: IPN.

Jacoby, L., Toth, J., Yonelinas, A., & Deubner, J. (1994). The relation between conscious and unconscious influences: Interdependence or redundancy? *Journal of Experimental Research: General, 123,* 216–219.

Kasten, H., & Krapp, A. (1986). Das Interessengenese-Projekt. *Zeitschrift für Pädagogik, 32,* 175–188.

Kerschensteiner, G. (1922). Der Interessenbegriff in der Pädagogik. *Pädagogische Blätter, 5,* 349–354.

Krapp, A. (1992). Das Interessenkonstrukt. Bestimmungsmerkmale der Interessenhandlung und des individuellen Interesses aus der Sicht einer Person-Gegenstands-Konzeption. In A. Krapp & M. Prenzel (Eds.), *Interesse, Lernen, Leistung* (S. 297–329). Münster: Aschendorff.

Krapp, A. (1998). Entwicklung und Förderung von Interessen im Unterricht. *Psychologie in Erziehung und Unterricht, 45,* 186–203.

Krapp, A. (1999a). Interest, motivation and learning: An educational-psychological perspective. *European Journal of Psychology in Education, 14,* 23–40.

Krapp, A. (1999b). Intrinsischen Lernmotivation und Interesse. Forschungsansätze und konzeptuelle Überlegungen. *Zeitschrift für Pädagogik, 45*(3), 387–406.

Krapp, A. (2000). Interest and human development during adolescence: An educational-psychological approach. In J. Heckhausen (Ed.), *Motivational psychology of human development* (pp. 109–128). London: Elsevier.

Krapp, A. (2002a). An educational–psychological theory of interest and its relation to self-determination theory. In E. Deci & R. Ryan (Eds.), *The handbook of self-determination research* (pp. 405–427). Rochester, NY: University of Rochester Press.

Krapp, A. (2002b). Structural and dynamic aspects of interest development: Theoretical considerations from an ontogenetic perspective. *Learning and Instruction, 12,* 383–409.

Krapp, A., & Fink, B. (1992). The development and function of interests during the critical transition from home to preschool. In K. A. Renninger, S. Hidi, & A. Krapp (Eds.), *The role of interest in learning and development* (pp. 397–429). Hillsdale, NJ: Erlbaum.

Krapp, A., Hidi, S., & Renninger, K. A. (1992). Interest, learning and development. In K. A. Renninger, S. Hidi, & A. Krapp (Eds.), *The role of interest in learning and development* (pp. 3–25). Hillsdale, NJ: Erlbaum.

Krapp, A., & Lewalter, D. (2001). Development of interests and interest-based motivational orientations. A longitudinal study in school and work settings. In S. Volet & S. Järvelä (Eds.), *Motivation in learning contexts: Theoretical advances and methodological implications* (pp. 201–232). London: Elsevier.

Krapp, A., & Prenzel, M. (Eds.) (1992). *Interesse, Lernen, Leistung.* Münster: Aschendorff.

Kuhl, J. (2000). A functional-design approach to motivation and self-regulation. The dynamics of personality systems interactions. In M. Boekaerts, P. R. Pintrich, & M. Zeidner (Eds.), *Handbook of self-regulation: Theory, research and applications* (pp. 451–502). San Diego, CA: Academic Press.

Kuhl, J. (2001). A functional approach to motivation. In A. Efklides, J. Kuhl & R. M. Sorrentino (Eds.), *Trends and prospects in motivation research.* London: Kluwer.

LeDoux, J. E. (1995). Emotion: Clues from the brain. *Annual Review of Psychology, 46,* 209–235.

Lehrke, M., Hoffmann, L., & Gardner, P. L. (Eds.). (1985). *Interests in science and technology education.* Kiel: IPN.

Lepper, M., & Henderlong, J. (2000). Turning 'play' into 'work' and 'work' into 'play': 25 years of research on intrinsic versus extrinsic motivation. In C. Sansone & J. M. Harackiewicz (Eds.), *Intrinsic and extrinsic motivation: The search for optimal motivation and performance* (pp. 257-307). New York: Academic Press.

Lewalter, D., Krapp, A., Schreyer, I., & Wild, K. -P. (1998). Die Bedeutsamkeit des Erlebens von Kompetenz, Autonomie und sozialer Eingebundenheit für die Entwicklung berufsspezifischer Interessen. In K. Beck & R. Dubs (Eds.), *Kompetenzentwicklung in der Berufserziehung* (pp. 143-168.). Stuttgart: Steiner.

Lewalter, D., & Schreyer, I. (2000). Entwicklung von Interessen und Abneigungen—zwei Seiten einer Medaille. In U. Schiefele & K. P. Wild (Eds.), *Interesse und Lernmotivation* (pp. 53-72). Münster: Waxmann.

Lewicki, P., Hill, T., & Czyzemska, M. (1992). Nonconscious acquisition of information. *American Psychologist, 47*, 796-801.

Lewin, K. (1936). *A dynamic theory of personality*. New York: McGraw-Hill.

McClelland, D. C., Koestner, R., & Weinberger, J. (1989). How do self-attributed and implicit motives differ? *Psychological Review, 96*, 690-702.

Markus, H., & Nurius, P. (1986). Possible selves. *American Psychologist, 41*, 954-969.

Murphy, P. K., & Alexander, P. (2000). A motivated exploration of motivation terminology. *Contemporary Educational Psychology, 25*, 3-53.

Nuttin, J. (1984). *Motivation, planning, and action*. Hillsdale, NJ: Erlbaum.

Perrig, W. J., & Grob, A. (Eds.) (2000). *Control of human behaviour, mental processes, and consciousness* (pp. 245-261). Mahwah, NJ: Erlbaum.

Piaget, J. (1978). *Grasp of consciousness*. London: Routledge and Kegan Paul.

Piaget, J. (1981). *Intelligence and affectivity*. Palo Alto, CA: Annual Reviews.

Piaget, J. (1985). *Equilibration of cognitive structures*. Chicago: University of Chicago Press.

Piaget, J. (1995). *Sociological studies*. London: Routledge.

Pintrich, P. R. (2000). The role of goal orientation in self-regulated learning. In M. Boekaerts, P. R. Pintrich, & M. Zeidner (Eds.), *Handbook of self-regulation: Theory, research and applications* (pp. 451-502). San Diego, CA: Academic Press.

Pintrich, P. R. (2003). Multiple goals and multiple pathways in the development of motivation and self-regulated learning. *British Journal of Educational Psychology Monograph Series II, Part 2* (Development and Motivation), 137-153.

Pintrich, P. R., & Schunk, D. H. (1996). *Motivation in education. Theory, research and applications*. Englewood Cliffs: Prentice-Hall.

Prenzel, M. (1988). *Die Wirkungsweise von Interesse*. Opladen: Westdeutscher Verlag.

Prenzel. M. (1992). Selective persistence of interest. In K. A. Renninger, S. Hidi, & A. Krapp (Eds.), *The role of interest in learning and development* (pp. 71-98). Hillsdale, NJ: Erlbaum.

Prenzel, M. (1998). Interest research concerning the upper secondary level, college, and vocational education: An overview. In L. Hoffmann, A. Krapp, K. A. Renninger, & J. Baumert (Eds.), *Interest and learning. Proceedings of the Seeon-Conference on interest and gender* (pp. 355-366). Kiel: IPN.

Prenzel, M., Kramer, K., & Drechsel, B. (1998). Changes in learning motivation and interest in vocational education: Halfway through the study. In L. Hoffmann, A. Krapp, K. A. Renninger, & J. Baumert (Eds.), *Interest and learning. Proceedings of the Seeon-Conference on interest and gender* (pp. 430-440). Kiel: IPN.

Rathunde, K. (1993). The experience of interest: A theoretical and empirical look at its role in adolescent talent development. In M. Maehr & P. R. Pintrich (Eds.), *Advances in motivation and achievement* (pp. 59-98). Greenwich, CT: JAI Press.

Rathunde, K. (1998). Undivided and abiding interest: Comparisons across studies of talented adolescents and creative adults. In L. Hoffmann, A. Krapp, K. A. Renninger, & J. Baumert (Eds.), *Interest and learning. Proceedings of the Seeon-Conference on interest and gender* (pp. 367-376). Kiel: IPN.

Rathunde, K., & Csikszentmihalyi, M. (1993). Undivided interest and the growth of talent: A longitudinal study of adolescents. *Journal of Youth and Adolescence, 22,* 1-21.

Reber, A. (1989). Implicit learning and tacit knowledge. *Journal of Experimental Psychology: General, 118*(3), 219-235.

Renninger, K. A. (1989). Individual patterns in children's play interests. In L. T. Winegar (Ed.), *Social interaction and the development of children's understanding* (pp. 147-172). Norwood, NY: Ablex.

Renninger, K. A. (1990). Children's play interests, representation, and activity. In R. Fivush & J. Hudson (Eds.), *Knowing and remembering in young children* (pp. 127-147). New York: Cambridge University Press.

Renninger, K. A. (1992). Individual interest and development: Implications for theory and practice. In K. A. Renninger, S. Hidi, & A. Krapp (Eds.), *The role of interest in learning and development* (pp. 361-395). Hillsdale, NJ: Erlbaum.

Renninger, K. A. (1998). The role of individual interest(s) and gender in learning: An overview of research on preschool and elementary school-aged children/students. In L. Hoffmann, A. Krapp, K. A. Renninger, & J. Baumert (Eds.), *Interest and learning: Proceedings of the Seeon-Conference on interest and gender* (pp. 165-174). Kiel: IPN.

Renninger, K. A. (2000). Individual interest and development: Implications for theory and practice. In C. Sansone & J. M. Harackiewicz (Eds.), *Intrinsic and extrinsic motivation: The search for optimal motivation and performance* (pp. 375-404). New York: Academic Press.

Renninger, K. A., & Hidi, S. (2002). Student interest and achievement: Developmental isues raised by a case study. In A. Wigfield & J. S. Eccles (Eds), *Development of achievement motivation* (pp. 173-195). New York: Academic Press.

Renninger, K. A., Hidi, S., & Krapp, A. (Eds.) (1992). *The role of interest in learning and development.* Hillsdale, NJ: Erlbaum.

Ryan, R. M. (1993). Agency and organization: Intrinsic motivation, autonomy and the self in psychological development. In J. Jacobs (Ed.), *Nebraska symposium on motivation: Development perspectives on motivation. Vol. 40. Developmental perspectives on motivation* (pp. 1-56). Lincoln, NE: University of Nebraska Press.

Ryan, R. M. (1995). Psychological needs and the facilitation of integrative process. *Journal of Personality, 63*(3), 397-427.

Sansone, C., & Harackiewicz, J. M. (2000). *Intrinsic and extrinsic motivation: The search for optimal motivation and performance.* New York: Academic Press.

Schick, A. (2000a). *Der Einfluss von Interesse und anderen selbstbezogenen Kognitionen auf Handlungen im Physikunterricht.* Berlin: Logos.

Schick, A. (2000b). Self-concept reflected in students' activities during physics instruction: The role of interest-oriented actions. *Journal of the Hellenic Psychological Society, 7,* 325-339.

Schiefele, H. (1978). *Lernmotivation und Motivlernen.* München: Ehrenwirth.

Schiefele, H. (1981). Interesse. In H. Schiefele & A. Krapp (Eds.), *Handlexikon zur Pädagogischen Psychologie* (pp. 192-196). München: Ehrenwirth.

Schiefele, H., Krapp, A., Prenzel, M., Heiland, A., & Kasten, H. (1983). *Principles of an educational theory of interest.* Paper presented at the 7th Meeting of the International Society for the Study of Behavioral Development in Munich.

Schiefele, U. (1991). Interest, learning and motivation. *Educational Psychologist, 26,* 299-323.

Schiefele, U. (1992). Topic interest and levels of text comprehension. In K. A. Renninger, S. Hidi, & A. Krapp (Eds.), *The role of interest in learning and development* (pp. 151-182). Hillsdale, NJ: Erlbaum.

Schiefele, U. (1996). *Motivation und Lernen mit Texten.* Göttingen: Hogrefe.

Schiefele, U. (1999). Interest and learning from text. *Scientific Studies of Reading, 3*(3), 257-279.

Schiefele, U. (2001). The role of interest in motivation and learning. In J. M. Collis & S. Messick (Eds.), *Intelligence and personality* (pp. 163-194). Mahwah, NJ: Erlbaum.

Schiefele, U., Krapp, A., & Winteler, A. (1992). Interest as a predictor of academic achievement: A meta-analysis of research. In K. A. Renninger, S. Hidi, & A. Krapp (Eds.), *The role of interest in learning and development* (pp. 183–212). Hillsdale, NJ: Erlbaum.

Schiefele U., & Wild, K. P. (Eds.) (2000). *Interesse und Lernmotivation*. Münster: Waxmann.

Sheldon, K. M., & Elliot, A. J. (1998). Not all personal goals are personal: Comparing autonomous and controlled reasons for goals as predictors of effort and attainment. *Personality and Social Psychology Bulletin, 24*, 546–557.

Smith, L. (1996). The social construction of rational understanding. In A. Tryphon & J. Vonèche (Eds.), *Piaget–Vygotsky: The social genesis of thought*. Hove: Psychology Press.

Smith, L. (2002a). *Reasoning by mathematical induction in children's arithmetic: Advances in learning and instruction series*. Oxford: Pergamon.

Smith, L. (2002b). Piaget's model. In U. Goswami (Ed.), *Blackwell handbook of childhood cognitive development*. Oxford: Blackwell.

Spangler, G., & Zimmermann, P. (1999). Emotion, Motivation und Leistung aus entwicklungs- und persönlichkeitspsychologischer Perspektive. In M. Jerusalem & R. Pekrun (Eds.), *Emotion, Motivation und Leistung* (pp. 85–103). Göttingen: Hogrefe.

Stern, W. (1918). *Die menschliche Persönlichkeit*. Munich: Barth.

Sun, R. (2002). *Duality of the mind*. Mahwah, NJ: Erlbaum.

Thorndike, E. L. (1935). *The psychology of wants, interests, and attitudes*. New York: Appleton-Century.

Todt, E. (1985). Elements of a theory of science interests. In M. Lehrke, L. Hoffmann, & P. L. Gardner (Eds.). *Interests in science and technology* (pp. 59–69). Kiel, Germany: IPN.

Todt, E., & Schreiber, S. (1998). Development of interests. In L. Hoffmann, A. Krapp, K. A. Renninger, & J. Baumert (Eds.), *Interest and learning. Proceedings of the Seeon-Conference on interest and gender* (pp. 25–40). Kiel: IPN.

Valsiner, J. (1986). Between groups and individuals: Psychologists' and laypersons' interpretations of correlational findings. In J. Valsiner (Ed.), *The individual subject and scientific psychology* (pp. 113–151). New York: Plenum.

Valsiner, J. (1992). Interest: A metatheoretical perspective. In K. A. Renninger, S. Hidi & A. Krapp (Eds.), *The role of interest in learning and development* (pp. 27–41). Hillsdale, NJ: Erlbaum.

Volet, S., & Järvelä, S. (Eds.). (2001). *Motivation in learning contexts: Theoretical advances and methodological Implications*. Amsterdam: Elsevier.

Vygotsky, L. (1978). *Mind and society*. Cambridge, MA: Harvard University Press.

Wheeler, M. A., Stuss, D. T., & Tulving, E. (1997). Toward a theory of episodic memory: The frontal lobes and autonoetic consciousness. *Psychological Bulletin, 121*, 331–3543.

Wigfield, A., & Eccles, J. (2002). *Development of achievement motivation*. New York: Academic Press.

Wild, K.-P., Krapp, A., Schreyer, I., & Lewalter, D. (1998). The development of interest and motivational orientations: Gender differences in vocational education. In L. Hoffmann, A. Krapp, K. A. Renninger, & J. Baumert (Eds.), *Interest and learning: Proceedings of the Seeon-Conference on interest and gender* (pp. 441–454). Kiel: IPN.

Development and Motivation, 85–102
BJEP Monograph Series II, 2
© 2003 The British Psychological Society

www.bps.org.uk

Developmental regulation across the life span: A control-theory approach and implications for secondary education

Jutta Heckhausen* and Susan P. Farruggia

University of California, Irvine, USA

This chapter integrates developmental and motivational theory and addresses phenomena at the interface of development and motivation. A life-span developmental approach to the study of motivational engagement and disengagement with important life goals is presented, and a set of relevant studies addressing developmental regulation at different points in the life span is discussed.

Heckhausen and Schulz (1995; Schulz & Heckhausen, 1996) have proposed a life-span theory of control, which conceptualizes primary and secondary control strategies in a life-span context. Primary control behaviour is directed at changing the external environment, while secondary control behaviour is targeted at internal processes to optimize motivational resources for primary control. Across the life span, primary control potential undergoes radical changes, with steep increases in childhood and adolescence, and decline in old age.

According to the life-span theory of control, the control system operates so as to optimize primary control across the life span. This is achieved by striving for those developmental goals that hold a high potential of controllability at a given phase of life, while disengaging from goals that have become exceedingly difficult to achieve. Opportunities for attaining important goals in life, such as starting a vocational career, finding a partner, and having a child, vary systematically across the life span. For each developmental goal, age gradients of opportunities can be identified.

A developmental deadline model was formulated to capture transitions from favourable to unfavourable opportunities for goal attainment (Heckhausen, 1999a, 2002). According to this model, cycles of goal engagement and disengagement follow the opportunities and constraints for goal attainment when coming up to and passing a deadline. The deadline model thus conceptualizes and generates predictions about consecutive phases of a goal engagement/disengagement cycle, which are characterized

---

*Requests for reprints should be addressed to Jutta Heckhausen, Department of Psychology and Social Behavior, University of California, Irvine, CA 92697-7085, USA (e-mail: heckhaus@uci.edu).

by specific combinations of primary and secondary control strategies. A set of studies about deadline-relevant transitions in adolescence and adulthood demonstrates overall adaptive patterns of goal engagement and disengagement (Heckhausen, Wrosch, & Fleeson, 2001; Wrosch & Heckhausen, 1999). In addition, inter-individual differences in the adaptive match of control strategies and deadline-related timing were found to predict both concurrent and future psychological well-being.

Finally, some implications of the life-span theory of control for developmental regulation of students enrolled in secondary education are discussed. The focus here is on the different instrumentality of educational performance for the school-to-work transition in different countries and how this may influence engagement with school-based learning in adolescent students.

This chapter addresses the question of to what extent and in which ways individuals actively influence their own development across the life span. It is a question about the ways in which major factors set the stage for the individual to take an active role in shaping their life course and optimizing development. Some of these factors include the biology of maturation and aging and societal institutions regulating important life-course transitions (e.g. school entry, marriage, retirement; Heckhausen, 1999a, 2001). This line of research calls for an integration of theory in life-span developmental and motivational psychology. A research programme along these lines is outlined.

The life-span theory of control

The need to produce outcomes and thus control one's environment is ubiquitous in human life (Heckhausen & Schulz, 1995). From the first hours of life, infants focus on and prefer behaviour-event contingencies. Once becoming aware of a contingency, they strive to produce and actively control it. This preference is shared with a wide array of mammals, and some would argue that it goes far beyond the mammalian strata (see recent review in Heckhausen, 2000; Heckhausen & Schulz, 1999; classic review in White, 1959). The functional value of this behavioural preference is obvious: it promotes behaviours that help the organism to successfully forage, seek shelter, compete for mates, fight off predators, and protect and care for its young. We refer to this striving to control outcomes in the environment as 'primary control striving' (see also Rothbaum, Weisz, & Snyder, 1982), and we assert that it holds functional primacy in the motivational system (Heckhausen & Schulz, 1995: Schulz & Heckhausen, 1996). Controlling outcomes in one's physical and social environment is central for the basic motivational systems—achievement, power and affiliation/intimacy. Thus, primary control striving is a universal motivational tendency in humans that underlies more specific motivational orientations.

Due to its fundamental role in motivating behaviour and its ubiquitous functionality in directing adaptive behaviour, primary control striving should maintain its role as a stable motivator of behaviour across the human life span. This primary control striving is illustrated in the solid and level line in Fig. 1. However, the potential for primary control undergoes radical changes across the life span. In infancy, primary control potential is very low, but increases at a rapid speed throughout childhood into adolescence and young adulthood, when it slows down, peaks and plateaus during midlife, and declines again slowly in young old age, and more radically in the old old

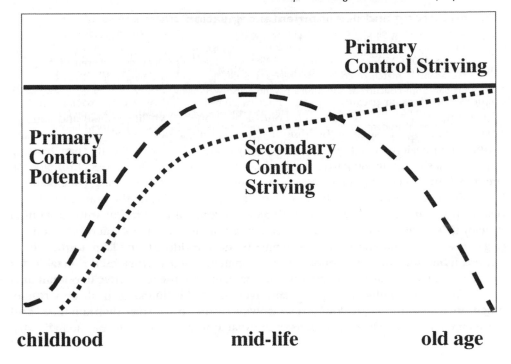

Figure 1. Hypothetical life-course trajectories of primary control potential, primary control striving, and secondary control striving (adapted from Heckhausen, 1999a).

and oldest old (Baltes, 1997). Thus, discrepancies exist between primary control striving and primary control potential in the earliest and latest parts of life. In childhood, this discrepancy is less of a problem because the child's control potential is constantly and rapidly increasing. What has been out of reach yesterday may be mastered today, and thus the striving for primary control is constantly fed by experiences of failure being outrun by success. In sharp contrast, primary control striving in advanced age has to come up against the challenges of loss and failure, thus potentially endangering the very motivational resources of primary control (e.g. hopefulness, self-esteem, motivational vitality). This requires a buffering mechanism that helps to protect motivational resources in spite of failure. Incidentally, the need to compensate for failure is, of course, not unique to old age. However, in old age, the need for self-protection should be especially pronounced. This is the function of secondary control; that is, control directed at the internal world of the individual, helping the individual to disengage from fruitless primary control goals, as indicated by the upturn in the curve for secondary control in Fig. 1.

Thus, the two types of control strivings are primary control striving, which is directed at attaining effects in the external world by one's own action, and secondary control, which is directed towards the internal world, and serves the function of protecting and enhancing motivational resources for primary control. Primary control striving holds functional primacy across the life span and is served by secondary control striving via its influence on motivational resources.

Control striving and developmental regulation

Given the vast ontogenetic potential of humans, the life course and developmental change throughout the life span provide a prime field of potential control. Especially under conditions of high social mobility in industrialized societies, the individual can exert a substantial influence on his or her own social trajectory, thus encountering chances and risks far greater than in societies characterized by greater social stability.

The opportunities to realize such control over one's own life course and achieve developmental goals such as building a family, establishing oneself in a career and saving for a pension are not evenly or arbitrarily distributed across the life span. Instead, opportunities for attaining particular life goals vary systematically across chronological age and form trajectories of increase, peak and plateau, and decrease (Heckhausen, 2000). Figure 2 shows how such trajectories vary in steepness and the time extension of peak opportunities. Some curves depict narrow time windows for attaining developmental goals such as entering school or finding a first job, and other curves (e.g. first child) embrace longer segments of the life span. This sequence of opportunities for attaining important developmental goals provides a timetable for the individual to activate and deactivate engagement with the respective developmental goals. To be sure, individual agents can divert from the timing of peak opportunity when investing in major life goals. However, the price for such off-time goal engagements is that under conditions of less-than-optimal opportunities, the individual

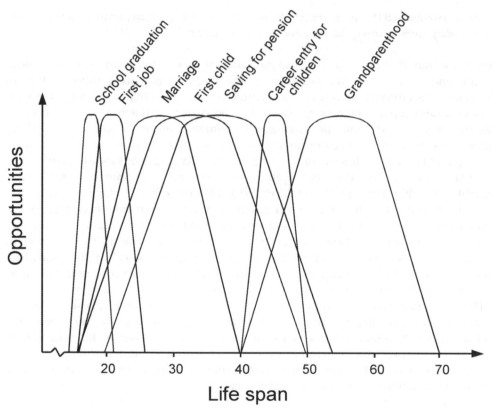

Figure 2. Age-graded sequencing of opportunity trajectories (hypothetical) for different developmental goals (adapted from Heckhausen, 2000).

has to invest extra resources to compensate for the untoward developmental ecology, resources that may be missed in other domains of functioning.

An important aspect of this model of time-structured goal opportunities across the life span is that, at the lower end of decreasing opportunities, goal attainment becomes close to impossible and so costly that further goal engagement becomes virtually futile. This is the point of a developmental deadline. Developmental deadlines prompt the individual to disengage from goal striving but also exert an influence before being passed. When coming up for a deadline, people are likely to anticipate it and experience urgency in achieving the goal before the deadline passes and opportunities are lost forever. In this way, developmental deadlines provide an exceptional challenge to developmental regulation, because they require the individual to shift from an urgent and intense engagement with a goal before hitting the deadline to disengagement and self-protection after passing the deadline.

Specifically, we expect the following three control strategies to be activated during goal engagement and particularly during phases of urgency when the deadline draws close. *Selective primary control* is directed at attaining effects in the environment by selectively investing behavioural resources such as effort, time and skills. *Compensatory primary control* involves attempts to recruit assistance and advice from others and to use technical devices and unusual means. It becomes important when internal resources are insufficient, and therefore compensatory means are needed. Finally, *selective secondary control* mobilizes volitional commitment to the chosen goal, by enhancing the perceived value of the goal and the perceptions about its attainability.

Goal disengagement by contrast, is achieved by using *compensatory secondary control* strategies. These strategies serve two different but complementary functions. First, goal disengagement is achieved by deprecating the value of the original and futile goal and enhancing the value of competing or alternative goals. This helps to free up behavioural and motivational resources for fruitful primary control pursuits. Second, the potentially negative effect of missing the deadline on motivational resources is buffered by using various self-protective strategies, such as attributing the failure to external causes and comparing oneself with others who are worse off.

An action-phase model of developmental regulation

How can we envisage the cycle of goal engagement and goal disengagement as the individual moves through a phase of waxing and waning opportunities for a particular developmental goal? In this regard, the key proposition of our theory is that shifts into goal engagement and from goal engagement to goal disengagement are not gradual but discrete and radical. The individual is either in a 'go' mode or in a 'stop and withdraw' mode. Specifically, the phases of the action cycle and the control strategies involved in each phase is represented in Fig. 3.

This model (Heckhausen, 1999a) expands and modifies the Rubicon model of action phases proposed by Heinz Heckhausen for action phases in general (H. Heckhausen, 1991: H. Heckhausen & Gollwitzer, 1987) to actions directed at developmental goals. During the predecisional phase, different developmental alternatives (e.g. careers) are compared with regard to their advantages and problems and using an information-processing mode of openness and impartialness. Once the decisional Rubicon has been passed, this open mode radically shifts to a mode of functioning suitable to maximize primary control of the chosen goal. To this end, selective primary control and selective

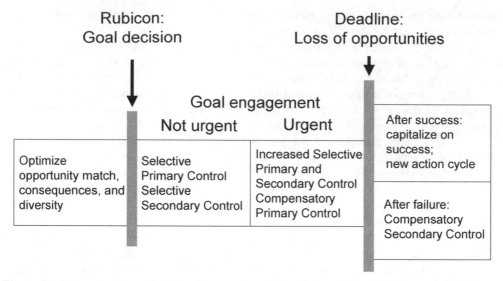

Figure 3. Action-phase model of developmental regulation (adapted from Heckhausen, 1999a)

secondary control are invested. As the individual agent moves closer to the deadline for the chosen goal, primary control striving enters a phase of urgency, during which all control strategies are invested with even greater intensity. In addition, compensatory primary control may be used, should internal behavioural resources be insufficient to reach the urgent goal. However, once the deadline is passed without achieving success, goal engagement becomes dysfunctional. In fact, a radical shift from goal engagement to disengagement is the most adaptive response to this shift in opportunities. This shift to disengagement is analogous to the lion chasing a prey; at first he goes full speed (urgent goal engagement), but when the prey turns out to be too fast and the gap widens, the lion will not gradually slow down but will stop in his tracks and turn around. It is active disengagement that achieves this rapid and radical shift from goal engagement to disengagement. This means that strategies of goal disengagement need to be an important part of compensatory secondary control, so that futile investments of behavioural and motivational resources are prevented. In addition, self-protective strategies of control should help minimize the long-term damage that failing the deadline could have on motivational resources (e.g. self esteem, and hope for success in future actions). In case of success when the goal has been attained before the deadline passed, the individual can build on the success in the same domain (e.g. strive for the next promotion, have a second child) or control resources may be switched over to another domain, which may have lain dormant during the urgent investment in the goal that has now been achieved. An example is a switch from career to family investment after achieving a long-awaited and time-sensitive promotion (e.g. tenure in an academic career).

Applying the action-phase model to life-course transitions

An ongoing research programme addresses the ways in which people at various ages and in different socio-cultural contexts respond to challenging transitions in their lives; transitions that affect their opportunities to control outcomes and attain goals in important domains of functioning (e.g. career, family). The general paradigm is one of identifying notable shifts in the opportunities for attaining important goals and then investigating whether individuals engage and disengage with the respective goals in congruence with the changes in opportunities. A first set of studies addressed the transition from favourable to unfavourable opportunities to attain important goals in adulthood, namely bearing a child and living with an intimate partner. These studies were cross-sectional because the changes in opportunities extend over long time periods that make longitudinal tracking difficult.

We conducted two studies on developmental regulation before and after passing the developmental deadline for childbearing (Heckhausen *et al.*, 2001). In an attempt to investigate women before and after the 'biological clock' runs out, we recruited childless women in the age ranges 30–35 years (pre-deadline urgency condition), 40–45 years (just after deadline), and 50–55 years (typically long after deadline). We investigated these women's self-reported control strategies with regard to the goal of bearing a child. The control strategies were measured using a domain-specific version of the Optimization in Primary and Secondary Control scales (OPS scales), which addresses the primary and secondary control strategies with regard to having a biological child. Sample items include 'I try everything possible to have my own children' for selective primary control; 'I try not to be distracted by other things from my wish for a child' for selective secondary control; 'When having a child proves difficult for me, I seek the advice of others (e.g. physicians)' for compensatory primary control, 'If I cannot realize my wish for a child, I can get it out of my mind' for the goal disengagement component of compensatory secondary control; and 'It is not my fault, if I do not have a child' for the self-protection component of compensatory secondary control.

The ratings for the control strategies in this study on the developmental deadline for childbearing indicate that the childless women in their early 30s were highly engaged with the goal of having a first child. They rated selective primary control and compensatory primary control, as well as selective secondary control, much higher than the childless women in their 40s or 50s. Conversely, women in their 40s and 50s rated strategies of compensatory secondary control significantly higher than the younger, pre-deadline women. Thus, the findings show that both pre-menopausal women and women in an age range of declining fertility or even post-menopause reported patterns of control strivings that were congruent with the opportunities for childbearing given at their respective ages.

Next, we investigated the question of whether such opportunity-congruent patterns of control strategies have implications for psychological well-being. In order to address this question, we investigated the association between control strategies and depressive symptoms measured by the Center for Epidemiological Studies Depression scale (CES-D; Radloff, 1977). Figure 4 shows the significant interaction between group and selective primary control on depressive symptoms by displaying the association between selective primary control (sample item: 'I try everything possible to have my own children') and depressive symptoms for the groups before the deadline (30–35 years of age) and after passing the deadline (40–45 years and 50–55 years of age).

Figure 4 shows that strong selective primary control striving is beneficial for women before the childbearing deadline in that they report fewer depressive symptoms than those women their age who express less control striving for a child. For the women who have passed the deadline, the relationship is the opposite; the more they strive for having a child, the more depressive symptoms they report. Thus, patterns of well-being

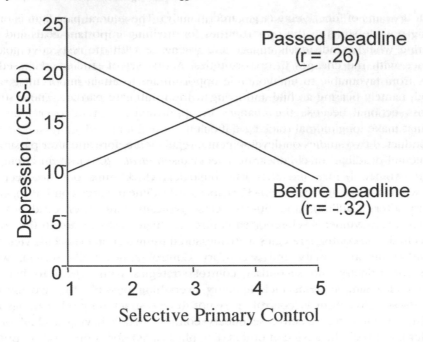

Figure 4. Selective primary control as a predictor of depressive symptoms in childless women who have and have not passed the childbearing deadline (adapted from Heckhausen *et al.*, 2001).

reflect the degree of congruence between opportunities and control striving, greater congruence is associated with relatively few depressive symptoms and incongruence is related to elevated depressive symptomatology.

In another study about the deadline for childbearing, we wanted to explore whether goal engagement and goal disengagement would be related to information processing biases, thus showing an implicit or subintentional effect of motivated information processing. In order to assess such implicit information processing biases, we used an incidental memory paradigm. We recruited pre- (27–33 years old) and post-deadline (40–46 years old) childless women. Subjects were asked to nominate five developmental goals for the next 5–10 years (goal questionnaire; see Heckhausen, 1997). Subjects also completed the Positive and Negative Affect scale (PANAS; Watson, Clark, & Tellegen, 1988). Incidental recall was measured by introducing the participants to sentences about children and babies and sentences not relevant to children or babies. The participants were asked to respond quickly and spontaneously to them in terms of the degree of agreement they felt with each sentence. The women then completed the PANAS and were subsequently asked to recall as many sentences as they could. Participants did not expect this memory task.

The findings of this study indicated that developmental goals varied as a function of age. Pre-deadline women reported more goals about childbearing than post-deadline women did, and post-deadline women mentioned more goals about developing the self, finding and maintaining friendships, and protecting one's health. Again, we questioned whether these differences in the motivational orientation towards the deadline-sensitive goal were associated with psychological well-being as reflected in positive and negative affect. Findings were significant for the passed-deadline group only: women who had passed the deadline were more likely to report negative affect when they had good recall for sentences containing statements about the positive value of living with children, the reasons that one is not to blame or that one is to blame for one's own childlessness, and the ways in which one can capitalize and build on having a child (e.g. become a grandparent). In sum, this study showed both intentional and subintentional evidence for opportunity-congruent goal engagement and disengagement. In addition, incongruence of implicit goal orientation with opportunities for goal attainment was associated with more negative affect.

Another study examining developmental deadlines in adulthood addressed the goal of establishing an intimate relationship (Wrosch & Heckhausen, 1999). Finding an intimate partner for a long-term relationship is possible throughout adulthood and thus seems an unlikely area to study deadline-related control behaviour. However, the probability of finding a new partner undergoes a linear decline across adulthood from about 80% in early adulthood to 20% in advanced midlife (Wrosch & Heckhausen, 1999). Thus, individuals have to adjust their control behaviour regarding intimate relationships accordingly if they want to avoid investing in a costly and relatively futile endeavour. It can be expected, therefore, that individuals set their own deadlines for disengaging in the search for an intimate partnership some time in midlife. In this study, recently separated and recently committed men and women were recruited from two age groups, 20–35 and 50–60 years of age. Presumably, participants in the younger group have a high probability of finding an intimate partner, while those in the older group have a low probability of finding an intimate partner. In this chapter, we focus on the findings for the recently separated women and men.

Similar to the childbearing study, subjects in the partnership study were expected to use control strategies and endorse goals that are congruent with the opportunities encountered n the respective age groups. The findings support this prediction. Young adults nominated more partner-related goals and provided higher ratings for the goal engagement control strategies, selective primary control, selective secondary control and compensatory primary control. Older adults reported using more strategies of compensatory secondary control, both the disengagement and the self-protective components.

An incidental-recall task was also included in the partnership study. Subjects rated positive and negative adjectives (e.g. happy and deceptive) with regard to the question, 'whether most people view their partnerships as …'. After a short interval, an unannounced test for the recall for these adjectives was conducted. The findings showed that young adults were more likely to remember relatively more positive than negative aspects of partnerships than late midlifers. In contrast, men and women in their 50s were more likely to recall relatively more negative than positive adjectives.

The partnership study involved a follow-up 18 months after the initial data collection that was mostly focused on psychological well-being. Would congruent goal engagement and goal disengagement be superior to an incongruent engagement pattern in bringing about positive well-being over the course of 18 months? Figure 5 displays the pattern of predictors for a change in positive affect over the longitudinal span. As can be seen in Fig. 5, compensatory secondary control strategies (sample items: 'I can lead a happy life without having a partner', 'It is not my fault if I do not have a partner') were beneficial for late midlifers but detrimental for young adults. If young adults gave up the goal of partnership after a recent separation, their positive affect was likely to decline over the course of the following 18 months. For women and men in their 50s, however, giving up on the goal of achieving an intimate partnership promoted positive affect over time.

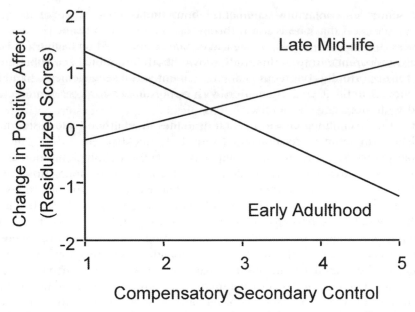

Figure 5. Compensatory secondary control as a predictor of change in positive affect over 18 months in recently separated women and men in early adulthood and late midlife (adapted from Wrosch & Heckhausen, 1999).

In sum, the cross-sectional studies addressing adults' control behaviour when navigating a transition from favourable to unfavourable opportunities for attaining an important goal of adult development supported the action-phase model of developmental regulation. When approaching a deadline, adults exhibited intense goal engagement involving the relevant control strategies. In contrast, after passing a deadline, the adults were likely to disengage using compensatory secondary control strategies. Moreover, the more this pattern of opportunity-congruent goal engagement and disengagement was exhibited, the better were psychological well-being and mental health. Engagement and disengagement with important life goals was also reflected in biased information processing, so that urgently engaged individuals also recalled more goal-relevant information, whereas disengaged individuals recalled less goal-relevant information or information that implied a negative aspect of the goal in question. In one study, evidence was found that the degree to which information processing was biased in congruence with the opportunity structure was associated with less negative affect. Thus, cycles of goal engagement not only comprise explicit intentions and behaviours accessible to self-report, but also involve implicit cognitive orientations that facilitate information processing in the service of the different action phases.

After establishing the phenomenon of pre- versus post-deadline difference in goal engagement in these cross-sectional studies, we took the next step of investigating switches between action phases across a longitudinal span. This is a challenging endeavour because changes in opportunities to attain important developmental goals usually take a long time. Moreover, given that most people attain the important goals during the time when opportunities are at their peak, prospective studies would have to start with very large samples in order to detect a sufficient number of individuals, who get close to or even pass a deadline without attaining the goal.

We therefore picked a transition that is highly predictable and happens during a relatively short time-span—the transition from school to work—and tracked adolescents' vocational goals and control strategies used to attain them. In the German system, the developmental task of entering the workforce is scaffolded by the institution of apprenticeship (Hamilton, 1990), which channels young people into vocational career paths and provides them with certificates of vocational qualifications. However, this has become a considerable challenge. Due to globalization and the economic strain associated with German reunification, apprenticeship positions have become hard to obtain. About 30% of a given cohort end up with no apprenticeship position when they graduate from school. Thus, German adolescents face the challenge of competing for an apprenticeship, which will shape their career and financial prospects for their entire future life, in a situation of scarce supply. The acuteness of the challenge is heightened by the implicit yet inescapable deadline for starting an apprenticeship. Blossfeld (1990) has demonstrated that German adolescents who do not start vocational training within 2 years of graduating from school will not stand a significant chance of ever receiving vocational training and thus will be doomed to unskilled work for their entire working life. Therefore, the urgent task for these adolescents is one of choosing and securing an apprenticeship position during a short period of time in 10th grade just before graduating from school. A particularly challenging aspect of this choosing and securing is to calibrate one's aspirations such that one's potential for a well-paid vocation is realized, yet overshooting one's potential is avoided in order not to risk failure to attain an apprenticeship altogether. Thus, the adolescents have to navigate the Scylla and Charybdis of under- and over-aspirations.

In order to track control striving and engagement for the goal of seeking an apprenticeship, we studied the senior classes in four middle-tier schools (called 'Realschulen') using a micro-sequential approach during 10th grade (bi-monthly data collections) and following them through 3 years after graduation (Heckhausen, 1999b). Longitudinal follow-ups and analyses in this study are still ongoing. An initial set of findings (Heckhausen & Tomasik, 2002) relates to the adjustments of vocational aspirations and their relation to school grades, a topic that will be revisited in the final section of this chapter. First, we examined more closely the jobs adolescents mentioned as their dream jobs and those they applied for, in particular with regard to their social prestige. We found that during the urgent phase of 10th grade, the adolescents adjusted their 'dream job' upwards and downwards towards a closer match with the apprenticeships they were considering applying for.

Next, we investigated possible explanations for an intriguing finding: adolescents who succeeded and those who failed to secure an apprenticeship did not differ in their school grades, even though it is known that employers scrutinize applicants' school grades. This scrutiny is high especially when selecting apprentices for more challenging vocational training positions. Was it that the young applicants selected vocations in accordance with their school performance? Maybe school grades served as guidelines for these adolescents to judge whether a certain apprenticeship is within or out of their league.

Figure 6 shows the relationship of school achievement and vocational aspiration by plotting the bivariate distribution of these two variables. The regression line representing the relationship for the sample reflects a positive relationship. Overall, the adolescents apply for apprenticeships at a level of social prestige that matches their school performance, thus demonstrating adaptive calibration of their vocational aspirations. Further analyses indicated that this adjustment of aspirations to the available resources (e.g. school grades) is particularly salient during the urgent and most active phases of application.

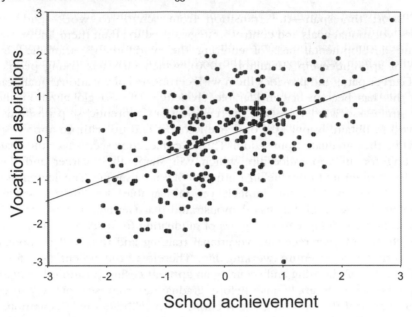

Figure 6. Bivariate distribution of school achievement and vocational aspiration (adapted from Heckhausen & Tomasik, 2002).

It is quite impressive to find this level of sophisticated adaptive goal engagement and goal calibration in these 15–16-year-old adolescents. Most likely, the institutional scaffolding of the school-to-work transition in the German system is a great help to these adolescents, because it makes salient what the challenges are and which behaviours and decisions are adaptive during the critical phase.

Characteristics of the labour market and educational system in other countries render the school-to-work transition a much riskier enterprise. A case in point is the USA, where institutional channelization of the transition into work is scarce (Hamilton, 1990; Heinz, 1999). Under such conditions, the navigation of the transition is up to the individual, their regulatory skills and social support. A longitudinal study of high school seniors from the Los Angeles metropolitan area is therefore under way to investigate adaptive and maladaptive motivational orientations, control strategies and social support systems (Heckhausen, Chen, Greenberger, & Dooley, 2002).

Implications for students' motivation in secondary schools

The association between secondary school achievement and post-secondary school employment success appears to be strong. Researchers have found that earning good grades in secondary school is associated with successful employment in the years immediately following school. However, the pathways from school to work vary greatly across societies. This variation may facilitate differences in the types of motivation (intrinsic versus extrinsic) and the degree of goal engagement that are required for a successful transition which differentially affect the behaviour of adolescents negotiating this transition in different societies.

Researchers in the USA, studying the school-to-work transition, have found strong connections between academic achievement and employment success. For instance, Cooksey and Rindfuss (2001) examined the work and school patterns of young adults in the USA. They found that the young adults, both male and female, who earned poor grades while in high school increased the likelihood of experiencing time away from the labour force due to unemployment or being between jobs. In addition, low grades in high school increased the probability of a young adult entering the workforce instead of going to college. Moreover, many young adults participated in both work and school, either simultaneously or going back and forth between phases of education and employment.

Rosenbaum and Kariya's (1991) findings, however, are not consistent with a strong relation and intermeshing between school and work. They compared the impact of school achievement on holding white-collar and desirable manual jobs for Japanese and US high school graduates. They found that for white-collar jobs, grades had a strong association for all Japanese participants and a medium association for the US female young adults, but no association for the US males. For manual jobs, grades again had a strong association for Japanese men, but no association for US men (only males were included in this analysis). A possible explanation for this difference in the findings for US participants is that Rosenbaum and Kariya (1991) broke down employment into two categories—white-collar jobs and desirable manual jobs—and Cooksey and Rindfuss (2001) looked at employment as a whole.

In our longitudinal study of the school-to-work transition in Germany, a strong association between academic achievement (grades in school) and an adolescent's aspirations for an apprenticeship with high social prestige was found (Heckhausen & Tomasik, 2002). Further, Heinz (1999) found a positive association between German adolescents' academic achievement and the prestige of the apprenticeship that they were able to secure.

Researchers in other countries have also examined the impact of academic achievement on employment success after the transition from school to work. Patton and colleagues (Patton, Creed, & Muller, 2002) investigated the distinctive character-istics of Australian adolescents who go into the labour force versus those who continue their education. Self-reported school achievement was higher for those who continued with their education than for those who went into the labour force. Caspi, Wright, Moffitt, and Silva (1998) studied the childhood and adolescent predictors of unemployment in the transition to adulthood for New Zealand young people. They found that failure to have a School Certificate (an optional examination taken at around age 15), low achievement in reading during the last year of compulsory education (age 15) and dropping out of school were all predictors of both unemployment and length of time unemployed for the first 5 years after the end of compulsory education. Bynner (1999) showed that for young adults in the UK, low literacy and low numeracy were related to an increased likelihood of being vocationally bound versus academically bound and also predicted an increased probablility of being unemployed.

It thus appears that secondary school achievement is closely related to the overall success in work life for young people in most industrialized countries. However, it is unclear what the mechanisms are that mediate this relationship. Is it mediated through institutionalized selection processes being based on school achievement? Or are good grades and success in work life simply two indicators of effective individual abilities and motivation? The consistently strong role that academic achievement plays in the school-to-work transition across different countries and institutional settings is striking, and suggests that this may be due more to individual differences creating a positive manifold than to institutional channelling.

Kerckhoff (2000) described the differences in the school-to-work transition of adolescents in four countries: Germany, the USA, the UK, and France. He examined the social and institutional contexts of each country and how these different environments are associated with different trajectories of youth who make the transition from secondary school into the workforce. He differentiates the four cultures on three domains: (1) stratification, which is also referred to as tracking, (2) educational standardization, referring to the degree of control the national government has over the schools, and (3) the type of educational credentials that secondary schools award; general, vocational, or both on separate tracks. Germany and the USA are on the extremes of the domains, with the UK and France falling in the middle. Germany is described as high on stratification, high on standardization and having a separate vocational credential (i.e. 'Hauptschule', 'Realschule') besides the general educational credential (i.e. 'Abitur'). Adolescents in Germany are tracked into schools based on their achievement when they are 10 years old (in two states of Germany, it is 12 years of age). Two-thirds of German adolescents participate in a 3-year apprenticeship, thus earning a certificate in a particular trade or industry and then go on to seek employment in the labour market for qualified jobs (Heinz, Kelle, Witzel, & Zinn, 1998). The USA is described as low on stratification, low on standardization and having a general credential only. US adolescents graduate from high school at age 18. They earn a general diploma without specific job training. The UK is described as having a medium degree of stratification and standardization, and as having both general and vocational credentials. Finally, France is described as having a medium degree of stratification and a high degree of standardization, and as having both general and vocational credentials (see Kerckhoff, 2000 for a more complete discussion).

The type of jobs that adolescents hold while still in formal schooling also differs. Typically, US adolescents are employed in part-time jobs while in high school (Hamilton, 1990). These jobs generally have few requirements, do not reinforce school learning and offer little training. Thus, they provide little preparation for adult work. German adolescents, however, typically do not hold jobs, although they do participate in apprenticeships. The German school system has two tracks—vocational and higher education (Hamilton, 1990). Young people who are in the vocational track participate in a 3-year apprenticeship that provides them with training to gain the skills required for adult work.

Rosenbaum (1996) also helps provide evidence for differences in the institutional support in the school-to-work transition. In the USA, employers do not take into consideration academic achievement (grades, class rank or test scores) when hiring high school graduates. According to Rosenbaum, employers generally do not even ask for this information when they hire someone. This is very different from the employment experiences of college graduates where grades directly affect the jobs that people get. Rosenbaum (1996) goes on to describe three consequences of US employers ignoring the grades of potential high school graduate hires: (1) they ignore a good indicator of the qualities of their potential workers, (2) students who plan on heading straight into the workforce will have less incentive to do well in school, and (3) approximately half of the high school graduates who do not go to college do not have jobs at the time of graduation, and of those who do have jobs, the majority continue in the same job that they had in high school. The unspoken message to work-bound high school students is that high school graduation and achievement in high school do not matter much because, regardless of these two factors, the jobs tend to remain the same.

An additional aspect to take into account when comparing different countries in their school-to-work transitions is the structure of opportunities and constraints provided by educational institutions and the labour market in these countries (Hurrelmann, 1996). All students in Germany attend school for at least 10 years. Then, as previously mentioned, most German adolescents participate in an apprenticeship. Securing an apprenticeship has a strong association with academic achievement (Heinz, 1999). When adolescents apply for apprenticeship positions, grades are a primary criterion used for selecting an applicant to fill a position. Those who follow the vocational route take a state-approved examination once they complete their apprenticeship at approximately 18 years of age.

The pathway from school to work is much less clear for adolescents in the USA than it is in other countries, such as Germany or Japan. There are no commonly accepted institutions of vocational training for different vocations, and thus it is unclear how vocational qualifications can be acquired. Also, as we have seen above, employers do not communicate that school achievement plays a major role in their decisions about who to hire. This lack of an obvious connection between secondary school achievement and employment is likely to have a dampening effect on adolescents' motivation to do well in school. Work-bound students in the USA, where grades do not appear to be instrumental in obtaining a job, are less likely to see the external reward (i.e. future employment) of doing well in school. If they do well in school, it is for intrinsic reasons of achievement motivation, reasons that are likely to keep them active and striving after graduating from high school too. For college-bound US students, the motivation to do well in school can be both intrinsic and extrinsic—students need good grades to go to college, earn scholarships, etc. However, for work-bound adolescents in countries where the connection between secondary school achievement and employment success is much stronger (e.g. Germany), students are motivated both intrinsically and extrinsically. School behaviour is an investment both in the self and in one's future success. The clarity of the pathway from school to work also promotes adaptive goal engagement. In the USA, the young people will have difficulty engaging in goal-directed behaviour, as they will not necessarily know what to do. In countries such as Germany and Japan, where the pathways are clearer, the behaviours (e.g. academic achievement) required for reaching a goal of employment are likely to be known.

Summary

Motivational and developmental psychology are integrated in this approach to studying individuals' efforts to regulate their own development across the life span. The life-span theory of control conceptualizes developmental regulation in terms of individuals' striving for primary control, while pursuing important developmental goals such as finding a partner, having children and starting an occupational career. Secondary control is conceptualized as assisting such primary control strivings by helping to focus motivational resources and volitional commitment, and by facilitating goal disengagement and self-protection when failure or loss have occurred or appear likely. Across the life course, such goal engagement and disengagement typically and adaptively follow waxing and waning opportunities for goal attainment. Just before opportunities run out at a certain age, and thus a deadline for goal attainment in a certain domain is passed, goal engagement becomes more urgent, and thus more resources are invested in primary control striving. Once the deadline is passed, goal engagement is deactivated, and self-protection buffers the negative effects of this control loss for motivational resources (e.g. self-esteem).

This model of developmental regulation was put to the test in a set of cross-sectional studies addressing goal engagement and control striving in deadline-prone developmental goals (i.e. childbearing, finding a partner). The findings indicate that control strivings and goal engagement and disengagement follow the urgent and the post-deadline opportunity structure. Moreover, indicators of biased and selective information processing show that subintentional processes also reflect this opportunity-congruent goal engagement and disengagement. In addition, these studies showed that opportunity-congruent goal engagement and disengagement are associated with positive psychological well-being, while non-synchronic engagement and disengagement are related to compromised psychological well-being.

The research programme then took another step to investigate opportunity matching goal engagement and disengagement in a longitudinal study, so that changes in opportunities and control strategies could be tracked as they occur over time. A first study addressed the school-to-work transition in German adolescents and revealed adaptive goal adjustments in these young adolescents. Work is under way to investigate developmental regulation during the school-to-work transition in US youth, too. These young people face an even greater challenge because few institutions of vocational training exist to pave the way and set some guidelines.

Finally, we discussed the implications of different educational systems for the developmental regulation of adolescents in the school-to-work transition. In particular, attention was paid to the questions of whether school achievement has instrumental value in this transition and whether adolescent intrinsic or merely extrinsic motivation is required. This area of research has been largely neglected and deserves particular attention in future research.

References

Baltes, P. B. (1997). On the incomplete architecture of human ontogeny: Selection, optimization, and compensation as foundation of developmental theory. *American Psychologist, 52*, 366–380.

Blossfeld, H.-P. (1990). Changes in educational careers in the Federal Republic of Germany. *Sociology of Education, 63*, 165–177.

Bynner, J. (1999). New routes to employment: Integration and exclusion. In W. Heinz (Ed.), *From education to work: Cross-national perspectives* (pp. 65–86). Cambridge: Cambridge University Press.

Caspi, A., Wright, B. R. E., Mofitt, T. E., & Silva, P. A. (1998). Early failure in the labor market: Childhood and adolescent predictors of unemployment in the transition to adulthood. *American Sociological Review, 63*, 424–451.

Cooksey, E. C., & Rindfuss, R. R. (2001). Patterns of work and school in young adulthood. *Sociological Forum, 16*, 731–755.

Hamilton, S. F. (1990). *Apprenticeship for adulthood: Preparing youth for the future*. New York: Free Press.

Heckhausen, H. (1991). *Motivation and action*. Berlin: Springer.

Heckhausen, H., & Gollwitzer, P. M. (1987). Thought contents and cognitive functioning in motivational versus volitional states of mind. *Motivation and Emotion, 11*, 101–120.

Heckhausen, J. (1997). Developmental regulation across adulthood: Primary and secondary control of age-related challenges. *Developmental Psychology, 33,* 176-187.

Heckhausen, J. (1999a). *Developmental regulation in adulthood: Age-normative and socio-structural constraints as adaptive challenges.* New York: Cambridge University Press.

Heckhausen, J. (1999b). Balancing for weaknesses and challenging developmental potential: A longitudinal study of mother-infant dyads in apprenticeship interactions. In: P. Lloyd, & C. Fernyhough, (Eds.), *Lev Vygotsky: Critical assessments Vol 3: The zone of proximal development* (pp. 81-100). London: Routledge.

Heckhausen, J. (2000). Evolutionary perspectives on human motivation. In J. Heckhausen & P. Boyer (Eds.), Evolutionary psychology: Potential and limits of a Darwinian framework for the behavioral sciences (Special issue). *American Behavioral Scientist, 43,* 1015-1029.

Heckhausen, J. (2002). Developmental regulation of life-course transitions: A control theory approach. In L. Pulkkinen & A. Caspi (Eds.), *Paths to successful development: Personality in the life course* (pp. 257-280). Cambridge: Cambridge University Press.

Heckhausen, J., Chen, C., Greenberger, E., & Dooley, D. (2002). *School-to-work transition in a multi-ethnic metropolitan sample of working and middle-class youth: Individuals' control striving and social network influences.* Unpublished project proposal, University of California, Irvine.

Heckhausen, J., & Schulz, R. (1995). A life-span theory of control. *Psychological Review, 102,* 284-304.

Heckhausen, J., & Schulz, R. (1999). The primacy of primary control is a human universal: A reply to Gould's critique of the life-span theory of control. *Psychological Review, 106,* 605-609.

Heckhausen, J., & Tomasik, M. J. (2002). Get an apprenticeship before school is out: How German adolescents adjust vocational aspirations when getting close to a developmental deadline. *Journal of Vocational Behavior, 60,* 199-219.

Heckhausen, J., Wrosch, C., & Fleeson, W. (2001). Developmental regulation before and after a developmental deadline: The sample case of 'biological clock' for childbearing. *Psychology and Aging, 16,* 400-413.

Heinz, W. R. (1999). Introduction: Transitions to employment in a cross-national perspective. In W. Heinz (Ed.), *From education to work: Cross-national perspectives* (pp. 1-21). Cambridge: Cambridge University Press.

Heinz, W. R., Kelle, U., Witzel, A., & Zinn, J. (1998). Vocational training and career development in Germany: Results from a longitudinal study. *International Journal of Behavioral Development, 22,* 77-101.

Hurrelmann, K. (1996). The social worlds of adolescents: A sociological perspective. In K. Hurrelmann & S. Hamilton (Eds.), *Social problems and social contexts in adolescence: perspectives across boundaries* (pp. 39-62). New York: Aldinbe de Gruyter.

Kerckhoff, A. C. (2000). Transition from school to work in comparative perspective. In M. Hallinan (Ed.), *Handbook of the sociology of education* (pp. 453-474). New York: Kluwer Academic/Plenum.

Patton, W., Creed, P. A., & Muller, J. (2002). Career maturity and well-being as determinants of occupational status of recent school leavers: A brief report of an Australian study. *Journal of Research on Adolescence, 17,* 425-435.

Radloff, L. S. (1977). The CES-D scale: A self-report depression scale for research in the general population. *Applied Psychological Measurement, 1,* 385-401.

Rosenbaum, J. E. (1996). Policy uses of research on the high school-to-work transition. *Sociology of Education, Special Issue,* 102-122.

Rosenbaum, J. E., & Kariya, T. (1991). Do school achievements affect the early jobs of high school graduates in the United States and Japan? *Sociology of Education, 64,* 78-95.

Rothbaum, F., Weisz, J. R., & Snyder, S. S. (1982) Changing the world and changing the self: A two-process model of perceived control. *Journal of Personality and Social Psychology, 42,* 5-37.

Schulz, R., & Heckhausen, J. (1996). A life span model of successful aging. *American Psychologist, 51,* 702-714.

Watson, D., Clark, L. A., & Tellegen, A. (1988). Development and validation of brief measures of positive and negative affect: The PANAS scales. *Journal of Personality and Social Psychology, 54,* 1063-1070.

White, R. W. (1959). Motivation reconsidered: The concept of competence. *Psychological Review, 66,* 297-333.

Wrosch, C., & Heckhausen, J. (1999). Control processes before and after passing a developmental deadline: Activation and deactivation of intimate relationship goals. *Journal of Personality and Social Psychology, 77,* 415-427.

103

Development and Motivation, 103–123
BJEP Monograph Series II, 2
© 2003 The British Psychological Society

www.bps.org.uk

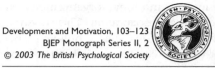

Two motivational systems that shape development: Epistemic and self-organizing

Kurt W. Fischer* and Michael W. Connell
Harvard Graduate School of Education, USA

Cognitive science, with its narrow focus on the structure of the mind, has largely lost sight of motivation. In this article, we propose that understanding the structure of the mind requires understanding the forces and biases that shape the mind—which are generally called 'motivation'. Development is not the execution of a program, the implementation of a blueprint or the unfolding of a pre-determined sequence. It is a dynamically equilibrated, self-organizing process that is both driven internally toward higher levels of complexity and simultaneously supported and shaped powerfully by the contexts to which it has adapted over evolutionary time and to which it is constantly adapting in real time (Baldwin, 1894; Fischer & Bidell, 1998; Heckhausen, 2000; Piaget, 1967/1971; van Geert, 1998; Vygotsky, 1978; Wiener, 1965). Understanding development requires identifying and characterizing the processes that allow a person to bootstrap themselves into acquiring the fundamental representations needed to build ever more complex knowledge. These processes provide the impetus to move toward higher levels of complexity, and they are shaped by internal and external constraints and influences, resulting in the diverse yet characteristic shapes that development and learning assume.

In this article, we argue that two kinds of motivation are key mechanisms that together drive and shape cognitive and emotional development: epistemic motivation, and self-organizing motivation. A concrete developmental phenomenon exemplifies each type of motivation: circular reactions for epistemic motivation and positive self-attribution bias for self-organizing motivation. Epistemic motivation promotes development of skills and knowledge of the world. Self-organization promotes construction and regulation of stable patterns of activities based on long-term goals and representations, especially those involving self and others.

These two motivational processes work through similar processes, although they act to shape distinct content. Both of them constitute broad developmental forces that

*Requests for reprints should be addressed to Kurt W. Fischer, Harvard Graduate School of Education, Larsen 702, Cambridge, MA 2138, USA (e-mail: kurt_fischer@harvard.edu).

have strong sensorimotor origins in early development and are realized in terms of specific goals and concerns of each developing individual. They function through particular emotional organizations that comprise similar processes of appraisal, feedback and adaptation. The concrete phenomena of circular reactions and positive self-attribution facilitate building specific dynamic models of the two kinds of motivation, which specify both common processes and differences in content. Based in emotion processes and neural networks, these models outline how the two related types of motivation participate in developmental processes operating across diverse time scales (seconds to years).

Epistemic motivation: Circular reactions in children and adults

In a classic portrait of infancy, a baby experiences an interesting event, such as seeing a mobile jiggle over her crib, and she works hard to make it happen again and again. This is the essence of the mechanism of epistemic motivation—a drive to repeat and master interesting events in the world, and thus to create knowledge. With Piaget's (1936/ 1952) classic observations, he tied a string from his baby's hand or foot to the mobile, and she moved her limb over and over to make the mobile move. For example, a baby girl in a crib with a low-hanging mobile moves her arms and legs around in apparently random motions, happening to jerk the string or kick the mobile and thus making the object spin and emit a sound like a musical chime. The motion and sound attract her attention, and she focuses on the mobile and kicks her legs more enthusiastically at the same time. These activities make it more likely that she will jiggle the mobile again, and over time, she repeats and varies her activities until she learns an effective way to kick her foot to create the interesting actions of the mobile.

Circular reactions in children

The relation between action and event is the key to circular reactions, and the phenomenon has been described extensively not only by Piaget but also by J. M. Baldwin (1894), Henri Wallon (1970) and Carolyn Rovee-Collier (Rovee-Collier & Sullivan, 1980). Response-contingent activity promotes positive emotions and leads directly to growth of knowledge and skills (Fischer, Shaver, & Carnochan, 1990; Krapp, 2003; Locke, 1993). 'Interesting' events create circular reactions, which lead people to persist until they master a skill or understand an event.

In Piaget's words, '. . . [W]hat Baldwin called the *circular reaction* [is] the first step toward all other accommodations. The child does something at random, and when he gets an interesting result, he repeats the action indefinitely. In this way, he learns to suck his thumb, to seize objects, to make noises by knocking hard things together, and so on. The circular reaction is therefore the utilization of chance.' (Piaget, 1927, *The first year of life in the child*, as cited in Gruber and Vonèche, 1977, p. 202). Piaget describes the circular reaction as a mechanism for explaining how infants develop initial sensorimotor knowledge that will serve as the foundation for all later knowledge.

Complex circular reactions in adults

Although most of the research literature attributes circular reactions primarily to the early years, research suggests that it is an important mechanism in development and learning throughout the human life span (Csikszentmihalyi, 1997; Fischer & Yan, 2002; Krapp, 2003; Yan & Fischer, 2002). The process seems to be more protracted in early development and therefore more obvious, but older children, adolescents and adults can all be captured in circular reactions by captivating contingencies. For example, creators of electronic games recognize the power of this mechanism of epistemic motivation when they create circular structures to their games to keep people playing, sometimes to the point of exhaustion. Computer programming can have the same qualities: how often have we been caught by a programming effort, as time passes unnoticed, until we end up disoriented and feeling strange from exhaustion as we finally break out of the programming activity? The difference between infant, child and adult circular reactions seems to be the complexity of the capturing activity. Infants can be captured more easily by ordinary events in the world, while adults are captured by complicated tasks and games that are usually socially constructed. The capturing comes not from the complexity of the action but from the motivational process that appraises it as interesting and worth repeating or varying. Studies of microdevelopment illustrate some such circular activities, as we will describe later. Developmental and educational scholars have appreciated neither the role of epistemic motivation in producing the circular reaction in the first place nor its role in driving and shaping development.

Research on microdevelopment in learning situations shows the pervasiveness of circular reactions in adult learning and problem-solving (Yan & Fischer, 2002). When adults encounter a novel, interesting task or situation, they commonly pursue it energetically until they reach some understanding or skill, or until they become tired or are obliged to pursue another goal. For example, when Granott (1994, 2002) placed adult teachers and graduate students in a room with Lego robots, which they had not seen before, they began exploring the robots energetically. Their explorations demonstrated a recurring, circular learning process, as shown in Fig. 1 for one dyad, named Ann and Donald. The scale labelled Skill Level is based on hierarchical complexity level as specified in skill theory, which is strongly grounded in empirical research demarcating distinct developmental levels (Dawson, 2002; Dawson & Gabrielian, 2003; Fischer, 1980; Fischer & Rose, 1994; http://gseacademic.harvard. edu/~hcs/base/index.shtml). They began with primitive, confused activities with one of the robots and gradually built up some understanding of the gadget over a few minutes of exploration, as shown in the Start panel. Soon, however, they encountered a change in the situation—a wire falling out and being put back inadvertently in a different place. Their 'skill' collapsed, falling down again to a primitive, confused level, and then gradually they built it up again over a few minutes, as shown in the panel Redo Gadget. Next, someone walked up and asked them to explain what they had done: their explanation again collapsed immediately to a very low level, as shown in the panel Explain, and then relatively quickly, they built up a more complex explanation. Finally, in the fourth panel Redo, they purposely removed a wire and put it back in a different place, and once again their skill fell down to a low level, and they gradually built it up until the session ended.

This example shows the dynamics of a circular reaction. Not only did the adults spontaneously stay with the task and repeatedly work with understanding and controlling the robot, even though they were free to do other activities at any time, but they also evidenced a recurring process of short-term learning and collapse of skill, thus showing a kind of repetition or circularity similar to the infant trying over and over to make a mobile jiggle and occasionally succeeding. The activity and skill are more complex than the infant's, and consequently the circularity is less obvious to an

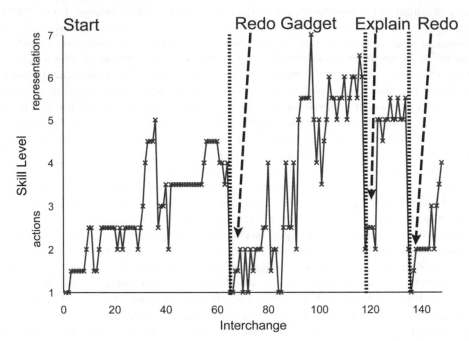

Figure 1. A circular reaction in an adult dyad exploring a Lego robot. Data from Granott (1994, 2002).

observer; but it is clearly present. We hypothesize that older children and adults regularly show circular reactions of this kind in their daily learning and problem-solving.

Even Charles Darwin demonstrated complex circular reactions as he struggled to understand variations in species and fossils. His notebooks clearly demonstrate both short-term circular reactions, such as trying to understand a particular species, fossil or formation (a kind of finch, a dinosaur bone, a coral reef) and longer-term ones, such as grappling with the nature of evolution (Fischer & Yan, 2002; Gruber, 1981; Keegan, 1989). Indeed, his notebooks show that he worked for years to understand the nature of species variation and evolution, building a series of different explanatory principles, several of which were abandoned while others were maintained and revised. Eventually, he constructed the successful principle of evolution by natural selection, which emerged from his earlier principles and also required repeated reconstruction. He 'discovered' it several times and then lost it, similar to the way that Ann and Donald lost their understanding of the Lego robot several times. Eventually in 1838 and 1839, he consolidated the principle into a skill that he could consistently formulate, generalize and use to explain many of his observations.

In general, circular reactions in both infants and adults depend on at least three components: (1) a process that spontaneously *generates* behaviours, (2) a mechanism for *detecting and appraising* interesting response-contingent configurations of the world (some set of criteria for what constitutes an interesting event) and (3) an intrinsic motivation to attend to and try to *repeat* an interesting behaviour once it has been observed. In older children and adults, a fourth component is required—a mechanism for appraising whether something is interesting, based on the person's long-term goals and knowledge. For example, Darwin appraised observations and ideas in terms of his goal of explaining the variations of species and his extensive knowledge of biology and geology.

Taken together, these last three components constitute what we call *epistemic motivation*—the intrinsic human ability to identify interesting events and the motivation to attend to them and to try to make them repeat. These components are essential to fundamental emotional/motivational processes in development and learning and provide clues about the nature of the motivational processes underlying regulation of behaviour and learning.

Model for epistemic motivation

Emotion and motivation organize a feedback process that controls immediate behaviour and shapes learning and development (Bickhard, 2003; Fischer *et al.*, 1990; Frijda, 1986; Heckhausen & Schulz, 1995; Higgins, Roney, Crowe, & Hymes, 1994; Lazarus, 1991; Scherer, 1984). This process of behaviour regulation forms the core of the models of epistemic motivation and self-organizing motivation. Figure 2 shows the general model as applied to epistemic motivation: a person acting in a specific context notices something important based on his or her concerns and goals (notable change) and appraises that change. Based on the appraisal, they select (unconsciously) a pattern of behaviour (action tendency), which is a script, not merely a single action. For example, the script for anger includes a focus on the problematic situation, a bias toward attributing blame, a pattern of facial expression and posture, and a tendency to act

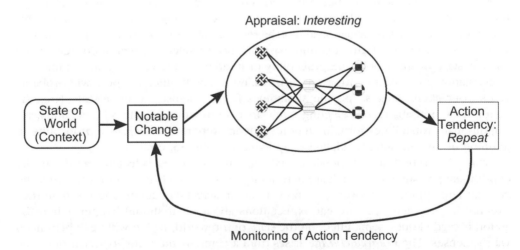

Key: *Notable Change*: Something happens that the person notices. *Appraisal*: Person evaluates the notable change with respect to its valence (positive or negative) and coping potential for the self. For epistemic motivation, it is evaluated as interesting. *Action Tendency*: Person has various probabilities for specific actions, such as for a baby kicking, hitting with hands, or lying still. *Monitoring*: Person can notice their own activity and appraise it, which becomes common later in development.

Figure 2. Model of motivational system applied to epistemic motivation. This general model of motivational/emotional feedback applies to a wide range of actions and contexts, including the circular reactions of epistemic motivation, as shown in the italicized examples. (Reference: Fischer *et al.*, 1990.)

aggressively. In epistemic motivation, the appraisal is that the change is interesting, and the action tendency is to attempt to repeat the event or activity. The action tendency thus leads to circular reactions.

As infants grow, they develop the capacity to monitor their action tendency and often adjust it before they carry out an overt act, as shown in the bottom of the figure (monitoring of action tendency). For example, a child can become anxious in reaction to feeling angry at Mother. For epistemic motivation, if a notable change is interesting but socially inappropriate, such as bumping into someone on the pavement, most people will not try to recreate it (except in slapstick comedies).

Mathematical models of neural networks capture an essential part of this model: In a context, a person processes input through the nervous system and acts, and the results of the action feed back to alter the values of elements in the neural network (Elman *et al.*, 1996; Grossberg, 1987). This feedback shapes the neural network and thereby influences future action tendencies, which is key to learning and development. The network component of the model is represented in Fig. 2 by the multi-node diagram under Appraisal. We describe the properties of neural networks below.

This model represents the type of feedback mechanism that we hypothesize to be common to both types of motivation, epistemic and self-organizing. Dealing with the full range of motivational phenomena requires an elaboration of the circuit, explicitly differentiating two kinds of knowledge stored in neural networks. On the one hand, people have knowledge about *how the world is*, which involves primarily epistemic motivation. On the other hand, they have knowledge about *how I and other people generally act or should act* in the world, which relates centrally to self- (and other-) organizing motivation.

The basic idea of the motivational model is that a person senses and appraises the world around them, and the appraisal informs possible actions. For example, jumping is not an option when crawling on hands and knees through a narrow tunnel. This context also provides information about the relative value of selecting any given action, which (in this model) translates into a probability of selecting that action given the current state of the world: the probability of jumping while crawling in a tunnel (or while standing in a room with a very low ceiling) is small, since jumping will probably crack your skull. Because people sometimes forget themselves or miscalculate, the conditional probability of selecting such an action will typically still be non-zero. Conditional probabilities form an action tendency repertoire, such as a probability of jumping of .01, waving .21, kicking .23, doing nothing .35, etc.

From this repertoire of possible actions, one action is selected based on the conditional probabilities, which are determined by personal history, motivational state, context and appraisal. Between the time a person selects an action and the time they execute it, they generate internal expectations about what should happen when the action is carried out—some effect on the state of the world, which will be experienced via the senses. The *notable change* arises from a comparison of the *expected* outcome with the *experienced* outcome resulting from the action. If the actual effects match expected effects, then there is no notable change, representations about the world do not change, and no surprise, interest or other behaviour-organizing affective states are induced. If, however, the expectations do not match the experience, then this difference serves as a feedback signal to drive learning, moving the expectations closer to the current experience.

For older children and adults, another component must be added to the model to expand epistemic motivation beyond the immediate interest of an event to include its relation to a person's long-term goals and knowledge. Emotion theorists often place these long-term representations in the same box with all the appraisals of the proximate aspects of the event. We suspect that a realistic model of motivational/emotional processes requires separate loops for short-term appraisal of current experience and long-term appraisal of expected outcomes and implications (represented in Fig. 6 later in this article). Many of the circular reactions of older children and adults depend on the interest sparked by long-term appraisal. Being caught in a circular computer game is mediated mainly by the short-term appraisal loop, but being caught in a search to explain an anomaly in a computer program or a pattern of variation in species is mediated mainly by the long-term loop. We will elaborate properties of this loop in the discussion of self-organizing motivation, which depends more obviously on the long-term loop than epistemic motivation.

Over time, the process of epistemic motivation outlined in Fig. 2 refines knowledge and skill to make them more accurate and more adaptive. In simulated neural networks, mechanisms of this kind have produced effective adaptive learning, without the need for any kind of explicit teacher (Elman *et al.*, 1996; Grossberg, 1987; Tesauro, 1995).

Neural networks

Artificial neural network models are computer simulations of neural processes based on data from neurobiology and neurochemistry. They are powerful tools for exploring how constraints and processes at the neural level might percolate up to constrain and shape mental/psychological and behavioural phenomena (Elman *et al.*, 1996; Grossberg, 1987; Quartz & Sejnowski, 1998). They avoid many of the flaws of classical cognitive science, which are based on the assumption of a language of thought, an encoding or copying of the world in the brain or mind (Bickhard, 2003; Bickhard & Terveen, 1995; Fischer & Bidell, 1998; Piaget, 1967/1971). Instead of a language of thought, cognition is based in action, and it can be illuminated by analysis of the neural bases of learning and action. In this chapter, we use artificial neural networks as a source of concepts and constraints for analysing the mechanisms that underlie motivation and for scaffolding interpretations of the concrete scenarios that exemplify each type of motivation— circular reactions and self-organizing bias. The neuroscientific foundations of the networks complement the cognitive and behavioural foundations of most research on motivation and development.

Virtually all of the many different types of artificial neural network models share two assumptions: (1) the neuron doctrine—the neuron is the atomic processing unit in biological neural systems, and (2) the network doctrine—that learning processes act upon synapses that connect neurons to one another, thereby producing the changes in neural circuitry for memory formation, skill acquisition or refinement, and other alterations in mental processing or overt behaviour. Every neural network model works with the properties of three components: nodes (simulated neurons), connections (type and strength) and learning rules that specify how synaptic properties change under what conditions (typically from some kind of experience). Figure 3 diagrams these elements for a generic neural network model.

The construction of these models is informed and constrained by principles of neuroscience, so that they are grounded in a way that purely cognitive or behavioural models are not. The use of neural network models to analyse motivation has been rare, and we hope to catalyse work on modelling motivation through this analysis. Neural network models can suggest novel hypotheses and provide data on the feasibility of a

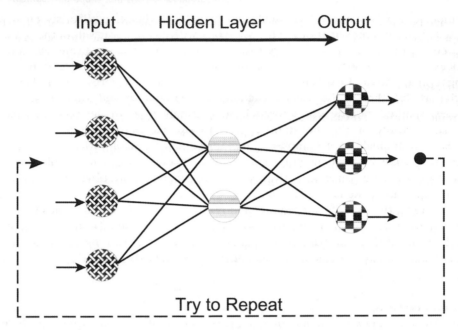

Figure 3. Generic artificial neural network model. Nine nodes (circles) are organized in three layers (input, hidden, output) and connected from left to right. Lines between nodes indicate connections, each with a specific synaptic weight (connection strength). The network changes its activity patterns as a result of learning rules that systemically modify synaptic weights based on experience. The network repeats its activity, as in a circular reaction, in order to learn appropriate activity patterns.

hypothesis concerning the mechanism(s) underlying, for example, development of epistemic motivation and self-organizing motivation. They have proved extremely fruitful in analysing other change phenomena, such as habituation, learning and cognitive and language development (Elman *et al.*, 1996; Grossberg, 1987; Mareschal & Johnson, 2002).

Indeed, neural networks have properties that seem to have direct analogues in human motivation. First, they show something akin to circular reactions. To adapt, learn or develop, they act, adjust and act again—over and over and over, just like people caught in a circular reaction, as indicated by the bottom arrow in Fig. 3. This property is central to what is called 'self-organization' in neural networks and other dynamic systems (Thelen & Smith, 1994; van Geert, 1991): through processing biases and bootstrapping mechanisms, they sustain persistent patterns, and over time, different kinds of patterns often emerge as a function of experience. In a similar way, the human being (with central contributions from the brain, of course) produces persistent and changing patterns of activity over time and experience. We propose that motivational processes, such as both epistemic and self-organizing motivation, specify key biases and organizing principles that create these properties and that are similar in neural networks.

Second, neural networks provide mechanisms for coordination of information across diverse contents, such as vision and movement (Bullock & Grossberg, 1988; Mareschal & Johnson, 2002) or emotion and cognition. An essential question for understanding human action and thought is how affect and behaviour organize each other. Neural network models are a valuable tool, which facilitates our understanding of how affective information (such as positive and negative evaluations of events and activities) shapes learning and knowledge. The circular reactions of epistemic motivation are one example of how motivation and emotion can drive and shape learning.

Appraisal and emotion

Feedback to modify the value of taking a particular action can take several forms. At one extreme, information can have a relatively innate, automatic effect, such as touching a hot stove and experiencing painful burning, which will sharply change the probabilities of action tendencies. For most of human experience, including epistemic and self-organizing motivation, the notable change derives from the comparison of expectation with experience, and it is proportional to the discrepancy between expectation and experience (Hebb, 1949; Heckhausen & Schulz, 1995; Kagan, 1970; McCall, Kennedy, & Appelbaum, 1977). Epistemic motivation functions not only in human beings but also in many animals (Hebb & Thompson, 1968), which show responses to moderate novelty such as interest and exploration. The ultimate result of epistemic motivation then is an increase in the probability of an action tendency that has produced an interesting outcome.

These examples highlight the role of emotion in the model in Fig. 2. The experience of a notable change or discrepancy between expectation and experience leads to an affective appraisal of the significance of the change for that person (Fischer *et al.*, 1990; Lazarus, 1991): Is it good for me or bad for me (evaluation)? How can I cope with it (coping potential)? One example is an appraisal that something is interesting, as in epistemic motivation. Another is that it is dangerous, as with the hot stove. The appraisal creates a signal that focuses and organizes attention and behaviour in a particular pattern—for epistemic motivation, interest in and exploration of the activities and events leading up to the interesting effect.

This kind of learning based on feedback of an evaluation (reinforcement/ punishment) signal has been shown to be surprisingly powerful in artificial neural network models learning to do complex but useful tasks. For example, neural network programs have learned to play backgammon at the level of a master based only on the program's experience of playing the game against itself (with two players both operated by the computer program). The only feedback was a simple evaluation signal—winning or losing the game (Tesauro, 1995).

Some commercial products have integrated motivation and neural networks into their programs to create more complex, human-like agents. For example, computer games such as 'The Sims' simulate characters that have personalities and act independently, seemingly showing 'free will'. The program even allows the human player to turn free will on or off for Sims characters. Each character has a set of motivational characteristics (like weight patterns in a neural network) that interact with properties of objects (also like patterns of weights) to produce goal-directed activities and learning. In this way, characters start with motivational patterns or 'personalities', and objects start with what J. J. Gibson (1979) called 'affordances'. Each character's appraisals of particular experiences affect the neural networks, so that the character's actions change based on its interactions with particular objects and other characters. We know of no efforts yet to program game characters to have epistemic motivation, although some robots have been programmed with partial epistemic motivation, trying to learn how to function in their particular environments—for example, how to move around effectively in a laboratory, office or home (Fischer, Yan, McGonigle, & Warnett, 2000; McGonigle, 2001; Nehmzow & McGonigle, 1994).

In epistemic motivation, the process in Fig. 2 eventually leads to change in the person's representations and skills and gradual decay of the orienting and perseveration of the circular reaction as he or she successfully assimilates the new information. As the person gains more experience with the contingency between their actions and their outcomes, expectations are refined so that eventually they expect that when they kick a leg (for example) in a certain manner, the mobile will swing and chime. Since expectation is aligned with experience at this point, the affective reaction diminishes right along with the 'error' or mismatch signal. As mastery is achieved, the person loses interest in the task and moves on to some other activity. This kind of model strikes us as a plausible, straightforward and elegant mechanism that the neural system can use to optimize learning—one that explains the emergence, maintenance and extinction of circular reactions.

Epistemic motivation serves to modify attention and behaviour to exploit surprising events and thus extract interesting information about the world. The feedback signal of notable change is adaptive for learning and development because unexpected activities and events produce a mismatch between the state of activities in the world and the person's representation of those events and activities in the nervous system. The feedback from that mismatch leads to repetition of the activity until the person's representation approximates the results of the activity. The function of this kind of motivational mechanism is to improve *knowledge and skill* (understanding how the world works).

Self-organizing motivation: Positive self-attribution bias

A second powerful pattern of behaviour captures the essence of self-organizing motivation, just as circular reactions capture the essence of epistemic motivation. When a person detects a notable change, they immediately appraise it as good or bad for the self (to be approached or avoided)—a part of the motivation process in Fig. 2 (Fischer *et al.*, 1990; Frijda, 1986; Higgins *et al.*, 1994; Lazarus, 1991). Generally, people are biased toward the positive, seeking events and activities that are good for the self and avoiding those that are bad. This positive bias goes far beyond immediate reactions, however, pervading the ways in which people represent themselves and others. Self-organizing motivation involves constant appraisal of ongoing activity in terms of its significance for representing oneself and important others, especially evaluating positive and negative aspects of self and others. In essence, self-organizing motivation creates a bias toward enduring appraisal of oneself in positive terms, although the process does also lead to negative biases, both transient and enduring.

People are typically biased to promote or positively represent themselves, including their family and ethnic or religious group, taking personal responsibility for what is good and valued in their lives. Early attachments to caregivers provide a basis for this positive bias in representation of the self as lovable, good and secure (Ainsworth, Blehar, Waters, & Wall, 1978; Ayoub, Fischer, & O'Connor, 2003; Bowlby, 1969). In contrast, people are biased to see others as responsible for what is bad, mean or to be avoided, and to project negative attributions onto out-groups. This prejudice develops early in infancy, when toddlers in their first pretend play typically show what is called 'affective splitting', representing themselves as good and nice and other people as bad and mean (Fischer & Ayoub, 1994). Harry Stack Sullivan (1953) and Daniel Stern (1985) described early versions of this affective splitting in young infants, who seem to organize their world in terms of good and bad activities from the start—good breast, bad breast (will not give milk); good Mother, bad Mother (witch); good me, bad me. This self-organizing bias toward the positive and its complement—the other/out-group-organizing bias toward the negative—are remarkably pervasive and powerful. Indeed, the general pattern of bias is often called the fundamental attribution error or the totalitarian ego (Greenwald, 1980; Unger & Crawford, 1992).

Positive and negative biases in representing self-in-relationships
Research with the Self-in-Relationships Interview illustrates the self-organizing bias in representations of self and others by children, adolescents and adults (Fischer *et al.*, 1997; Fischer, Wang, Kennedy, & Cheng, 1998; Harter & Monsour, 1992). For example, in a study in Suzhou, China, a 17-year-old girl named Jin described herself in her important relationships (with mother, father, best friend, teachers, etc.), listing several characteristics for each relationship (Wang, 1997). Then she created the diagram in Fig. 4a, organizing the characteristics with the most important in the centre of the concentric rectangles and the least important in the outer rectangle. She grouped the characteristics that she saw as belonging together by drawing a line around them, and she indicated important relations between characteristics or groups by drawing a line between them. The relations were designated as showing similarity, opposition or conflict, as shown in Fig. 4a by numbers, letters, and arrowheads, respectively. Most children and teenagers produced sophisticated, complex self-descriptions analogous to Jin's. Children and teenagers in the USA, South Korea, Taiwan and China all showed the same sophistication, despite claims in the literature that Asian adolescents do not show sophisticated self-descriptions (Kitayama, Markus, & Matsumoto, 1995).

The diagrams show dramatically the self-organizing evaluative bias, as illustrated in Fig. 4b. The person rated each of their self-descriptions as positive (+), negative (−), or neither/ambivalent (+/−). Consistently across studies using this interview, people indicate that most of their characteristics are positive, and the relatively few negative responses are mostly marginalized as not important. Figure 4b highlights this pattern by stripping away everything from the diagram except the pluses and minuses. Jin created 18 positive descriptions, 5 negative, and 1 neither/ambivalent, and she made the central rectangle (most important) overwhelmingly positive, with negatives relegated to the less important and least important rectangles. Younger children usually show an even stronger positive bias, leaving out all negative characteristics unless they are specifically asked to include them and hardly ever placing any negative or ambivalent characteristics in the central rectangle as most important. Older children and adults often place one or a few ambivalent or negative characteristics in the centre as most important, while at the same time placing mostly positive characteristics there, maintaining a general positive bias in importance.

In many situations, the self-organizing bias fits this strongly positive pattern, but different meanings and contexts can change the bias dramatically. For example, in pretend play, many 2- and 3-year-old children prefer and enjoy taking the role of a mean, aggressive character, who often has more power and controls the action in a story or game. They also tend to understand these vivid negative roles (being mean) better than positive roles (being nice) (Fischer & Ayoub, 1994; Fischer *et al.*, 1997; Hand, 1982; Hencke, 1996). These young children seem to trade power and vividness for goodness. Even for adults, negative events and creatures can be vivid and attractive: Satan in Milton's *Paradise Lost* and Darth Vader in *Star Wars* are more vivid and perhaps more interesting than God or Obi-Wan Kenobe.

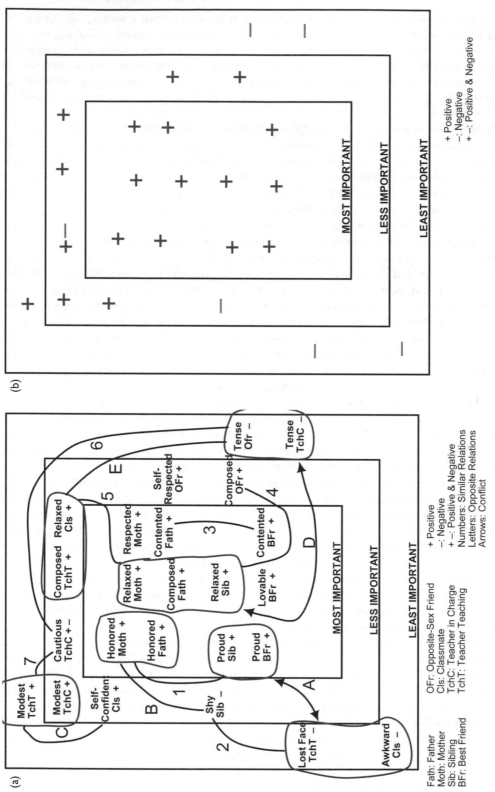

Fath: Father   OFr: Opposite-Sex Friend   + Positive
Moth: Mother   Cls: Classmate   −: Negative
Sib: Sibling   TchC: Teacher in Charge   + −: Positive & Negative
BFr: Best Friend   TchT: Teacher Teaching   Numbers: Similar Relations
                                                      Letters: Opposite Relations
                                                      Arrows: Conflict

Figure 4. (a) Diagram of Self-in-Relationships by 17-year-old Jin. (b) Positive bias in Jin's Self-in-Relationships diagram.

People can sometimes switch between positive and negative states. Sullivan (1953) describes babies as organizing all their current experience around either a positive or negative state, whichever they are experiencing at the moment. Harter (1982) describes young children as feeling 'all good' or 'all smart' at one moment and 'all bad' or 'all dumb' at another. In a pattern called hidden family violence, children and parents act as victims and tyrants in their abusive homes but as 'perfect' good students and citizens in their public personas (Fischer & Ayoub, 1994). In dissociative identity disorder (multiple personality), people seem to organize each identity (personality) around a predominant emotional state, usually with a one-sided valence of mostly negative or positive; different identities are organized around different emotional states (Bower, 1981; Fischer & Ayoub, 1994; Osgood, Jeans, Luria, & Smith, 1976). However, in pretend play and in most other situations, children generally stop choosing negative roles for self by 4 or 5 years of age, although they are still attracted to stories about evil characters (usually vanquished eventually by good characters). As the model of self-organizing motivation is developed, it will need to predict these sorts of variations in choices about positive and negative self and other.

The vast majority of children show a positive self-organizing bias similar to that of 17-year-old Jin in Fig. 4, and this pattern seems to hold even in cultures that emphasize modesty, such as China, Taiwan and Korea (Fischer *et al.*, 1998). However, there is one circumstance that leads to a striking reversal of the bias—extreme child abuse, especially sexual abuse (Calverley, 1995; Fischer & Ayoub, 1994; Raya, 1996; Westen, 1994). In one study, for instance, adolescents who had been severely abused showed a dramatic reversal of the pattern in Fig. 4b (Calverley, Fischer, & Ayoub, 1994; Fischer *et al.*, 1997): they produced predominantly negative characteristics and placed them in the central core of the Self-in-Relationships diagram, as shown in Fig. 5(a and b) for Alison. In this study, the effect of abuse was to shift the affective organization to a negativity bias, while maintaining the same level of developmental complexity as other girls of the same age. (Note: some studies using the Self-in-Relationships Interview have used circular diagrams, as in Fig. 5, and others have used rectangles, as in Fig. 4.)

Alison was a 17-year-old American girl who had been sexually and physically abused repeatedly since the age of 4 years by her father and several other men. She saw herself as empty, sad, used, unlovable, bad, different, lonely, desperate and scared, all of which she categorized as very important characteristics. In general, she described herself in preponderantly negative terms, with 20 negative categorizations, only 4 positive ones and no neither/ambivalent ones. What a sad, woeful representation of self! The only ray of hope in Fig. 5 is that Alison sees her positive characteristics as important (all with her friends, none with her parents or the real me). Like Alison, many of the sexually abused adolescent girls in this study categorized their negative self-descriptions as most important, but, unlike her, many did not see their positive characteristics as important, relegating most or all of them to the less important and least important circles. This negative affective bias seems to stem from the experience of extreme abuse, especially the kind of personal violation that comes with sexual abuse (Waller, Putnam, & Carlson, 1996; Waller & Ross, 1997; Westen, 1994). Self-organizing motivation may be biased toward positive self-attributions in most people, but in extreme cases, it can be reset to a predominantly negative bias.

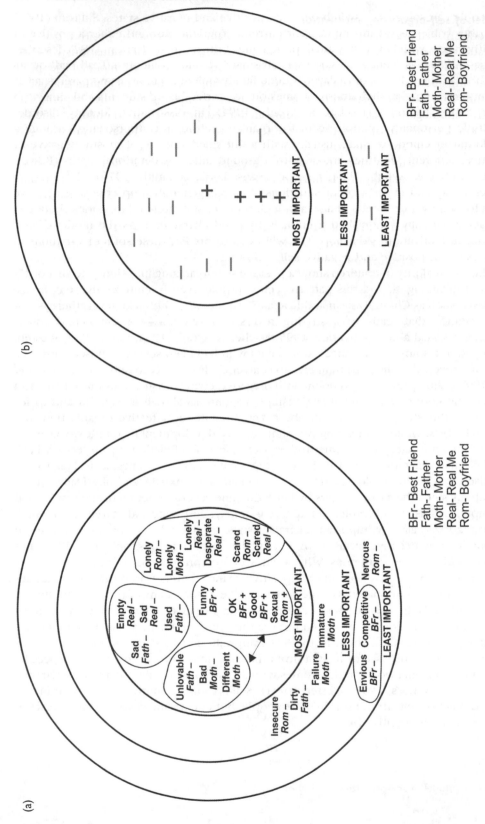

Figure 5. (a) Diagram of Self-in-Relationships by 17-year-old Alison, who had been severely abused. (b) Negative bias in Alison's Self-in-Relationships diagram.

Model of self-organizing motivation

A model of self-organizing motivation must explain the normative positive bias that pervades not only self-in-relationships but also many other self-evaluations, but the consistency of the positive bias makes it obvious and easy to model. The more interesting and challenging scientific task is explaining the variations in affective bias— the shift to a negative bias with abuse, the affective splitting and other variations in positive and negative bias across situations in abused and non-abused children, and the common attribution of negative characteristics to people different from the self, especially people from out-groups.

Self-organizing motivation involves an evaluative bias toward a positive or negative valence of representation of self and others. Such a bias generally fits with the centrality of evaluation in the appraisal process that forms the core of the model for motivation and emotion in Fig. 2. As children develop, they move beyond that simple model to include an additional loop (at least one) that appraises how the event or activity relates to long-term goals and knowledge, shown in Fig. 6. The second loop is important for advanced forms of epistemic motivation, such as Darwin's search for a principle to explain evolution, and it is essential for self-organizing motivation. The baby's initial division of experience and action into good versus bad develops by the end of the second year to include representations of self and others as independent agents. By 2 or 3 years of age, most children constantly appraise events not only in terms of evaluation for proximate aspects but also in terms of long-term relevance to these representations of self and others.

The general model of self-organizing motivation in Fig. 6 specifies how this more complex process occurs. The person detects a notable change, as in emotion processes in general (Fig. 2), and quickly appraises this change in terms of both short-term

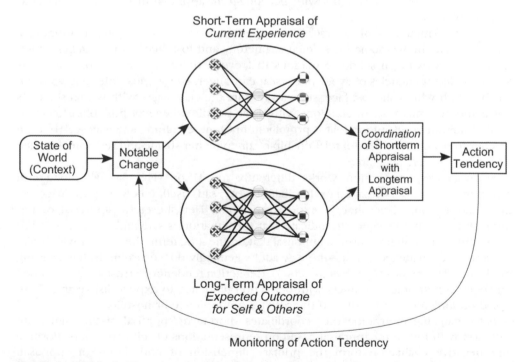

Figure 6. Model of self-organizing motivation.

implications of current experience and long-term implications of the expected outcome over time. These two appraisals are coordinated to produce an action tendency that combines short-term and long-term appraisals. Consider a new college student attending the beginning of her first year at a highly competitive college, such as Harvard, or Oxford University. Attending the first meeting of her physics class, she appraises the immediate situation—I understand what the lecturer says, I am treated respectfully—resulting in a short-term appraisal that everything is going well. At the same time, she appraises the situation in terms of long-term expectations—everybody here is so smart, which is different from my old school; there, I worked hard and did not always understand the material, especially physics—resulting in a long-term appraisal that maybe people are going to discover that I am not really so smart. The coexistence of the two kinds of appraisals leads to complexly motivated actions. Perhaps she says as little as possible to avoid disturbing the immediately positive situation and being found out as not really smart. Perhaps she assertively criticizes another student's mistaken answer to a question to show how smart she is.

In the self-in-relationships studies, Jin's long-term representation of herself as honoured, respected, contented and lovable (Fig. 4a) biases her toward positive emotions in many situations and towards action tendencies based in her confidence and security. Researchers on attachment describe this pattern as a secure internal working model for attachment that provides a strong basis for effective action in the world (Ainsworth *et al.*, 1978; Ayoub *et al.*, 2003; Bowlby, 1969). Across diverse situations, Jin carries with her this positive self-representation as a core component of her long-term appraisal process, resulting in action tendencies of approach and exploration: she often acts confidently to learn in school, to interact happily with friends and to share her inner feelings with her mother and best friend. Her immediate appraisal of a situation as safe and supportive typically fits with her long-term appraisal of herself as honoured and lovable.

In some situations, of course, she experiences negative long-term appraisals, knowing that she has sometimes acted shamefully and lost face with a teacher or felt tense and awkward in school. Situations that evoke these long-term representations lead to action tendencies of avoidance, escape or anger: she spends little time with the teacher with whom she lost face, stays away from the classmates with whom she feels tense and minimizes her interactions with these people whenever possible. However, in the tradition of restitution that is prominent in Chinese culture, she may seek out the teacher to restore a respectful relationship by undoing her shame and restoring her face (Mascolo, Fischer, & Li, 2003).

Self-organizing motivation works differently for Alison (Fig. 5a). Her long-term representation of herself as unlovable, bad, empty, sad, used, lonely, scared, insecure, dirty and a failure leads her to expect the worst. Her short-term appraisal of her interactions with a teacher can indicate that the situation is safe and positive, but her long-term representations lead to appraisal that, in the long term, the teacher will dislike her and take advantage of her—the way adults generally do, according to her working model of relationships (Ayoub *et al.*, 2003). Her action tendency to trust a teacher based on short-term appraisal conflicts with her action tendency to expect dislike and abuse based on long-term appraisal, and the result is ambivalence or hostility.

Self-organizing motivation thus coordinates short-term appraisal of the immediate situation with long-term appraisal based on representations of self and others. Positive and negative evaluation form the primary dimension of both kinds of appraisal. Processes that combine the two kinds of appraisal lead to the varied array of motivational–emotional patterns of action that we have described. As scientists, we face the challenge of building models that can capture and explain these remarkable variations in human behaviour.

Conclusion: The roles of motivation in development

The two types of motivation—epistemic and self-organizing—as well as the phenomena that illustrate them (circular reactions and positive attribution bias) involve common mechanisms while simultaneously differing in the ways that they shape behaviour. Both involve appraisal that coordinates experience with expectation, and both use the discrepancy as an information signal that shapes action, learning and long-term development. Both depend on a process of extraction of regularities from experience that is modelled effectively by artificial neural networks. From a developmental perspective, the two mechanisms of motivation coordinate cognitive and affective facets of experience (action, attention, knowledge, social relationships, environmental affordances) into hierarchically organized adaptive activities, representations and strategies, working together to shape activity and development.

Epistemic and self-organizing motivation differ in the systems being coordinated, especially the dimension of expectation appraised—novelty and interest in the first case and relevance to self-representation in the second. In epistemic motivation and circular reactions, the motivation is to repeat interesting phenomena and gain control of them, which drives the process of knowledge acquisition. In self-organizing motivation and self-attribution bias, the motivation is to match and sustain long-term values and representations of self, usually as positive.

An important component of the process for both types of motivation is short-term appraisal of proximate aspects of an event or activity in contrast to long-term appraisal of implications of an event for broad goals and representations. Epistemic motivation in infancy and early childhood depends primarily on short-term appraisal of proximate aspects (at time scales of seconds), but with development, it comes to be driven also by long-term appraisal, such as career or family goals (at time scales of days and months). Self-organizing motivation emerges with the capacity to represent self and others, although it has an early sensorimotor precursor in the affective organization of behaviour in terms of positive and negative evaluation (good for me versus bad for me). The dimension of affective evaluation remains central at all times, usually with a positive bias involving self; but some circumstances evoke negative biases. Extreme sexual abuse in childhood seems to shift the general self-organizing bias from positive to negative.

In general, epistemic motivation begins with discrepancies between experience and expectation that drive changes to representations about the nature of the world, exploiting surprising events to extract interesting information about the world. Its function is to improve knowledge, to create more effective representations of how one can act effectively in the world. However, self-organizing motivation begins with discrepancies that appraise the match between experience and evaluative representations of self and others. With experience and development, these representations become relatively stable, reflecting the expected evaluations of different courses of action in terms of characteristics of oneself and other people. Its function seems to be to predict and stabilize how the person will interact with the world, especially other people. The normative pattern centres on a positive bias for self and attribution of negative characteristics as less important or as belonging to other people. These two kinds of motivational systems pervade human activity, where they work together to shape long-term development. We have presented a framework that researchers can use to begin to articulate the two systems and specify how they shape development and how they contribute to the wide variations among human beings in knowledge of the world and evaluation of self and others (Fischer & Bidell, 1998; Heckhausen, 2003; Mascolo *et al.*, 2003).

Acknowledgements

The authors thank Catherine Ayoub, Nira Granott, Susan Harter, Rebecca Hencke, Brendan McGonigle, Gil Noam, Pamela Raya, Phillip Shaver, Paul van Geert, Lianquin Wang, Malcolm Watson, and Zheng Yan for their contributions to the work on which this article is based. The research reported here was supported by Frederick P. and Sandra P. Rose, the Spencer Foundation, NICHD grant No. HD32371, and Harvard University.

References

Ainsworth, M. D., Blehar, M., Waters, E., & Wall, S. (1978). *Patterns of attachment: A psychological study of the strange situation*. Hillsdale, NJ: Erlbaum.

Ayoub, C. C., Fischer, K. W., & O'Connor, E. E. (2003). Analyzing development of working models for disrupted attachments: The case of family violence. *Attachment and Human Development, 5*.

Baldwin, J. M. (1894). *Mental development in the child and the race*. New York: MacMillan.

Bickhard, M. H. (2003). An integration of motivation and cognition. *British Journal of Educational Psychology, Monograph Series II, Part 2* (Development and Motivation), 41–56.

Bickhard, M. H., & Terveen, L. (1995). *Foundational issues in artificial intelligence and cognitive science: Impasse and solution*. Amsterdam: Elsevier North-Holland.

Bower, G. H. (1981). Emotional mood and memory. *American Psychologist, 36*, 129–148.

Bowlby, J. (1969). *Attachment and loss. Vol. 1: Attachment*. New York: Basic Books.

Bullock, D., & Grossberg, S. (1988). Neural dynamics of planned arm movements: Emergent invariants and speed–accuracy properties during trajectory formation. *Psychological Review, 95*, 49–90.

Calverley, R. (1995). *Self-representation and self-understanding in sexually abused adolescent girls*. Unpublished doctoral dissertation, Harvard University, Cambridge, MA.

Calverley, R., Fischer, K. W., & Ayoub, C. (1994). Complex splitting of self-representations in sexually abused adolescent girls. *Development and Psychopathology, 6*, 195–213.

Csikszentmihalyi, M. (1997). *Finding flow: The psychology of engagement with everyday life*. New York: Basic Books.

Dawson, T. L. (2002). New tools, new insights: Kohlberg's moral reasoning stages revisited. *International Journal of Behavior Development, 26*, 154–166.

Dawson, T. L., & Gabrielian, S. (2003). Developing conceptions of authority and contract across the lifespan: Two perspectives. *Developmental Review, 23*.

Elman, J. L., Bates, E. A., Johnson, M. K., Karmiloff-Smith, A., Parisi, D., & Plunkett, K. (1996). *Rethinking innateness: A connectionist perspective on development*. Cambridge, MA: Bradford Books.

Fischer, K. W. (1980). A theory of cognitive development: The control and construction of hierarchies of skills. *Psychological Review, 87*, 477–531.

Fischer, K. W., & Ayoub, C. (1994). Affective splitting and dissociation in normal and maltreated children: Developmental pathways for self in relationships. In D. Cicchetti & S. L. Toth (Eds.),

Rochester symposium on developmental psychopathology: Vol. 5. Disorders and dysfunctions of the self (pp. 149–222). Rochester, NY: Rochester University Press.

Fischer, K. W., Ayoub, C. C., Noam, G. G., Singh, I., Maraganore, A., & Raya, P. (1997). Psychopathology as adaptive development along distinctive pathways. *Development and Psychopathology, 9,* 751–781.

Fischer, K. W., & Bidell, T. R. (1998). Dynamic development of psychological structures in action and thought. In R. M. Lerner (Ed.) & W. Damon (Series Ed.), *Handbook of child psychology: Vol. 1. Theoretical models of human development* (5th ed., pp. 467–561). New York: Wiley.

Fischer, K. W., & Rose, S. P. (1994). Dynamic development of coordination of components in brain and behavior: A framework for theory and research. In G. Dawson & K. W. Fischer (Eds.), *Human behavior and the developing brain* (pp. 3–66). New York: Guilford.

Fischer, K. W., Shaver, P. R., & Carnochan, P. (1990). How emotions develop and how they organise development. *Cognition and Emotion, 4*(2), 81–127.

Fischer, K. W., Wang, L., Kennedy, B., & Cheng, C. (1998). Culture and biology in emotional development. In D. Sharma & K. W. Fischer (Eds.), *Socioemotional development across cultures. New directions for child development, 81,* 21–43. San Francisco: Jossey-Bass.

Fischer, K. W., & Yan, Z. (2002). Darwin's construction of the theory of evolution: Microdevelopment of explanations of species variation and change. In N. Granott & J. Parziale (Eds.), *Microdevelopment: Transition processes in development and learning* (pp. 294–318). Cambridge: Cambridge University Press.

Fischer, K. W., Yan, Z., McGonigle, B., & Warnett, L. (2000). Learning and developing together: Dynamic construction of human and robot knowledge. In J. Weng & I. Stockman (Eds.), *Workshop on development and learning: Proceedings of an NSF/DARPA workshop* (pp. 50–59). East Lansing, MI: Michigan State University.

Frijda, N. H. (1986). *The emotions.* Cambridge: Cambridge University Press.

Gibson, J. J. (1979). *The ecological approach to visual perception.* Boston: Houghton-Mifflin.

Granott, N. (1994). Microdevelopment of co-construction of knowledge during problem-solving: Puzzled minds, weird creatures, and wuggles. *Dissertation Abstracts International, 54*(10B), 5409.

Granott, N. (2002). How microdevelopment creates macrodevelopment: Reiterated sequences, backward transitions, and the zone of current development. In N. Granott & J. Parziale (Eds.), *Microdevelopment: Transition processes in development and learning* (pp. 213–242). Cambridge: Cambridge University Press.

Greenwald, A. G. (1980). The totalitarian ego: Fabrication and revision of personal history. *American Psychologist, 35,* 603–618.

Grossberg, S. (1987). Competitive learning: From interactive activation to adaptive resonance. *Cognitive Science, 11,* 23–63.

Gruber, H. E. (1981). *Darwin on man* (2nd ed.). Chicago: University of Chicago Press.

Gruber, H. E., & Vonèche, J. (Eds.) (1977). *The essential Piaget: An interpretive reference and guide.* New York: Basic Books.

Hand, H. H. (1982). The development of concepts of social interaction: Children's understanding of nice and mean. *Dissertation Abstracts International, 42*(11), 4578B.

Harter, S. (1982). Cognitive-developmental considerations in the conduct of play therapy. In C. E. Schaefer & K. H. O'Connor (Eds.), *Handbook of play therapy* (pp. 119–160). New York: Wiley.

Harter, S., & Monsour, A. (1992). Developmental analysis of conflict caused by opposing attributes in the adolescent self-portrait. *Developmental Psychology, 28,* 251–260.

Hebb, D. O. (1949). *The organization of behavior.* New York: Wiley.

Hebb, D. O., & Thompson, W. R. (1968). The social significance of animal studies. In G. Lindzey (Ed.), *Handbook of social psychology* (Vol. 2, pp. 729–774). Reading, MA: Addison-Wesley.

Heckhausen, J. (2000). Evolutionary perspectives on human motivation. *American Behavioral Scientist, 43,* 1015–1029.

Heckhausen, J., & Farruggia, S. P. (2003). Developmental regulation across the life span: A control-theory approach and implications for secondary education. *British Journal of Educational Psychology, Monograph Series II, Part 2* (Development and Motivation), 85–102.

Heckhausen, J., & Schulz, R. (1995). A life-span theory of control. *Psychological Review, 102*, 284–304.

Hencke, R. W. (1996). *Self stories: Effects of children's emotional styles on their appropriation of self-schemata.* Unpublished doctoral dissertation, Harvard University, Cambridge, MA.

Higgins, E. T., Roney, C., Crowe, E., & Hymes, C. (1994). Ideal versus ought predilections for approach and avoidance: Distinct self-regulatory systems. *Journal of Personality and Social Psychology, 66*, 276–286.

Kagan, J. (1970). Attention and psychological change in the young child. *Science, 170*, 826–832.

Keegan, R. T. (1989). How Charles Darwin became a psychologist. In D. B. Wallace & H. E. Gruber (Eds.), *Creative people at work: Twelve cognitive case studies* (pp. 107–125). New York: Oxford University Press.

Kitayama, S., Markus, H. R., & Matsumoto, H. (1995). Culture, self, and emotion: A cultural perspective on "self-conscious" emotions. In J. Tangney & K. W. Fischer (Eds.), *Self-conscious emotions: The psychology of shame, guilt, embarrassment, and pride* (pp. 439–464). New York: Guilford.

Krapp, A. (2003). Interest and human development: An educational-psychological perspective. *British Journal of Educational Psychology, Monograph Series II, Part 2* (Development and Motivation), 57–84.

Lazarus, R. S. (1991). *Emotion and adaptation.* New York: Oxford University Press.

Locke, J. L. (1993). *The child's path to spoken language.* Cambridge, MA: Harvard University Press.

Mareschal, D., & Johnson, S. P. (2002). Learning to perceive object unity: A connectionist account. *Developmental Science, 5*, 151–185.

Mascolo, M. J., Fischer, K. W., & Li, J. (2003). Dynamic development of component systems of emotions: Pride, shame, and guilt in China and the United States. In R. J. Davidson, K. Scherer, & H. H. Goldsmith (Eds.), *Handbook of affective science* (pp. 375–408). Oxford: Oxford University Press.

McCall, R. B., Kennedy, C. B., & Appelbaum, M. I. (1977). Magnitude of discrepancy and the distribution of attention in infants. *Child Development, 48*, 772–785.

McGonigle, B. (2001). Getting artificial agents to control themselves. In O. Holland & D. MacFarland (Eds.), *Artificial ethology.* Oxford: Oxford University Press.

Nehmzow, U., & McGonigle, B. (1994). Achieving rapid adaptations. In D. Cliff, P. Husbands, J.-A. Meyer, & S. W. Wilson (Eds.), *From animals to animats 3: Proceedings of the third international conference on simulation of adaptive behavior.* Cambridge, MA: MIT Press.

Osgood, C. E., Jeans, R. F., Luria, Z., & Smith, S. W. (1976). The three faces of Evelyn: A case report. *Journal of Abnormal Psychology, 85*, 247–286.

Piaget, J. (1952). *The origins of intelligence in children* (M. Cook, trans.). New York: International Universities Press. (Originally published, 1936.)

Piaget, J. (1971). *Biology and knowledge: An essay on the relations between organic regulations and cognitive processes* (B. Walsh, trans.). Chicago: University of Chicago Press. (Originally published, 1967.)

Quartz, S. R., & Sejnowski, T. J. (1998). The neural basis of cognitive development: A constructivist manifesto. *Behavioral and Brain Sciences, 20*, 537–556.

Raya, P. (1996). *Pretense in pair-play therapy: Examining the understanding of emotions in young at-risk children.* Unpublished doctoral dissertation, Harvard University, Cambridge, MA.

Rovee-Collier, C. K., & Sullivan, M. W. (1980). Organization of infant memory. *Journal of Experimental Psychology: Human Learning and Memory, 6*, 798–807.

Scherer, K. R. (1984). Emotion as a multicomponent process: A model and some cross-cultural data. In P. Shaver (Ed.), *Review of personality and social psychology, 5*, 37-63. Beverly Hills, CA: Sage.

Stern, D. N. (1985). *The interpersonal world of the infant: A view from psychoanalysis and developmental psychology*. New York: Basic Books.

Sullivan, H. S. (1953). *The interpersonal theory of psychiatry*. New York: Norton.

Tesauro, G. (1995). Temporal difference learning and TD-Gammon. *Communications of the ACM, 38*(3), 58-68.

Thelen, E., & Smith, L. B. (1994). *A dynamic systems approach to the development of cognition and action*. Cambridge, MA: MIT Press.

Unger, R., & Crawford, M. (1992). *Women and gender: A feminist psychology*. New York: McGraw-Hill.

van Geert, P. (1991). A dynamic systems model of cognitive and language growth. *Psychological Review, 98*, 3-53.

van Geert, P. (1998). A dynamic systems model of basic developmental mechanisms: Piaget, Vygotsky, and beyond. *Psychological Review, 105*, 634-677.

Vygotsky, L. (1978). *Mind in society: The development of higher psychological processes* (M. Cole, V. John-Steiner, S. Scribner, & E. Souberman, trans.). Cambridge, MA: Harvard University Press.

Waller, N. G., Putnam, F. W., & Carlson, E. B. (1996). Types of dissociation and dissociative types: A taxometric analysis of dissociative experiences. *Psychological Methods, 1996*, 300-321.

Waller, N. G., & Ross, C. A. (1997). The prevalence and biometric structure of pathological dissociation in the general population: Taxometric and behavior genetic findings. *Journal of Abnormal Psychology, 106*, 499-510.

Wallon, H. (1970). *De l'acte à la pensée [From action to thought]*. Paris: Flammarion.

Wang, L. (1997). *The development of self-conscious emotions in Chinese adolescents*. Unpublished doctoral dissertation. Cambridge, MA: Harvard Graduate School of Education.

Westen, D. (1994). The impact of sexual abuse on self structure. In D. Cicchetti & S. L. Toth (Eds.), *Rochester symposium on development and psychopathology: Vol. 5. Disorders and dysfunctions of the self* (pp. 223-250). Rochester, NY: University of Rochester.

Wiener, N. (1965). *Cybernetics, or control and communication in the animal and the machine* (2nd ed.). Cambridge, MA: MIT Press.

Yan, Z., & Fischer, K. W. (2002). Always under construction: Dynamic variations in adult cognitive development. *Human Development, 45*, 141-160.

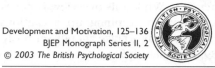

Development and Motivation, 125–136
BJEP Monograph Series II, 2
© 2003 The British Psychological Society

www.bps.org.uk

Taking agency seriously in the theories-of-mind enterprise: Exploring children's understanding of interpretation and intention

Bryan W. Sokol[1]* and Michael J. Chandler[2]

[1]Simon Fraser University, Burnaby, Canada
[2]University of British Columbia, Vancouver, Canada

If generativity were the proper measure of all things, there would be little about the theories-of-mind enterprise, and its guiding 'child as scientist' metaphor, with which to find fault. As it is, our recent work on children's understanding of the interpretive nature of the knowing process (see, e.g., Carpendale & Chandler, 1996; Chandler, Sokol, & Hallett, 2001; Lalonde & Chandler, 2002) has led us to a less generous reading. In particular, we mean to argue that the ubiquity of this metaphor, and the 'causal' language that commonly attends it, works to distort the way in which young people actually understand human thought and action. Specifically, we hope to persuade you that, in its push to situate children's conceptions of others' beliefs and desires within a 'scientistic' framework of folk psychological 'laws' (e.g. Gopnik & Wellman, 1994), the theories-of-mind enterprise has promoted an impoverished conception of agency, that, to borrow from the Enlightenment philosopher Thomas Reid (1788/1863), works to wrongly locate the 'active powers of man' outside, or external to, the individual. The upshot of such an externalist view, as Blasi (1995, p. 235) points out, is that 'the idea that knowledge belongs to, [and] is an intrinsic possession of the conscious person, who intentionally pursues it' is lost, and all talk of subjectivity, at least as it is commonly understood to operate in the personal construction of meaning, takes a backseat to more spurious, 'object-centred' notions that work to reduce genuine interpretive diversity to mundane instances of simple ignorance and *mis*-interpretation (see Carpendale & Chandler, 1996, p. 1693). To show this more clearly, we will first have to say more about an already well-trafficked distinction in the theories-of-mind literature between *passive* 'copy theories' and more *active* 'interpretive' conceptions of mental life (Chandler & Boyes, 1982; Wellman,

Requests for reprints should be addressed to Bryan W. Sokol, Department of Psychology, Simon Fraser University, 8888 University Drive, Burnaby, BC, Canada V5A 1S8 (e-mail: bryan_sokol@sfu.ca).

1990), as well as outlining why children's false belief understanding falls importantly short of being the developmental milestone that best captures this active–passive dimension. While this overview is necessarily brief, it will hopefully provide sufficient justification for running up a cautionary flag meant to warn off those who, like ourselves, mean to take agency seriously (e.g. Bickhard, 2003; Blasi, 1995; Greenwood, 1989; Russell, 1996).

Mental action versus mere activity

A frequent and widely accepted claim in theories-of-mind circles is that young children are first committed to a 'causal', or passive (Pillow, 1988, 1995), conception of the knowing process. By this account, young people first begin the epistemic enterprise by effectively treating their own and others' minds as 'passive recorders' that simply 'bear the scars of information which has been imbossed upon them' by the external world (Chandler & Boyes, 1982, p. 391). An example of such a 'copy theory' at work can be seen in children's early attempts at deception in which they rely on relatively straightforward efforts to keep others in the dark about certain critical details of a situation. The easiest of these to achieve—and so typically the earliest to be seen, even in children as young as 2½ or 3 years old (Chandler, Fritz, & Hala, 1989; Hala & Chandler, 1996)—is that of simple secret keeping. These instances of basic deception turn on little more than efforts to withhold key information by keeping one's own council or some other rough equivalent of hiding one's light under a bushel. Still, because such 'clamming up' activities have been construed in certain functionalist quarters (see Mitchell, 1986; Sodian, Taylor, Harris, & Perner, 1991) as reflecting more of a pre-programmed behavioural response to adversity than a conscientious effort to deceive, learning with some confidence whether young children really do understand the knowing process from a copy-theorist perspective generally requires evidence of a more active and outward sort, typically involving discernible attempts to dis-inform others. What is important to realize here, though, is that even the bulk of these more active attempts to dupe others, similarly evident in the efforts of young pre-schoolers to mislead, turn on the same basic principle of ignorance and, particularly, the notion that others only 'believe what they see' or have otherwise gained informational access to. That is, while secret-keeping strategies are effective because another's state of ignorance is preserved by preventing new and *relevant* facts from coming to light, tactics of disinformation essentially work to achieve the same effect by introducing all *but* the relevant details of a situation. While perhaps in some ways this latter strategy takes on a more sophisticated form, it clearly remains well within the bounds of a copy-theorist framework.

All of this speaks to the *process* of knowing or, more precisely, to what children seem to initially make of it—that much is clear. Still, what remains more or less hidden in the background of this description is exactly where such a copy theory of mind leaves children in terms of their understanding of the *source* of the mind's activity and their consequent notions of *epistemic agency*. A copy theory, we would argue, naturally leads children to view epistemic agency as originating outside, or external to, the individual (see also Bickhard, 2003). This follows from the fact that, based on such a view, the mind is, as Rorty (1979) claims, no more than a 'mirror of nature' that essentially reflects internally on the mind's eye what can be seen externally in the world outside our skins. Although some (e.g. Perner & Davies, 1991) have claimed that the mind, even in this evident state of passive accommodation, is nevertheless 'doing' something, it is no more 'active'—we would counter—than is any other mirror or reflective surface when light strikes it. The mind's activity, in this case, is neither a process that is initiated nor controlled by an active subject, and is akin instead to what philosophers of action (e.g. Frankfurt, 1988; Taylor, 1966; Velleman, 2000) have characterized as behavioural re-actions, or mere internal events, that pale in comparison with more 'full-blooded' (Velleman, 1993) and 'meaningful' (Moya, 1990) real *actions* belonging to, and initiated by, autonomous, self-moving agents. For the young copy-theorist, mental life amounts to 'psychological and physiological *events*' that, as Velleman (1993) notes, may be said to 'take place inside a person', but then (and here's the catch) 'the person serves merely as the arena for these events: he takes no active part' (p. 189). In other words, for those children who hold a copy theory of mind, it is best to say that they recognize the mere *activities* of epistemic 'patients' rather than the meaning-making *actions* of knowing 'agents'.

By contrast, when children come to hold what we have termed an 'interpretive' view of the knowing process, they relinquish their earlier causal conceptions of the mind in favour of a more fully agentive understanding of mental life. Rather than viewing the mind as passively accommodating to the impact of the surrounding world, young people who subscribe to such an interpretive conception understand themselves and others as actively transforming the world by assimilating experience to the mind's existing knowledge structures. By this interpretive account, then, the epistemic process is viewed as being made up of two complementary parts, including not only the 'objective' uptake of information from the world, but also the 'subjective' *action* of giving such input meaning. That is, children holding such an interpretive theory of mind no longer view the knowing process as just another simple instance of what some have called 'mechanical agency' (Bandura, 1986, p. 12), where all activity or movement originates from outside of persons. Rather, they attribute the mind's activity to an autonomous and inherently active subject, who, by personally engaging the world, does more than simply react in some mechanistic fashion, but purposefully pursues and constructs their own meaning from their experience. Such young interpretive theorists, we claim, in coming to regard themselves and others as what Scholastic philosophers once described as 'prime movers', have begun to lay the conceptual groundwork for appreciating the fullness and depth of real actions, as opposed to mere activities or other behavioural contingencies that omit the participation of an active subject.

To quickly summarize, then, the boundary conditions for these two categories of epistemic agency are set by the following contrastive features. On the one hand, there are passive, externalistic and mechanically oriented copy theories that children, at the very beginning of their efforts to piece together some coherent understanding of mental life, appear to possess. On the other hand, there are more active, internalistic and autonomous interpretive views to which older children eventually come when earlier, outdated folk theories of minds and persons are no longer seen to adequately capture the fullness of human actions. Although these definitional matters seem clear enough, translating them from theory into some suitable operational practice has nevertheless met with difficulties. The biggest of these, or so we argue, has to do with matters of 'false belief' understanding, and whether the standard 'unexpected change' and 'unexpected contents' procedures so commonly employed in gauging this epistemic insight are, in fact, adequate tests for crediting children with making the conceptual leap from a copy theory to an interpretive theory of mind. As it turns out, there is no shortage of researchers (e.g. Meltzoff & Gopnik, 1993, p. 335; Ruffman, Olson, & Astington, 1991, p. 90; Wellman, 1990, p. 244) who have said 'yes' to this question, and so would claim, like Perner (1991), that success on false-belief tests is enough to conclude confidently that children 'understand knowledge as representation with all its essential characteristics. One such characteristic is *interpretation*' (p. 275, italics in original). We, however, do not share such confidence and instead argue that simple false-belief understanding falls far short of qualifying as the·interpretive achievement that so many others make it out to be.

False beliefs about false belief

To better illustrate our suspicions, consider first how the typical scenario used to measure children's understanding of false belief is little more than a twist on the old cliché: 'seeing is believing'. In Wimmer and Perner's (1983) now classic 'unexpected transfer' task, a puppet character, Maxi, is out of the room when, unbeknownst to him, his chocolate bar is taken from the cupboard where he put it and left in another place entirely. Child participants in this task who are old enough to appreciate that a person has to at least 'see' an event occur in order to know something about it, and who are equally capable of reversing this logic by recognizing that 'not seeing' has the consequence of leaving one ignorant about particular matters, have all the cognitive prerequisites necessary for understanding what it means to hold a false belief about reality. The working definition of belief in this task, then, is merely a matter of sorting out what aspects of reality a person has been exposed to, and so has had an opportunity to passively register in their mind. That is, despite certain holdout arguments to the contrary (e.g. Perner, 1991), the Maxi task and others like it (i.e. those involving 'unexpected contents' such as the Smarties task of Perner, Leekam, & Wimmer, 1987) require no more than a passive copy theory of mind. By contrast, coming to appreciate that people can, and commonly do, interpret one and the same object or event, differently requires (in addition to simple false-belief understanding) some basic and new-found comprehension of how the knowing process is informed by an active, mind-to-world contribution on the part of autonomous human agents. The stimulus conditions available in the typical false-belief test simply do not meet such rigorous interpretive standards.

Our second consideration in this list of suspicions turns on putting these new criteria to the test by drawing on empirical evidence from our own studies of children's interpretive competence (Carpendale & Chandler, 1996; Chandler & Lalonde, 1996; Lalonde & Chandler, 2002). Put in brief, this programme of research demonstrates that, while 3- or 4-year-olds may well appreciate that those given access to *different* information will hold differing beliefs, it is typically not until they are 7 or 8 years old that such children also recognize that those having the *same* information can also make different interpretive sense of it. In our own efforts, then, to replace the typical false-belief procedure with a more suitable measure, we have found that children's understanding of interpretive diversity is best gauged using ambiguous visual stimuli, such as Roger Price's (1953) famous 'ship-witch' droodle (see Fig. 1). The 'restricted' droodle image seen in this diagram, not unlike a Rorschach inkblot, may elicit from casual observers any number of legitimate beliefs about what it really is. In the context of our experiments with young school-aged children, for instance, participants have credited various puppet observers with interpretations that diverge as dramatically as 'two knife points', 'sharks' teeth', and 'dolphin fins', to name only a few (see Lalonde,

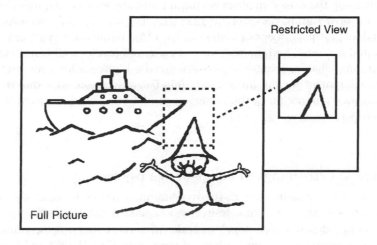

Restricted View

Full Picture

Figure 1. The 'ship-witch' droodle.

1997; Lalonde & Chandler, 2002). Children said to hold an interpretive theory of mind, in fact, quite readily make diverse attributions about others' beliefs in such ambiguous situations. However, children holding a non-interpretive view, or simple copy theory of mind, regularly attribute the *same* belief to independent observers and, if told otherwise, insist that those with a contrary view are simply mistaken. That is, while such non-interpretive children may recognize that observers are ignorant about what the droodle really is (i.e. they succeed at comprehending simple false belief), they nevertheless imagine that everyone (or everyone with any sense) will think that the ambiguous image is exactly the same thing. For these young children, the formation of belief—the essence of the knowing process—remains rooted in the causal push of external, 'objective' reality. The mind, by default, mechanically reflects external experience, even when it remains unclear. By contrast, interpretive children are found to treat the ambiguity of these drawings very differently. For them, the droodle procedure presents the ideal circumstances under which the inherent, 'subjective' action of the mind can show itself, and thus allow autonomous epistemic agency to proceed unchecked by finding different meanings in one and the same thing.

Keeping all of this straight about what does and does not constitute a minimal test of children's interpretive competence obviously depends on having a robust definition of agency in place to sustain the various distinctions we have made here. What seems to be missing from most contemporary work on children's theories of mind, however, is precisely this. Notions of agency, if they are evoked at all, remain closely tied to the well-rehearsed matters of 'psychological causality' (Whiteman, 1967) or so-called 'causal cognition' (Sperber, Premack, & Premack, 1995) where all talk of action is quickly collapsed onto the particular mental states or events that allegedly cause them. On such causal accounts, nothing is thought about 'omitting the agent's participation from the history of his action' (Velleman, 1993, p. 193), nor to the fact that such a 'curious omission', as White (1995, p. 68) calls it, is symptomatic of the field's singular infatuation with epistemic states like belief or desire, while ignoring 'children's understanding of the *person* whose mental states and representations they are' (p. 69, our emphasis) and to which they actively belong. Hobson (1993) has similarly argued that, by maintaining the classic dualism between mind and matter, the theories-of-mind enterprise, as it now stands, fails to recognize that 'the concept of "persons" is more fundamental than . . . the concept of "minds" ' (p. 115). While the term 'person' here is being contrasted to 'mind' and 'mental states', we could just as well insert 'agent' into these descriptions. That is, agents, or persons, are the higher-order constructs needed to make any account of mental life meaningful. To understand why this is the case, however, a closer examination of the dominant model of action in current theories-of-mind research is necessary.

The inherent shortcomings of belief–desire psychology

It is now generally commonplace in theory-of-mind quarters to hear human action described in terms of an individual's desires and beliefs. Wellman (1990), for instance, argues that 'belief–desire psychology' provides the basic organizing principles for understanding children's early conceptions of mind, and Kim (1996), in his influential text, *Philosophy of mind*, has stated quite explicitly that 'it seems essential to our concept of action that our bodies are moved in appropriate ways by our wants and beliefs' (p. 8). As it turns out, these are only some of the more recent expressions of a view whose intellectual history stretches at least as far back as the empiricist philosophies of Hobbes (see his *Leviathan*, Part 1, Chapter 6) and Hume (*A Treatise of Human Nature*; see McNaughton, 1988, pp. 21, 37–38), if not Aristotle (see Smith & Rogers, 2003). Regardless, though, of whatever distinguished names might be attached to such a belief–desire framework of action, our argument here aims to demonstrate that it carries along with it an impoverished view of human agency—one that closely resembles the copy theory of mind just discussed. This essential shortcoming becomes clear upon consideration of what exactly the separate components of belief and desire are meant to bring to the construction of actions.

Among those who make their living studying the mind, beliefs and desires are typically considered to be contrasting mental states (e.g. Astington & Gopnik, 1991) that differ according to the opposing 'directions of fit' that are said to obtain between the mind and the world. Trading upon language popularized by Searle (1983), beliefs are said to 'fit' with the world, relating to it by reproducing or re-presenting the world's contents inside the mind. Desires, by contrast, reverse this relationship and, instead of representing things as they currently stand, work to transform the world to how one wishes it to be—that is, by having the world 'fit' with the ambitions of the mind. On this account, it should be clear that beliefs are taken to serve as the quintessential *representational* state, while desires perform a more *motivational* function. This fundamental contrast is perhaps most evident in the distinct roles that these mental states are said to play in explanations of human action. That is, desires are typically seen as providing the motive force, or hydraulic push, that drives behaviour; while beliefs are taken as supplying the information that properly channel, or guide, this force (see, e.g., Harris, Johnson, Hutton, Andrews, & Cooke, 1989). Beliefs, here, as McNaughton (1988) has noted, are 'motivationally inert; they are merely passive responses to the way the world is' (p. 107); while desires, by contrast, 'are active; directed as they are towards obtaining something, they are intrinsically "pushy" ' (p. 107). No matter how familiar all this may sound, however, there are inherent difficulties with treating human beings like hydrostatic machines—the most obvious being that it throws agency out the window.

Agency lost

The problem, then, with belief–desire psychology is that it too easily allows human action to be construed as the mechanized output of what Harré (1982) has called 'subpersonal components' in the agent's mind. With these isolated parts now taking centre stage in action-explanations, the integrative role of the agent or person, to whom any such component beliefs and desires necessarily belong, is reduced to that of a bit-part and effectively explained away. Having said this, we do not want to be misunderstood as suggesting that the attribution of beliefs and desires, as usual parts of everyday action-explanation, is a mistake. Adults and children do quite regularly evoke such mental states in their common-sense accounts of behaviour, and no doubt use them to reasonably explain and predict others' actions. Rather, our objection arises when these loosely held notions of 'explain' and 'predict' employed in our ordinary day-to-day accounting practices are co-opted by the scientific community and re-read as 'causal' laws that mechanistically 'determine' human action. No doubt, ordinary people (young and old) do say, or are quick to agree, that we all act as we do because of the beliefs we hold or the desires we have. They do so, however, without being burdened, as is the case with most members of the scientific community, with empiricist or reductionist ambitions to depopulate the mind of any and all remnants of will or agency. That is, freed from any professional obligations to adhere to Morgan's Canon, the beliefs and desires of which they (your ordinary child- or person-on-the-street) speak are those closely held beliefs and heartfelt desires of active agents. When all of this is dropped from our professional accounting practices with extreme prejudice, the result is a 'theory-theory' that is only a pale shadow of those real flesh-and-blood theories of mental life it is meant to describe. The end result, in fact, begins to take on an uncanny resemblance to the classical 'black box' accounts that are so much a part of the professional histories of psychologists.

The overall posture of the current theories-of-mind literature seems to set up the conditions for this inadvertent manoeuvre. That is, by adopting the widely held view that beliefs and desires are analogous to 'theoretical constructs' (e.g. Perner, 1991, p. 108) that, in turn, 'provide *causal* explanations' (Gopnik & Wellman, 1994, p. 260, emphasis added) for others' behaviour, it is all too easy to slip into making claims such as: it is 'what actors think—their representation of the world ... [that] inevitably *determines* their actions' (Gopnik & Wellman, 1994, p. 264, emphasis added); or, even worse, into imagining that a simple 'practical syllogism ... works if no unusual circumstances intervene' (Perner, 1991, p. 108) to establish a psychological law (e.g. If Homer wants the beer, and thinks it is in the fridge, then he'll go there) that is adequate to capture the essence of human action. Such a privileging of impersonal, causal language to describe everyday experience has been characterized by Dewey (1989/ 1925, p. 21) as the very sort of 'intellectualism' that, when allowed to proceed unchecked (as it has been in the theories-of-mind literature), wrongly supplants our primary experience of agency as the basis for understanding human action. As a result, we are left, in Campbell's (1995) words, with a 'fragmented ... picture of human action that fits a machine better than an organism' (p. 34).

Similar early warning bells can be heard in the two-century-old cautionary remarks of the Enlightenment philosopher, Thomas Reid (1788/1863). He argued, in particular, that though 'we reason from men's motives [i.e. their beliefs and desires] to their actions, and, in many cases, with great probability' we never do so 'with absolute certainty' (p. 612). This is because human actions are not simply logical outcomes that follow necessarily from the identification of one or another belief–desire combination.

That is, although people may generally acknowledge, as recent research by Malle (1999) suggests, that beliefs and desires constitute 'an agent's reasons for choosing to act a certain way' (p. 24), they are not, by themselves, 'an empirically sufficient condition for the performance of the action' (Hacker, 1996, p. 581). Reasons, or any other serial combination of beliefs and desires, are at best 'enabling' factors that, while perhaps partially constitutive of human actions, are not the sole 'stimulus' conditions (Greenwood, 1988, pp. 100–101) for behaviour that, as Dent (1984, p. 99) says, 'like a weighty brick, fall upon one and impart a certain push to one's body'. Rather, actions are widely understood, at least among everyday folk, to be the natural purview of agents—or persons—who demonstrate self-motivation and exert self-control. Despite whatever claims to the contrary (e.g. Davidson, 1980), an agent's *reasons* must be set apart from the language of mere *causes* (see Chisholm, 1976; Taylor, 1966) if agency, in any robust sense, is to be maintained.

It is, perhaps, *not* our job as empirical scientists to attempt ultimately to sort out these philosophical questions of whether people really are or are not 'agents'. Still, we contend that it *is* our job to describe fairly what children and adults ordinarily suppose happens in the exercise of mental life, and to work to avoid imposing whatever prejudicial conceptual commitments we, or others, might hold regarding causal theories of mind onto the folk accounts of our research participants. If we are right about all this, then it becomes necessary to re-work the standard practice by which belief–desire psychology is applied to folk conceptions of action. More specifically, we must allow for an account that, as Duff (1990, p. 130) has suggested, sees 'persons and actions … [as] logically *basic* categories [that] cannot be explained by an analysis which seeks to reduce them to supposedly simpler elements' (see also Taylor, 1958, p. 215). In other words, beliefs and desires need to be re-integrated into a conceptual framework that at least potentially treats human agency as the primary unit of analysis, instead of something to be analysed away.

The new frontier of intentions

Having strenuously objected to any account of children's theories of mind that makes beliefs little more than the 'passive responses to the way the world is' (McNaughton, 1988, p. 107), our deconstructive efforts would end here were it not for more recent work meant to incorporate some of the foregoing ideas about agency into our ongoing programme of empirical research. More specifically, taking our cue from Wren (1974, p. 33) that the 'core of agency is *intention*' (our emphasis), we have begun to explore how young persons' interpretive competence (as measured by the 'droodles' procedure described earlier) may be used as a marker for further advances in their growing understanding of the multi-layered nature of intention.

Although not alone in this newfound interest in intentionality (see, e.g., Malle, Moses, & Baldwin, 2001; Zelazo, Astington, & Olson, 1999), many of those contributing to this new literature appear to have brought along with them much of the 'causal' language that previously characterized their earlier work on beliefs and desires. For instance, intentions are commonly said to '*cause* the actions they represent' (Astington, 2001, p. 88, emphasis added) and to 'underlie and *cause* bodily movements' (Meltzoff, Gopnik, & Repacholi, 1999, p. 24, emphasis added). The central problem with these causal accounts of intention is again to be found in what they leave out. That is, nothing about them suggests, as Kenny (1963, p. 94) once remarked, that 'an intention (in the sense of making a decision) is itself a human *action*' (our emphasis). Our point here is that intentions, by being subsumed into an exclusively causal framework, ultimately come to be seen as static mental *entities* rather than *actions* or *processes* undertaken by autonomous agents.

To quickly summarize how we have tried to capture this active dimension of intentions in our own work, we have borrowed from Bratman's (1987) characterization of human beings as fundamentally 'planning agents' (p. 2). According to Bratman, we recognize in ourselves not only the ability to act purposively, but more significantly as being constituted by our capacity to form and execute plans. On this view, then, although some of our actions may be described as fulfilling 'present-directed' *desires*, or wants, much of what we do follows from more deliberative, 'future-directed' prior *intentions*, or plans. As a result, even though both intentions and desires may be seen more generally as motivational 'pro-attitudes' (Davidson, 1980), there is a great deal to suggest that collapsing them into a single category is a mistake (Astington, 2001). Specifically, intentions implicate a kind of internalized, autonomous epistemic agency in a way that simple desires, by themselves, do not. In fact, desires, it is commonly said, refer only to specific *outcomes* or end-states of actions (see Malle & Knobe, 2001) that exist quite apart from, or external to, the agent's deliberations. This central difference between such externalistic desires and more autonomous intentions is the whole point, we would argue, behind the notion of 'deviant' or 'wayward' causal chains that philosophers of action (e.g. Chisholm, 1966; Moya, 1990, Searle, 1983) often use to illustrate how an individual's desires may be fulfilled without meeting the conditions of their more active deliberations.

As it turns out, our research (for more details, see Sokol, Chandler, & Jones, in press) has shown that children who can be credited with an interpretive theory of mind are significantly better than their non-interpretive, copy-theorist, counterparts at recognizing this fundamental distinction between intentions and desires. These results support, then, our claims that an active conception of mental life serves as a prerequisite for understanding intentions as mental actions, as opposed to more passive mental states such as desire that lack such agentive features. This also bring us to our final take-home message that any research effort that has the habit of systematically explaining agency away is likely to overlook not only the active dimension of intentions but also the bulk of what makes human mental life so unique. If nothing else, our argument here should make us all wary of the prospect that the causal language currently dominating the theories-of-mind enterprise prevents us from putting our best foot forward when it comes to exploring matters of agency and human action.

References

Astington, J. W. (2001). The paradox of intention: Assessing children's metarepresentational understanding. In B. F. Malle, L. J. Moses, & D. A. Baldwin (Eds.), *Understanding intentions and intentionality: Foundations of social cognition* (pp. 85–103). Cambridge, MA: MIT Press.

Astington, J. W., & Gopnik, A. (1991). Developing understanding of desire and intention. In A. Whiten (Ed.), *Natural theories of mind: Evolution, development, and simulation of everyday mindreading* (pp. 39–50). Oxford: Blackwell.

Bandura, A. (1986). *Social foundations of thought and action: A social cognitive theory*. Englewood Cliffs, NJ: Prentice-Hall.

134   *Bryan W. Sokol and Michael J. Chandler*

Bickhard, M.H. (2003). An integration of motivation and cognition. *British Journal of Educational Psychology, Monograph Series II, Part 2* (Development and Motivation), 41–56.

Blasi, A. (1995). Moral understanding and the moral personality: The process of moral integration. In W.M. Kurtines & J.L. Gewirtz (Eds). *Moral development: An introduction* (pp. 229–253). Barton: Allyn & Bacon.

Bratman, M. E. (1987). *Intention, plans, and practical reason.* Cambridge, MA: Harvard University Press.

Campbell, J. (1995). *Understanding John Dewey: Nature and cooperative intelligence.* Chicago: Open Court.

Carpendale, J. I., & Chandler, M. J. (1996). On the distinction between false belief understanding and subscribing to an interpretive theory of mind. *Child Development, 67,* 1686–1706.

Chandler, M. J., & Boyes, M. (1982). Social-cognitive development. In B. B. Wolman (Ed.), *Handbook of developmental psychology* (pp. 387–402). Englewood Cliffs, NJ: Prentice-Hall.

Chandler, M., Fritz, A. S., & Hala, S. (1989). Small-scale deceit: Deception as a marker of two-, three-, and four-year-olds' early theories of mind. *Child Development, 60,* 1263–1277.

Chandler, M. J., & Lalonde, C. (1996). Shifting from an interpretive theory of mind: 5- to 7-year olds' changing conceptions of mental life. In A. J. Sameroff & M. M. Haith (Eds.), *The five to seven year shift: The age of reason and responsibility* (pp. 111–139). Chicago: University of Chicago Press.

Chandler, M. J., Sokol, B. W., & Hallett, D. (2001). Moral responsibility and the interpretive turn: Children's changing conceptions of truth and rightness. In B. F. Malle, L. J. Moses & D. A. Baldwin (Eds.), *Intentions and intentionality: Foundations of social cognition* (pp. 345–365). Cambridge, MA: MIT Press.

Chisholm, R. M. (1976). *Person and object: A metaphysical study.* London: Allen & Unwin.

Davidson, D. (1980). *Essays on actions and events.* Oxford: Clarendon Press.

Dent, N. J. H. (1984). *The moral psychology of the virtues.* Cambridge: Cambridge University Press.

Dewey, J. (1989). *Experience and nature.* La Salle, IL: Open Court. (Original work published 1925.)

Duff, R. A. (1990). *Intention, agency, and criminal liability: Philosophy of action and the criminal law.* Oxford: Blackwell.

Frankfurt, H. G. (1988). *The importance of what we care about: Philosophical essays.* Cambridge: Cambridge University Press.

Gopnik, A., & Wellman, H. M. (1994). The theory theory. In L. A. Hirschfeld & S. A. Gelman (Eds.), *Mapping the mind: Domain specificity in cognition and culture* (pp. 257–293). New York: Cambridge University Press.

Greenwood, J. D. (1988). Agency, causality, and meaning. *Journal of the Theory of Social Behaviour, 18,* 95–115.

Greenwood, J. D. (1989). *Explanation and experiment in social psychological science: Realism and the social constitution of action.* New York: Springer.

Hacker, P. M. S. (1996). *Wittgenstein: Mind and will. An analytical commentary on the Philosophical Investigations, Vol. 4.* Oxford: Blackwell.

Hala, S., & Chandler, M. J. (1996). The role of strategic planning in accessing false-belief understanding. *Child Development, 67,* 2948–2966.

Harré, R. (1982). *Personal being: A theory of individual psychology.* Oxford: Blackwell.

Harris, P. L., Johnson, C. N., Hutton, D., Andrews, G., & Cooke, T. (1989). Young children's theory of mind and emotion. *Cognition and Emotion, 3,* 379–400.

Hobson, R. P. (1993). *Autism and the development of mind.* Hove, UK: Erlbaum.

Kenny, A. (1963). *Action, emotion, and will.* London: Routledge and Kegan Paul.

Kim, J. (1996). *Philosophy of mind.* Boulder, CO: Westview.

Lalonde, C. E. (1997). *Children's understanding of the interpretive nature of the mind.* Unpublished doctoral dissertation, University of British Columbia, Vancouver, Canada.

Lalonde, C. E., & Chandler, M. J. (2002). Children's understanding of interpretation. *New Ideas in Psychology*, *20*, 163-198.

McNaughton, David. (1988). *Moral vision: An introduction to ethics*. Oxford: Blackwell.

Malle, B. F. (1999). How people explain behavior: A new theoretical framework. *Personality and Social Psychology Review*, *3*, 23-48.

Malle, B. F., & Knobe, J. (2001). The distinction between desire and intention: A folk-conceptual analysis. In B. F. Malle, L. J. Moses, & D. A. Baldwin (Eds.), *Understanding intentions and intentionality: Foundations of social cognition* (pp. 45-67). Cambridge, MA: MIT Press.

Malle, B. F., Moses, L. J., & Baldwin, D. A. (Eds.) (2001). *Intentions and intentionality: Foundations of social cognition*. Cambridge, MA: MIT Press

Meltzoff, A., & Gopnik, A. (1993). The role of imitation in understanding persons and developing a theory of mind. In S. Baron-Cohen, H. Tager-Flusberg, & D. J. Cohen (Eds.), *Understanding other minds: Perspectives from autism* (pp. 335-366). Oxford: Oxford University Press.

Meltzoff, A. N., Gopnik, A., & Repacholi, B. M. (1999). Toddler's understanding of intentions, desires, and emotions: Exploring the dark ages. In P. D. Zelazo, J. W. Astington, & D. R. Olson (Eds.), *Developing theories of intention: Social understanding and self-control* (pp. 17-41). Hillsdale, NJ: Erlbaum.

Mitchell, R. W. (1986). A framework for discussing deception. In R. W. Mitchell & N. S. Thompson (Eds.), *Deception: Perspectives on human and nonhuman deceit* (pp. 3-31). Albany, NY: SUNY Press.

Moya, C. J. (1990). *The philosophy of action: An introduction*. Cambridge: Polity.

Perner, J. (1991). *Understanding the representational mind*. Cambridge, MA: The MIT.

Perner, J., & Davies, G. (1991). Understanding the mind as an active information processor: Do young children have a 'copy theory of mind'? *Cognition*, *39*, 51-69.

Perner, J., Leekam, S. R., & Wimmer, H. (1987). Three-year-olds' difficulty with false beliefs: The case for a conceptual deficit. *British Journal of Developmental Psychology*, *5*, 125-137.

Pillow, B. H. (1988). The development of children's beliefs about the mental world. *Merrill-Palmer Quarterly*, *34*, 1-32.

Pillow, B. H. (1995). Two trends in the development of conceptual perspective taking: An elaboration of the passive-active hypothesis. *International Journal of Behavioral Development*, *18*, 649-676.

Price, R. (1953). *Droodles*. New York: Simon & Schuster.

Reid, T. (1863). Essays on the active powers of man. In *The works of Thomas Reid, D.D.* (6th ed., Vol. 2, pp. 509-679). Edinburgh: Maclachlan and Stewart. (Original work published 1788.)

Rorty, R. (1979). *Philosophy and the mirror of nature*. Princeton, NJ: Princeton University Press.

Ruffman, T., Olson, D. R., & Astington, J. W. (1991). Children's understanding of visual ambiguity. *British Journal of Developmental Psychology*, *9*, 89-102.

Russell, J. (1996). *Agency: Its role in mental development*. Hove, UK: Erlbaum.

Searle, J. R. (1983). *Intentionality: An essay in the philosophy of mind*. Cambridge: Cambridge University Press.

Smith, L., & Rogers, C. (2003). Introduction. *British Journal of Educational Psychology Monograph Series II, Part 2* (Development and Motivation), 1-11.

Sodian, B., Taylor, C., Harris, P. L., & Perner, J. (1991). Early deception and the child's theory of mind: False trails and genuine markers. *Child Development*, *62*, 468-483.

Sokol, B. W., Chandler, M. J., & Jones, C. (in press). From mechanical to autonomous agency: The relationship between children's moral judgments and their developing theories of mind. In J. A. Baird & B. W. Sokol (Eds.), *Mind, morals, and action: The interface between children's theories of mind and socio-moral development*. San Francisco: Jossey-Bass.

Sperber, D., Premack, D., & Premack, A. J. (Eds.) (1995). *Causal cognition*. Oxford: Clarendon.

Taylor, R. (1958). Determinism and the theory of agency. In S. Hook (Eds.), *Determinism and freedom in the age of modern science* (pp. 211-218). New York: New York University Press.

Taylor, R. (1966). *Action and purpose*. Englewood Cliffs, NJ: Prentice-Hall.

Velleman, J. D. (1993). What happens when someone acts? In J. M. Fischer & M. Ravizza (Eds.), *Perspectives on moral responsibility* (pp. 188-210). Ithaca, NY: Cornell University Press.

Velleman, J. D. (2000). *The possibility of practical reason*. Oxford: Clarendon.

Wellman, H. M. (1990). *The child's theory of mind*. Cambridge, MA: MIT Press.

White, P. A. (1995). *The understanding of causation and the production of action: From infancy to adulthood*. Hove, UK: Erlbaum.

Whiteman, M. (1967). Children's conceptions of psychological causality. *Child Development, 38,* 143-155.

Wimmer, H., & Perner, J. (1983). Beliefs about beliefs: Representation and constraining function of wrong beliefs in young children's understanding of deception. *Cognition, 13,* 103-128.

Wren, T. E. (1974). *Agency and urgency: The origin of moral obligation*. New York: Precedent.

Zelazo, P. D., Astington, J. W., & Olson, D. R. (Eds.) (1999). *Developing theories of intention: Social understanding and self-control*. Hillsdale, NJ: Erlbaum.

Development and Motivation, 137–153
BJEP Monograph Series II, 2
© 2003 The British Psychological Society

www.bps.org.uk

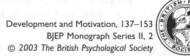

Multiple goals and multiple pathways in the development of motivation and self-regulated learning

Paul R. Pintrich*

The University of Michigan, USA

Current research in motivation has focused on the role of goals and self-regulatory activities as key components of achievement. A central assumption of all models of regulation is that some goal, standard, criterion or reference value exists that can serve as a gauge against which to assess the operation of the system and then guide regulatory processes. In self-regulated learning research, there have been two general classes of goals that have been discussed under various names such as target and purpose goals (e.g. Harackiewicz, Barron, & Elliot, 1998; Harackiewicz & Sansone, 1991), or task-specific goals and goal orientations (e.g. Garcia & Pintrich, 1994; Pintrich & Schunk, 2002; Wolters, Yu, & Pintrich, 1996). The general distinction between these two classes of goals is that target- and task-specific goals represent the specific outcome the individual is attempting to accomplish. In academic learning contexts, it would be represented by goals such as 'wanting to get 8 out of 10 correct on a quiz' or 'trying to get an A in a mid-term exam', etc. These goals are specific to a task and are most similar to the goals discussed by Locke and Latham (1990) for workers in an organizational context, such as 'wanting to make ten more widgets an hour' or 'wanting to sell five more cars in the next week'.

In contrast, purpose goals or goal orientations reflect the more general reasons that individuals do a task and are related more to the research on achievement motivation (Elliot, 1997; Urdan, 1997). It is an individual's general orientation (or 'schema' or 'theory') for approaching the task, doing the task and evaluating their performance on the task (Ames, 1992; Dweck & Leggett, 1988; Pintrich, 2002a, 2002c). In this case, purpose goals or goal orientations refer to *why* individuals want to get 8 out of 10 correct, *why* they want to get an A, or *why* they want to make more widgets or sell more cars as well as the standards or criteria (8 out of 10 correct, an A) they will use to

*Requests for reprints should be addressed to Paul R. Pintrich, Combined Program in Education and Psychology, 1406 SEB, 610 East University Street, The University of Michigan, Ann Arbor, MI 48109, USA (e-mail: pintrich@umich.edu).

evaluate their progress towards the goal. The inclusion of the reasons why an individual is pursuing a task allows for an integration of the achievement motivation literature into our models of self-regulated learning, since the achievement motivation literature is concerned with what, why and how individuals are motivated to achieve in different settings (Pintrich & Schunk, 2002).

The what, why and how of motivation form a general theory or orientation to the task which can influence many of the different processes of self-regulation (Meece, 1994). For example, if individuals are motivated to master and learn the material, they should orient their monitoring processes to cues that show progress in learning and invoke certain types of cognitive strategies for learning (e.g. deeper processing strategies, one type of pathway to learning) in order to make progress towards their goal of learning and mastery. In contrast, if they are oriented to demonstrating their superiority over others in terms of grades or scores on academic tasks, their monitoring and control processes may be qualitatively different as they monitor others' work and grades and attempt to regulate their motivation and cognition to demonstrate their superiority (another type of developmental pathway to learning). In addition, these different goal orientations may be linked to motivational beliefs such as self-efficacy for the task, as well as students' value and interest in the task (Ames, 1992). Finally, these goal orientations may be linked to attempts to regulate help-seeking behaviour or other aspects related to controlling the context (Pintrich, 2000c: Ryan, Midgley, & Pintrich, 2001).

The purpose of this chapter is to discuss how goal orientations, not specific target goals, are linked to various motivational and self-regulatory processes over the course of development. In addition, the chapter will explore the possibility that there are multiple goal orientations operating that lead to different trajectories or pathways in the development of motivation, self-regulated learning and achievement. The chapter begins with a description of four different types of goal orientation that moves beyond the normative mastery–performance goal model. The next section outlines four possible patterns of multiple goals and their relation to different trajectories of development. The chapter concludes with some suggestions for future theory and research.

A model of goal orientations

There are a number of different models of goal orientation that have been advanced by different achievement motivation researchers (see Ames, 1992; Dweck & Leggett, 1988; Harackiewicz *et al.*, 1998; Maehr & Midgley, 1991; Nicholls, 1984; Pintrich, 1989; Pintrich & De Groot, 1990; Wolters *et al.*, 1996). These models vary somewhat in their definition of goal orientation and the use of different labels for similar constructs. They also differ on the proposed number of goal orientations and the role of approach and avoidance forms of the different goals. Finally, they also differ on the degree to which an individual's goal orientations are more personal, based in somewhat stable individual differences, or the degree to which an individual's goal orientations are more situated or sensitive to the context and a function of the contextual features of the environment. Most of the models assume that goal orientations are a function of both individual differences and contextual factors, but the relative emphasis along this continuum does vary between the different models. In addition, given developmental differences between individuals and across contexts, the role and operation of these goal orientations may vary by age and normative age-associated contexts.

Most models propose two general goal orientations that concern the reasons or purposes that individuals are pursuing when approaching and engaging in a task. In Dweck's model, the two goal orientations are labelled *learning* and *performance* goals (Dweck & Leggett, 1988), with learning goals reflecting a focus on increasing competence, and performance goals involving either the avoidance of negative judgments of competence or attainment of positive judgments of competence. Ames (1992) labels them *mastery* and *performance* goals, with mastery goals orienting learners towards 'developing new skills, trying to understand their work, improving their level of competence, or achieving a sense of mastery based on self-referenced standards' (Ames, 1992, p. 262). In contrast, performance goals orient learners to focus on their ability and self-worth, to determine their ability in reference to besting other students, surpassing others, and to receiving public recognition for their superior performance (Ames, 1992).

Maehr and Midgley and their colleagues (e.g. Anderman & Midgley, 1997; Kaplan & Midgley, 1997; Maehr & Midgley, 1991, 1996; Middleton & Midgley, 1997; Midgley, Arunkumar, & Urdan, 1996; Midgley *et al.*, 1998) have mainly used use the terms *task* goals and *performance* goals in their research programme, which parallel the two main goals from Dweck and Ames. Task-focused goals involve an orientation to mastery of the task, increasing one's competence, and progress in learning which are similar to the learning and mastery goals of Dweck and Ames. Performance goals involve a concern with doing better than others and demonstrating ability to the teacher and peers, similar to the performance goals discussed by Dweck and Ames.

In a similar but somewhat different vein, Nicholls and his colleagues (Nicholls, 1984, 1989; Thorkildsen & Nicholls, 1998) have proposed *task-involved* and *ego-involved* goals or *task orientation* and *ego orientation*. In this research, the focus and operationalization of the goals have been on when individuals feel most successful, which is a somewhat different perspective than the more general reasons or purposes learners might adopt when approaching or performing a task. Nevertheless, they are somewhat similar to the goals proposed by others in that task-involved goals are defined as experiencing success when individuals learn something new, gain new skills or knowledge, or do their best. Ego-involved goals involve individuals feeling successful when outperforming or surpassing their peers or when avoiding looking incompetent. This model is probably the most different from the other models due to its emphasis on when and how individuals feel most successful in contrast to more general purposes or goals for engaging in academic tasks. The nature and meaning of success may show important developmental changes with age and changes in contexts that could lead to different developmental trajectories or outcomes as a function of these different task- and ego-involved orientations.

Finally, Harackiewicz and Elliot and their colleagues (e.g. Elliot, 1997; Elliot & Church, 1997; Elliot & Harackiewicz, 1996; Harackiewicz, Barron, Carter, Lehto, & Elliot, 1997; Harackiewicz *et al.*, 1998) have investigated two general goal orientations, a *mastery orientation* and a *performance orientation*. In their work, a mastery goal orientation reflects a focus on the development of knowledge, skill and competence relative to one's own previous performance and are thus self-referential. Performance goals concern a striving for demonstrating competence by trying to outperform peers on academic tasks. These two general orientations are in line with the other definitions of goals discussed in this chapter. More importantly, however, Elliot and his colleagues (e.g. Elliot, 1997; Elliot & Church, 1997) also make a distinction between two different types of performance goals, a *performance-approach* goal and a *performance-*

avoidance goal. They suggest that individuals can be positively motivated to try to outperform others, to demonstrate their competence and superiority, reflecting an approach orientation to the general performance goal. In contrast, individuals also can be negatively motivated to try to avoid failure, to avoid looking dumb or stupid or incompetent; what they label an avoidance orientation to the performance goal.

In the same vein, Midgley and her colleagues (Middleton & Midgley, 1997; Midgley *et al.*, 1998) have separated out both approach and avoid ability goals, paralleling the work by Elliot and his colleagues on approach and avoid performance goals. Other researchers (e.g. Urdan, 1997; Wolters *et al.*, 1996) have examined what they have called *relative ability goals*, but this construct seems to reflect the same construct as the performance-approach goal of Elliot and his colleagues. Finally, Skaalvik and his colleagues (Skaalvik, 1997; Skaalvik, Valas, & Sletta, 1994) also have proposed two dimensions of performance or ego goals, a *self-enhancing ego orientation*, where the emphasis is on besting others and demonstrating superior ability, as in the performance-approach goal, and *self-defeating ego orientation*, where the goal is to avoid looking dumb or to avoid negative judgments, as in the performance-avoidance orientation. The performance-approach orientation focused on besting others, and superior performance relative to peers is similar to the performance and ego orientation in the models of Dweck, Ames and Nicholls. In addition, although not formally separated out as two distinct performance or ego goals in the models of Dweck and Nicholls, both of those models did include concerns of avoiding judgments of incompetence or feeling dumb or stupid in their conceptualizations of performance and ego orientations, similar to the performance-avoidance orientation of Elliot and Midgley or the self-defeating ego orientation of Skaalvik.

In order to organize the literature on mastery and performance goals, it seems helpful to propose a general framework that allows for the classification of the two goals and their approach and avoidance versions. Table 1 represents one attempt at such a taxonomy. The columns in Table 1 reflect the general approach–avoidance distinction that has been a hallmark of achievement motivation research (Atkinson, 1957; McClelland, Atkinson, Clark, & Lowell, 1953; Elliot, 1997) since its inception, as well as more recent social cognitive perspectives on approaching and avoiding a task (e.g. Covington & Roberts, 1994; Harackiewicz *et al.*, 1998; Higgins, 1997). In

Table 1. A model of goal orientations

	Approach focus	Avoidance focus
Mastery orientation	Focus on mastering task, learning, understanding	Focus on avoiding misunderstanding, avoiding not learning or not mastering task
	Use of standards of self-improvement progress	Use of standards of not being wrong, not doing it incorrectly relative to task
Performance orientation	Focus on being superior, being the smartest, best at task, besting others	Focus on avoiding inferiority, not looking stupid or dumb
	Use of normative standards, getting best or highest grades, or best performer in class	Use of normative standards of not getting the worst grades, being lowest performer in class

particular, recent social cognitive models of self-regulation such as Higgins (1997) explicitly use this distinction of approach–avoidance (or promotion–prevention focus in his terms) to discuss different self-regulatory processes. An approach or promotion focus leads individuals to move towards positive or desired end-states, to try to promote them to occur; while an avoidance or prevention focus leads individuals to move away from negative or undesired end-states, to prevent them from occurring (Higgins, 1997). As such, there should be some important distinctions between approaching and avoiding certain goals with concomitant influences on self-regulated learning. For example, a promotion or approach orientation might be expected to have some generally positive relations with cognition, motivation and behaviour, while a prevention or avoidance orientation should be negatively related to these aspects of self-regulated learning.

The rows in Table 1 reflect two general goals that students might be striving for, and represent the general goals of mastery and performance that have been proposed by every one of the different models discussed here. All the models agree that mastery-approach goals are represented by attempts to improve or promote competence, knowledge, skills and learning, and that standards are self-set or self-referential, with a focus on progress and understanding. In all the models discussed, mastery goals have only been discussed and researched in terms of an approach orientation, that is, that students were trying to approach or attain this goal, not avoid it. As such, most models have only proposed the first cell in the first row in Table 1; it is not clear whether there is an mastery-avoidance goal theoretically, and there has been little explicit empirical research on an mastery avoidance goal.

However, there may be occasions when students are focused on avoiding misunderstanding or avoiding not learning or not mastering the task. Some students who are more 'perfectionistic' may use standards of not getting it wrong or not doing it incorrectly relative to the task. These students would be concerned not about doing it wrong because of comparisons with others (a performance-avoidance goal), but rather in terms of their own high standards for themselves. Both Pintrich (2000a, 2002c) and Elliot (1999) have suggested that mastery-avoid goals may be operating for some individuals. Elliot and McGregor (2001) have examined the feasibility of a four-goal model as shown in Table 1 and in factor analyses have found empirical support for the differentiation of the four goals. Moreover, it appears that mastery-avoid goals are mainly related to negative outcomes (Elliot and McGregor, 2001) such as more anxiety and less adaptive approaches to studying and learning.

The second row in Table 1 reflects the general performance goal orientation that all the models propose, but the approach and avoidance columns allow for the separation of the goal of trying to outperform or best others using normative standards from the goal of avoiding looking stupid, dumb or incompetent relative to others. This distinction has been formally made in the work of Elliot, Midgley, Skaalvik and their colleagues, and all the studies have shown that there are differential relations between other motivational and cognitive outcomes and a performance-approach goal and a performance-avoid goal (Harackiewicz *et al.*, 1998; Middleton & Midgley, 1997; Midgley *et al.*, 1998: Skaalvik, 1997). In Dweck's model, the performance orientation included both trying to gain positive judgments of the self as well as trying to avoid negative judgments (Dweck & Leggett, 1988). In Nicholls' model, ego-involved or ego orientation also included feeling successful when doing better than others did or avoiding looking incompetent (Nicholls, 1984; Thorkildsen & Nicholls, 1998). Accordingly, most of the models do recognize the possibility that students could be seeking to gain positive judgments of the self by besting or outperforming others as well as trying to avoid looking stupid, dumb or incompetent, although Dweck and Nicholls did not separate them conceptually or empirically as did Elliot, Midgley and Skaalvik. In this case, within this performance row in Table 1, in contrast to the mastery row in Table 1, there is no doubt that both performance-approach and avoidance goal orientations are possible, that students can adopt them and that they can have differential relations to other motivational or cognitive outcomes.

In terms of developmental progressions, these four different goal orientations may be evoked by features of the context and tasks. The extent to which the context and tasks change, over time, and are associated with normative age-related changes, would then result in developmental differences in the goals. For example, if secondary schools are more focused on competition and the use of evaluation structures and norm-referenced grading practices (i.e. grading on a curve) than elementary schools, it might be expected that older students would adopt more performance-oriented goals (both approach and avoidance forms) in comparison with younger students (Pintrich & Schunk, 2002). Besides the developmental differences in levels of goal adoption, this type of contextual effect could moderate the role of goal orientations and their links to outcomes. If contexts associated with more performance goal-inducing features are more pervasive in secondary and post-secondary classrooms, performance goals could play a more adaptive role in these settings. For example, Harackiewicz and her colleagues (e.g. Harackiewicz *et al.*, 1998) have consistently shown that performance-approach goals are associated with higher levels of achievement in post-secondary classrooms that are often characterized by normative grading practices. In contrast, if elementary classrooms are more mastery-oriented, the adoption of mastery approach goals may be more adaptive in these contexts.

Besides these context-developmental effects, if the goal orientations are conceptualized as more stable individual differences, there might be developmental and individual differences over time that have important implications for developmental trajectories. In terms of cognitive development, Dweck (1999) has shown that children's theories of ability and intelligence are related to goal adoption and that younger children are more likely to adopt incremental theories which lead to the adoption of mastery goals, in contrast with older children, who often adopt more entity theories accompanied by performance goals. Pintrich and Zusho (2001) have discussed other cognitive developmental factors, such as the development of a theory of mind and epistemological beliefs and theories, that might lead to different goal adoption and patterns of self-regulation. In terms of social developmental differences, if some children, by temperament or through parental socialization processes, are more approach- or avoidant-oriented, then these general orientations could have implications not just for the adoption of the four different goals, but also for how children regulate towards these goals. These developmental questions are relatively unexplored, and there is a clear need for more research on these various possibilities.

The role of multiple goals in the development of motivation, self-regulated learning and achievement

These four goals should lead to different outcomes, as they direct individuals' attention to different criteria or lead them to focus on different aspects of the learning task. In normative models of goal orientation that only examined the two mastery and performance goals, mastery goals have been related to a number of adaptive outcomes including higher levels of efficacy, task value, interest, positive affect, effort and persistence, the use of more cognitive and metacognitive strategies, as well as better performance. In contrast, under the normative goal model, performance goals are generally seen as less adaptive in terms of subsequent motivation, affect, strategy use and performance (Ames, 1992; Dweck & Leggett, 1988; Pintrich, 2000c; Pintrich & Schunk, 2002; Urdan, 1997).

However, there may be situations where performance goals, particularly performance-approach goals, may not be maladaptive. For example, Harackiewicz and Elliot and their colleagues (e.g. Elliot, 1997; Elliot & Church, 1997; Elliot & Harackiewicz, 1996; Harackiewicz *et al.*, 1997, 1998) have shown that performance-approach goals can result in better performance and achievement, while mastery goals are linked to more intrinsic interest in the task. In both correlational and experimental research where mastery, performance-approach and performance-avoid goals are compared, maladaptive patterns of intrinsic motivation and actual performance occur only in the performance-avoid groups (Elliot, 1997; Elliot & Church, 1997; Elliot & Harackiewicz, 1996; Harackiewicz *et al.*, 1998). Given this finding, one key issue concerns the interactive relations between mastery-approach and performance-approach goals (Barron & Harackiewicz, 2001; Harackiewicz, Barron, Pintrich, Elliot, & Thrash, 2002: Kaplan & Middleton, 2002; Midgley, Kaplan, & Middleton, 2001).

In the experimental work, the different goal orientation groups have been compared with each other in between-subjects designs, not allowing for the possibility of examining multiple goals and their interactions. For example, it may be that, in the reality of the classroom, students can endorse both mastery and performance-approach goals and different levels of both of these goals (Meece & Holt, 1993; Pintrich & Garcia, 1991). In fact, in some classroom work, mastery and performance-approach goals are orthogonal or slightly positively related to each other (Pintrich & Schunk, 2002). If the two goals are somewhat orthogonal, this raises the possibility that students could endorse different levels of both goals at the same time. Moreover, different patterns in the levels of the two goals may lead to differential outcomes. That is, there may be an interaction between mastery and performance-approach goals for different motivational or cognitive outcomes. Barron and Harackiewicz (2001) have suggested four potential patterns for these interactive relations. These four patterns are illustrated through a discussion of some of the empirical work we have undertaken in our research programme at the University of Michigan.

The *additive goal* effects pattern suggests that mastery and performance-approach goals can have independent positive effects on the same outcomes (Barron & Harackiewicz, 2001). For example, in the Wolters *et al.* (1996) study, in a two-wave correlational study of middle-school students in mathematics, English and social studies classrooms, we found that both mastery-approach and performance-approach goals were positively related to self-efficacy, task value, cognitive strategy use and self-regulation at wave 2, even after controlling for the wave 1 measure of the outcome in regression analyses. In other words, mastery-approach and performance-approach goals both lead to positive changes in motivational and self-regulatory outcomes, independent of each other, since they were both entered as predictors in the same regression equations. Zusho, Pintrich, and Schnabel (2002), in a correlational study of university students (including both Caucasian and Asian-Americans), found that mastery and performance-approach goals both predicted efficacy and interest for a mathematics task. We used structural equation modelling to demonstrate that students who were focused on both learning the task as well as trying to do better than others had higher judgments of their competence and higher levels of interest, again showing that both goals had independent relations with the same outcomes, in line with the additive effects hypothesis.

The second type of interaction discussed by Barron and Harackiewicz (2001) is what they call the *specialized goal* interaction pattern. In this case, there are different or specialized effects for mastery-approach and performance-approach goals, with mastery-approach predicting some outcomes, and performance-approach predicting other outcomes. Work by Harackiewicz and her colleagues (e.g. Harackiewicz *et al.*, 1998) with university students has consistently shown that mastery-approach goals are positively related to interest and intrinsic motivation but that performance-approach goals are positive predictors of actual achievement, as indexed by grades or performance in courses overall (GPA). In our own work with university students, we have also found evidence for specialized goal effects. For example, Zusho, Pintrich, and Coppola (in press), in a three-wave short-term longitudinal study in university chemistry courses, found that even after controlling for wave 1 measures of outcomes, mastery-approach goals positively predicted the increase in the use of more elaboration strategies (a deeper processing approach to learning). In contrast, performance-approach goals positively predicted an increase in the use of rehearsal strategies (a shallower approach to learning). Interestingly, in this case, in these chemistry courses, the use of rehearsal strategies was positively related to actual achievement in the course (in terms of grades). This finding that performance-approach goals were related to rehearsal, at least complements Harackiewicz *et al.*'s (1998) findings regarding the strong link between performance-approach goals and achievement. At the same time, however, we did find that performance-approach goals were related to an increase in anxiety over the course of the term.

In another two-wave correlational study of university students, in Germany in educational psychology classes, Pintrich, Zusho, Schiefele, and Pekrun (2001) found that mastery-approach goals were related to an increase in interest in the course material over time, partialling out earlier interest at wave 1, paralleling the findings from Harackiewicz *et al.*'s programme of research (Harackiewicz *et al.*, 1998). In addition, in line with normative goal theory, the results also revealed that mastery-approach goals led to an increase in the use of elaboration and self-regulatory learning strategies over time. Finally, paralleling our study in American chemistry courses, performance-approach goals were related to an increase in anxiety over the course of the year. In addition, in this same study, there also was evidence for the additive effects hypothesis, with both mastery-approach and performance-approach having independent and positive effects on students' reports of how much effort they exerted in the course. Students reported that they increased their effort over the course of the year as a function of endorsing both mastery and performance-approach goals.

The third pattern hypothesized by Barron and Harackiewicz (2001) is termed the *interactive goal* effect. For example, given the positive patterns found for the separate main effects of mastery goals and performance-approach goals (cf. Dweck & Leggett, 1988; Harackiewicz *et al.*, 1998), it could be predicted from a multiple goal theory perspective that having high levels of both of these goals would be the most adaptive. In this case, following the logic of multiplicative interaction effects, if there are two positive main effects for mastery and performance-approach goals, it may be that a focus on mastery along with a focus on trying to best others at the same time (a high mastery–high performance pattern) would result in enhanced positive outcomes. That is, as suggested by Harackiewicz *et al.* (1998), it may not matter what type of goals are pursued, but rather that the goals lead to affective and cognitive involvement in the task. In this enhancement view, with mastery goals leading to intrinsic task involvement, and performance-approach goals leading to involvement based on competition and trying harder to best others, the overall net effect would be a boost in involvement in the task, with a variety of positive outcomes.

On the other hand, normative goal theory would suggest that any concern with performance, even an performance-approach orientation, could have negative effects on involvement due to distractions fostered by attention on comparisons with others or to negative judgments regarding the self. Under this dampening or reduction perspective, the overall level of involvement that would be fostered by a mastery goal would be less when students simultaneously endorse an performance-approach goal. This lower level of overall involvement would then result in less positive outcomes. Accordingly, under this normative model, it would be hypothesized that the most adaptive pattern of multiple goals would be a high mastery, low performance-approach combination.

The search for these types of interaction has been mixed; some studies find them, many studies do not (see Harackiewicz *et al.*, 2002), and when the interactions are found, the pattern of results is mixed. For example, in the Wolters *et al.* (1996) study, using regression-based interaction terms, we did not find many significant interactions between mastery and performance-approach goals, but the few that did emerge seem to favour the normative goal theory prediction. In other classroom studies with more person-centred analyses (e.g. using median splits or clustering procedures) to create groups of students, in contrast with variable-centred analyses, the findings also have been mixed. For example, Meece and Holt (1993) observed that a high mastery–low performance group of elementary students had the most adaptive pattern of cognitive strategy use as well as actual achievement, in line with normative goal theory predictions. Pintrich and Garcia (1991), also using cluster analysis with a sample of college students, found that the high mastery–low performance group had the most adaptive profile. At the same time, we noted that their low mastery–high performance group did display some positive signs of motivation and cognition, at least in contrast to the low mastery–low performance group. We suggested that in the absence of a mastery goal, at least a concern with performance motivated their college students to engage in their courses to some degree. In contrast, Bouffard, Boisvert, Vezeau, and Larouche (1995), in another study of college students, using median splits to form groups, found that the highest levels of motivation, cognitive strategy use, self-regulation and achievement were displayed by the high mastery–high performance group. The next best pattern was the high mastery–low performance group, followed by the low mastery–high performance group, and the least adaptive pattern was found for the low mastery–low performance group. These results are more in line with a multiple goal perspective that proposes a more adaptive role for performance goals.

Pintrich (2000b), also using a median split analysis of the four goal groups, found very consistent evidence in favour of the multiple goals perspective. Students were junior high students in the seventh and eighth grades, and were in mathematics classrooms. The design was a three-wave longitudinal study with measures administered twice in one year and then once in the second year, so that students were sampled twice in seventh or eighth grade and then once in either eighth grade or ninth grade. All students remained in the same building, the school was a 7–9th-grade junior high, and there was no transition to a new school. An array of 13 different dependent measures was used as outcomes, including motivation, self-regulation, affect and actual achievement. The analyses used a repeated-measure ANOVA with the three waves comprising the within-subject factor and the four goal groups as the between-subject factor. The results showed that the high mastery–high performance group had the highest levels of self-efficacy, task value, risk-taking, cognitive strategy use and self-regulation over time. At the same time, the high mastery–high performance group did not really differ in terms of negative affect or anxiety in comparison with the high mastery–low performance group. Finally, although the statistical test for achievement (as indexed by grade in maths) was not significant at conventional levels, there was a trend ($p < .08$), that the high–high group had the highest level of achievement.

One factor that adds to the complexity of the results in discussing the adaptive role of performance-approach goals is that in Dweck's original model (Dweck & Leggett, 1988), the links between performance goals and other cognitive, motivational and achievement outcomes were assumed to be moderated by efficacy beliefs. That is, if students had high perceptions of their competence to do the task, then performance goals should not be detrimental for cognition, motivation and achievement, and these students should show the same basic pattern as mastery-oriented students. Performance goals were assumed to have negative effects only when efficacy was low. Students who believed they were unable and who were concerned with besting others or wanted to avoid looking incompetent did seem to show the maladaptive pattern of cognition, motivation and behaviour (Dweck & Leggett, 1988).

Other more correlational research that followed this work did not always explicitly test for the predicted interaction between performance goals and efficacy or did not replicate the predicted moderator effect. For example, Kaplan and Midgley (1997) and Miller, Behrens, Greene, and Newman (1993) did not find an interaction between performance-approach goals and efficacy on cognitive outcomes such as strategy use. Harackiewicz and Elliot and their colleagues (Harackiewicz *et al.*, 1998), using both experimental and correlational designs, did not find moderator or mediator effects of efficacy in relation to the effects of mastery or performance-approach goals on other outcomes such as actual performance or intrinsic motivation.

Correlational studies have also revealed a mixture of findings with regard to the linear relations between performance goals and efficacy. For example, Anderman and Midgley (1997) showed that performance-approach goals were positively related to perceptions of competence for sixth graders, but unrelated to perceptions of competence for fifth grades. Wolters *et al.* (1996) found that performance-approach goals were positively related to self-efficacy for junior high students, but Middleton and Midgley (1997) found in another sample of junior high students that performance approach goals were unrelated to efficacy, but performance-avoid goals were negatively related to efficacy. In two studies of junior high students, Skaalvik (1997) showed that performance-approach goals were positively related to efficacy, and performance-avoid goals were negatively related to efficacy.

It seems possible that students who are focused on performance-approach goals would have higher perceptions of efficacy as long as they are relatively successful in besting others and demonstrating their high ability. Some of the conflicting findings might be due to differences in the samples and who is represented in the performance-approach groups (e.g. actual high vs. low achievers). In contrast, students oriented to avoiding looking incompetent or stupid would seem likely to have lower perceptions of self-efficacy. In fact, for these students, they seem to have some consistent self-doubts or concerns about their own competence, reflecting a schema that should generate low efficacy judgments. In addition, it may be that this relation may be moderated by the classroom context. In many of the studies, the positive relations are found in junior high classrooms, but not in elementary classrooms. The literature suggests that junior high classrooms are more performance-oriented than elementary classrooms, which are generally more mastery-oriented (see review by Midgley, 1993). In this case, then, in junior high classrooms, there may be good reasons for efficacy to be positively related to performance-approach goals, but not in elementary classrooms which are generally more mastery-oriented (Anderman & Midgley, 1997).

The role of context as a moderator of the interactive relations between goals is highlighted in the fourth interaction pattern suggested by Barron and Harackiewicz (2001). In the *selective goal* effect, they suggest that students would actively select which type of goal to adopt, depending on the affordances of the situation. For example, students might adopt a mastery-approach goal in a small seminar or in a small group-learning situation with adaptive outcomes resulting. In contrast, in a large lecture course with a more competitive, norm-referenced grading system in place, the adoption of a performance-approach goal might be more adaptive in this context. In our own research, we have not specifically examined this type of selective goal process, but certainly in much of the research on college and university students, the context is a norm-referenced grading context (e.g. Harackiewicz *et al.*, 1998; Zusho *et al.*, in press). There is certainly a need for more research on this selective goal pattern, following the same individuals across different contexts to examine their goal adoption and outcomes.

As noted above, this selective goal effect could also be a function of normative developmental changes in context. If many post-secondary, and even secondary, classrooms are characterized by performance goal stresses, it may be adaptive to adopt personal performance-approach goals in these settings. In this case, there would be developmental-contextual differences in how the goals operate and how individuals regulate towards those goals and the outcomes associated with those goals. In addition, if there are some stable individual differences in goals that are associated with various cognitive or social developmental factors, then children of different ages will come to the classroom context with different goals. The interaction of these personal goals with the different contextual affordances and how individuals negotiate and regulate these potential differences is an important future research question. In addition, given some of the general developmental limitations of young children's ability to self-regulate (Pintrich & Zusho, 2001), younger children may have a much more difficult time 'selecting' the appropriate goals in different contexts. The potential for mismatches or disruptions between a young children's personal goals and the contextual affordances would seem to be much higher than it may be for post-secondary students, who are assumed to be much more capable at self-regulation. The work on multiple goals has not considered these types of developmental differences, and there is a clear need for future research on these issues.

Conclusions and future directions for research

The model presented here seems to have empirical support in a number of different contexts from middle-school through to university settings as well as in different domains such as mathematics, English, social studies, psychology and chemistry. There is a clear need for more research on the role of mastery-avoid goals, but there is strong support for the approach–avoid distinction in reference to performance goals. The basic model in Table 1 can be used to organize research in this area and to classify the different goal orientations that students might adopt in achievement contexts. Moreover, there are important relations between the goals and various motivational, affective, cognitive, self-regulatory and achievement outcomes. The model provides an important framework for understanding what goals students might be focused on in achievement settings and how these goals may shape the development of their subsequent motivation and achievement.

Nevertheless, there are still many important questions that remain unanswered in this programme of research. First, the issue of how these different goals are represented cognitively must be considered. Motivation researchers have not actively explored this question and, consequently, this research on goals has not been tied that closely to the larger research programmes on cognition in general, or the cognitive developmental research on children's cognition and learning. In the original normative goal theory work, the two general mastery and performance goals were considered to be general 'theories' or schemas or orientations that students operated under that focused their attention and learning. The assumption was that a constellation of related beliefs and ideas about goals, effort, ability, success and failure were part of what was activated in a mastery or performance goal orientation. However, this assumption was never explicitly examined experimentally, at least not in the same manner as cognitive or cognitive developmental psychologists would examine other presumed knowledge structures. This is a serious gap in the social cognitive motivational literature (Pintrich, 2000a) and limits its impact in terms of linking up with other more general models of children's cognition and learning.

In addition, the current multiple goals perspective, which has provided strong support for at least three, if not all four, possible goal orientations (see Table 1), complicates this issue of representation even more than the normative goal model of two general mastery and performance goals. In particular, it is not clear how students represent multiple goals simultaneously and how they may operate together to produce differential outcomes. For example, the approach–avoid distinction is an important one to consider in this work, but it does raise questions of how students can go towards and away from a goal at the same time. For example, it is not clear what it means to be both focused on doing better than others and being the smartest, and at the same time, also be focused on not appearing stupid or dumb relative to others. Although psychoanalytic and drive theories may allow for both approach and avoid behavioural tendencies, in cognitive models that assume that certain kinds of knowledge structures are activated which then guide behaviour, it is not clear how both approach and avoid goals may operate at the same time. It may be that the standards (see Table 1) for both approach and avoid goals can be held simultaneously, and students can search for information relative to their success on both approach and avoid dimensions at the same time. At some level, the multiple goals perspective may be more in line with a general node-network or association model of cognition, rather than a schema model of knowledge structures However, this is an empirical question that needs to be examined in experimental research.

Besides the approach–avoid distinction, the multiple goals model explicitly assumes that mastery and performance goals can interact. In the research discussed here, the interaction that has been examined empirically is the interaction between mastery-approach and performance-approach goals. In this case, it seems easier to understand that students might be going towards their goal of achievement, but that the standards might include a focus on self-improvement and mastery and at the same time include a focus on doing better than others. This seems intuitively plausible, and the actual research does show that students can be characterized in terms of multiple goals for mastery-approach and performance-approach goals. However, there is still a need for more research on how these two goals interact, how they may lead to different outcomes, and how best to index the interaction. In fact, the interaction between mastery-approach and performance-approach goals is not found all that often (see Harackiewicz *et al.*, 2002). Previous research has used different methods to index the interaction from multiplicative terms in regression models, to median splits and ANOVAs, to cluster analysis procedures, and the results are decidedly mixed. Some of the confusion may be due to different methods, but if the interactions are reliable and stable, they should obtain regardless of the methodology and analysis procedures used in the research. Finally, although the interaction between mastery-approach and performance-approach goals has been the focus of much of the research, it would still be useful to explore the other potential interactions between all four of the goals in Table 1. It is not clear whether they are all viable or sensible two-way interactions, but there is a need for empirical research to examine these possibilities.

The search for these interactions and the role of multiple goals also highlights the idea of different pathways for development of motivation and learning. It may be that students can obtain similar outcomes through different goals and means. For example, Pintrich (2000b) found that students who were high in both mastery-approach and performance-approach had similar outcomes to those who were high in mastery-approach, but low in performance-approach goals. These groups of students were focused on different goals, but achieved at the same level and seemed to be motivated in similar ways. In addition, the principle of equifinality (Shah & Kruglanski, 2000) suggests that the same goals can be achieved in multiple ways or through different actions, highlighting the importance of examining different self-regulatory strategies and different developmental pathways that students might use to accomplish similar goals. Finally, as some of the data suggest that students who are high in performance-approach goals might be more anxious, future research needs to examine multiple outcomes, not just interest and achievement, as we track the different developmental goals, experiences, and pathways that students take as they move through different educational contexts. In addition, the role of developmental differences in the shaping of these different pathways has not been examined fully. We have studies that characterize college students or middle-school students, or elementary students, but we do not have very many longitudinal studies of individuals over longer periods of time across multiple contexts. There is a clear need for both microgenetic studies of individuals across smaller time periods and longitudinal studies that follow students over many years, not just 1 or 2 years as they make the transition from elementary to middle school. These longitudinal studies will help us understand the different developmental pathways that individuals can take through school as well as the relative adaptive nature of different goal orientations.

The role of context in creating and shaping multiple goals and pathways is also important and has not been fully investigated. The selective goal pattern of interaction that allows for students selecting different goals to focus on, depending on the context, is one kind of multiple goals pattern that highlights the important role of context. This pattern may be the most reflective of a situational perspective on motivation which stresses the powerful role of context in shaping goals and learning, as well as moderating the relations. Although goal theory does emphasize the role of context in shaping goals, much of the work has focused on personal goals and their role in learning and motivation and has not examined the role of context as a potential moderator of these relations. For example, the findings that personal performance-approach goals are linked to higher levels of achievement in university students may be partially a function of the more competitive nature of college classrooms in the USA. In this case, given the competitive reward and evaluation structure, students who focus on doing better than other students do seem to achieve at higher levels. In contrast, in many elementary and middle-school classrooms, the context may not be very competitive at all, and in these contexts, then, mastery-approach goals can lead to achievement. This type of developmental-contextual moderator effect needs to be examined in more detail in future research.

Beyond the reward and evaluation structure of the context, recent research suggests the importance of the affective climate of the classroom as a potential moderator of the role of goals. For example, Turner, Midgley, Meyer, and Patrick (2003), in a qualitative study, examined two elementary classrooms that were both high in mastery and performance classroom goals. These were classrooms where there was a strong focus on learning and understanding, but also on competition and doing better than others. However, in one of these classrooms, the affective climate, as evidenced in teacher discourse, made the competition fun, and the teachers and peers were still supportive of one another. In contrast, in the second classroom, the affective climate was not supportive, and there was often use of teacher sarcasm in response to student mistakes or low performance. In the first classroom, the student outcomes were generally positive and adaptive, reflecting a positive interaction between a classroom stress on both mastery and performance goals, in line with a multiple goals perspective. In the second classroom, however, the student outcomes were much less adaptive, and were more reflective of normative goal theory predictions about the maladaptive outcomes of performance goals. This small-scale qualitative study does need to be replicated with more classrooms and at different grade levels (e.g. middle-school, college, etc.), but it does present important evidence on how the affective climate of the classroom can moderate the effects of mastery and performance goals. There is a clear need for much more research on how not just affective climate, but other classroom factors, may moderate the role of goals in motivation and learning.

There is clearly much research to be done, but a goal theory perspective does offer important insights into the development of student motivation and learning in classroom contexts. The multiple goals perspective, although it complicates theoretical predictions and necessitates much more complex research designs, does offer the potential to reflect more accurately the nature and development of student motivation and learning in classroom contexts.

References

Ames, C. (1992). Classrooms: Goals, structures, and student motivation. *Journal of Educational Psychology*, *84*, 261–271.

Anderman, E., & Midgley, C. (1997). Changes in achievement goal orientations, perceived academic competence, and grades across the transition to middle-level schools. *Contemporary Educational Psychology*, *22*, 269–298.

Atkinson, J. (1957). Motivational determinants of risk-taking behavior. *Psychological Review*, *64*, 359–372.

Barron, K. E., & Harackiewicz, J. (2001). Achievement goals and optimal motivation: Testing multiple goal models. *Journal of Personality and Social Psychology, 80,* 706–722.

Bouffard, T., Boisvert, J., Vezeau, C., & Larouche, C. (1995). The impact of goal orientation on self-regulation and performance among college students. *British Journal of Educational Psychology, 65,* 317–329.

Covington, M. V., & Roberts, B. (1994). Self-worth and college achievement: Motivational and personality correlates. In P. R. Pintrich, D. R. Brown, & C. E. Weinstein (Eds.), *Student motivation, cognition and learning: Essays in honor of Wilbert J. McKeachie* (pp. 157–187). Hillsdale, NJ: Erlbaum.

Dweck, C. S. (1999). *Self-theories: Their role in motivation, personality, and development.* Philadelphia, PA: Psychology Press/Taylor & Francis.

Dweck, C. S., & Leggett, E. L. (1988). A social-cognitive approach to motivation and personality. *Psychological Review, 95,* 256–273.

Elliot, A. J. (1997). Integrating the 'classic' and 'contemporary' approaches to achievement motivation: A hierarchical model of approach and avoidance achievement motivation. In M. L. Maehr & P. R. Pintrich (Eds.), *Advances in motivation and achievement* (Vol. 10, pp. 143–179). Greenwich, CT: JAI Press.

Elliot, A. J. (1999). Approach and avoidance motivation and achievement goals. *Educational Psychologist, 34,* 169–189.

Elliot, A. J., & Church, M. (1997). A hierarchical model of approach and avoidance achievement motivation. *Journal of Personality and Social Psychology, 72,* 218–232.

Elliot, A. J., & Harackiewicz, J. M. (1996). Approach and avoidance achievement goals and intrinsic motivation: A mediational analysis. *Journal of Personality and Social Psychology, 70,* 461–475.

Elliot, A. J., & McGregor, H. (2001). A 2 × 2 achievement goal framework. *Journal of Personality and Social Psychology, 80,* 501–519.

Garcia, T., & Pintrich, P. R. (1994). Regulating motivation and cognition in the classroom: The role of self-schemas and self-regulatory strategies. In D. H. Schunk & B. J. Zimmerman (Eds.), *Self-regulation of learning and performance: Issues and educational applications* (pp. 127–153). Hillsdale, NJ: Erlbaum.

Harackiewicz, J. M., Barron, K. E., Carter, S. M., Lehto, A. T., & Elliot, A. J. (1997). Predictors and consequences of achievement goals in the college classroom: Maintaining interest and making the grade. *Journal of Personality and Social Psychology, 73,* 1284–1295.

Harackiewicz, J. M., Barron, K. E., & Elliot, A. J. (1998). Rethinking achievement goals: When are they adaptive for college students and why? *Educational Psychologist, 33,* 1–21.

Harackiewicz, J. M., Barron, K. E., Pintrich, P. R., Elliot, A. J., & Thrash, T. (2002). Revision of achievement goal theory: Necessary and illuminating. *Journal of Educational Psychology, 94,* 638–645.

Harackiewicz, J. M., & Sansone, C. (1991). Goals and intrinsic motivation: You can get there from here. In M. L. Maehr & P. R. Pintrich (Eds.), *Advances in motivation and achievement: Goals and self-regulation* (Vol. 7, pp. 21–49). Greenwich, CT: JAI Press.

Higgins, E. T. (1997). Beyond pleasure and pain. *American Psychologist, 52,* 1280–1300.

Kaplan, A., & Middleton, M. (2002). Should childhood be a journey or a race? Response to Harackiewicz *et al.* (2002). *Journal of Educational Psychology, 94,* 646–648.

Kaplan, A., & Midgley, C. (1997). The effect of achievement goals: Does level of perceived academic competence make a difference? *Contemporary Educational Psychology, 22,* 415–435.

Locke, E. A., & Latham, G. P. (1990). *A theory of goal setting and task performance.* Englewood Cliffs, NJ: Prentice-Hall.

Maehr, M. L., & Midgley, C. (1991). Enhancing student motivation: A school-wide approach. *Educational Psychologist, 26,* 399–427.

Maehr, M. L., & Midgley, C. (1996). *Transforming school cultures.* Boulder, CO: Westview.

McClelland, D., Atkinson, J. W., Clark, R. A., & Lowell, E. L. (1953). *The achievement motive.* New York: Appleton-Century-Crofts.

Meece, J. (1994). The role of motivation in self-regulating learning. In D. H. Schunk & B. J. Zimmerman (Eds.), *Self-regulation of learning and performance: Issues and educational applications* (pp. 25–44). Hillsdale, NJ: Erlbaum.

Meece, J., & Holt, K. (1993). A pattern analysis of students' achievement goals. *Journal of Educational Psychology, 85,* 582–590.

Middleton, M., & Midgley, C. (1997). Avoiding the demonstration of lack of ability: An underexplored aspect of goal theory. *Journal of Educational Psychology, 89,* 710–718.

Midgley, C. (1993). Motivation and middle level schools. In M. L. Maehr & P. R. Pintrich (Eds.), *Advances in motivation and achievement: Motivation and adolescence* (Vol. 8, pp. 217–274). Greenwich, CT: JAI Press.

Midgley, C., Arunkumar, R., & Urdan, T. (1996). 'If I don't do well tomorrow, there's a reason': Predictors of adolescents' use of academic self-handicapping strategies. *Journal of Educational Psychology, 88,* 423–434.

Midgley, C., Kaplan, A., & Middleton, M. (2001). Performance-approach goals: Good for what, for whom, under what circumstances, and at what cost? *Journal of Educational Psychology, 93,* 77–86.

Midgley, C., Kaplan, A., Middleton, M., Maehr, M. L., Urdan, T., Anderman, L., Anderman, E., & Roeser, R. (1998). The development and validation of scales assessing students' achievement goal orientations. *Contemporary Educational Psychology, 23,* 113–131.

Miller, R., Behrens, J., Greene, B., & Newman, D. (1993). Goals and perceived ability: Impact on student valuing, self-regulation, and persistence. *Contemporary Educational Psychology, 18,* 2–14.

Nicholls, J. (1984). Achievement motivation: Conceptions of ability, subjective experience, task choice, and performance. *Psychological Review, 91,* 328–346.

Nicholls, J. (1989). *The competitive ethos and democratic education.* Cambridge, MA: Harvard University Press.

Pintrich, P. R. (1989). The dynamic interplay of student motivation and cognition in the college classroom. In M. Maehr & C. Ames (Eds.), *Advances in motivation and achievement. Vol. 6: Motivation enhancing environments* (pp. 117–160). Greenwich, CT: JAI Press.

Pintrich, P. R. (2000a). An achievement goal theory perspective on issues in motivation terminology, theory, and research. *Contemporary Educational Psychology, 25,* 92–104.

Pintrich, P. R. (2000b). Multiple goals, multiple pathways: The role of goal orientation in learning and achievement. *Journal of Educational Psychology. 92,* 544–555.

Pintrich, P. R. (2000c). The role of goal orientation in self-regulated learning. In M. Boekaerts, P. R. Pintrich, & M. Zeidner (Eds.), *The handbook of self-regulation: Theory, research, and applications* (pp. 451–502). San Diego, CA: Academic Press.

Pintrich, P. R., & De Groot, E. V. (1990). Motivational and self-regulated learning components of classroom academic performance. *Journal of Educational Psychology, 82,* 33–40.

Pintrich, P. R., & Garcia, T. (1991). Student goal orientation and self-regulation in the college classroom. In M. L. Maehr & P. R. Pintrich (Eds.), *Advances in motivation and achievement: Goals and self-regulatory processes* (Vol. 7, pp. 371–402). Greenwich, CT: JAI Press.

Pintrich, P. R., & Schunk, D. H. (2002). *Motivation in education: Theory, research and applications.* Upper Saddle River, NJ: Prentice-Hall Merrill.

Pintrich, P. R., & Zusho, A. (2001). The development of academic self-regulation: The role of cognitive and motivational factors. In A. Wigfield & J. Eccles (Eds.), *The development of achievement motivation* (pp. 249–284). San Diego, CA: Academic Press.

Pintrich, P. R., Zusho, A., Schiefele, U., & Pekrun, R. (2001). Goal orientation and self-regulated learning in the college classroom: A cross-cultural comparison. In F. Salili, C-Y. Chiu, & Y-Y. Hong (Eds.), *Student motivation: The culture and context of learning* (pp. 149–169). New York: Plenum.

Ryan, A., Pintrich, P. R., & Midgley, C. (2001). Avoiding seeking help in the classroom: Who and why? *Educational Psychology Review*, *13*, 93–114.

Shah, J., & Kruglanski, A. (2000). Aspects of goal networks: Implications for self-regulation. In M. Boekaerts, P. R. Pintrich, & M. Zeidner (Eds.), Handbook of self-regulation (pp. 85–110). San Diego, CA: Academic Press.

Skaalvik, E. (1997). Self-enhancing and self-defeating ego orientation: Relations with task avoidance orientation, achievement, self-perceptions, and anxiety. *Journal of Educational Psychology*, *89*, 71–81.

Skaalvik, E., Valas, H., & Sletta, O. (1994). Task involvement and ego involvement: Relations with academic achievement, academic self-concept and self-esteem. *Scandinavian Journal of Educational Research*, *38*, 231–243.

Thorkildsen, T., & Nicholls, J. (1998). Fifth graders' achievement orientations and beliefs: Individual and classroom differences. *Journal of Educational Psychology*, *90*, 179–201.

Turner, J., Midgley, C., Meyer, D., & Patrick, H. (2003). Teacher discourse and students' affect and achievement-related behaviors in two high mastery/high performance classrooms. *Elementary School Journal*, *103*, 357–382.

Urdan, T. (1997). Achievement goal theory: Past results, future directions. In M. L. Maehr & P. R. Pintrich (Eds.), *Advances in motivation and achievement* (Vol. 10, pp. 99–141). Greenwich, CT: JAI Press.

Wolters, C., Yu, S., & Pintrich, P. R. (1996). The relation between goal orientation and students' motivational beliefs and self-regulated learning. *Learning and Individual Differences*, *8*, 211–238.

Zusho, A., Pintrich, P. R., & Coppola, B. (in press). Skill and will: The role of motivation and cognition in the learning of college chemistry. *International Journal of Science Education*.

Zusho, A., Pintrich, P. R., & Schnabel, K. (2002). *Motives, goals, and self-regulation on a mathematics achievement task*. Manuscript submitted for publication.

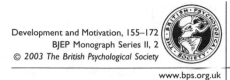

Development and Motivation, 155–172
BJEP Monograph Series II, 2
© 2003 The British Psychological Society

www.bps.org.uk

Achievement motivation in real contexts

Julian Elliott* and Neil Hufton

University of Sunderland, School of Education and Lifelong Learning, UK

This paper draws upon changing circumstances in Russia to raise a series of questions about the meaningfulness of much current work in the field of achievement motivation. Russian children of the former Soviet Union have traditionally been described as highly motivated students whose levels of achievement often exceeded those of Western countries such as England and the USA. Despite the massive social and economic disruption that followed in the 1990s, it appeared that this commitment was largely maintained. More recently, however, there are increasing signs of educational polarization, alienation and evidence of a more visible underclass for whom education appears to have little value. The paper discusses some major influences in the lives of Russian children that appear to be resulting in decreased achievement motivation and performance. In so doing, it raises larger questions about the capacity of current achievement motivation theory and methodology to provide rich and meaningful understandings about those factors that lead individuals, communities, cultures and nations to commit to academic study.

Introduction

> In times of dramatic social changes, it is particularly true that adolescents are the last children of the old system and the first adults of the new (Van Hoorn, Komlosi, Suchar, & Samuelson, 2000, p. 4).

Russia has long enjoyed a reputation for high educational standards, a phenomenon noted both by organizations such as the World Bank (Canning, Moock & Heleniak, 1999) and the Organization for Economic Cooperation and Development (OECD, 1998) and by academic researchers (Alexander, 2000; Bucur & Eklof, 1999). Similarly, in our own 5-year cross-cultural study of motivation and education practice in Sunderland (UK), St Petersburg (Russia) and eastern Kentucky (USA), we have noted particularly

*Requests for reprints should be addressed to Julian G. Elliott, University of Sunderland, School of Education and Lifelong Learning, Hammerton Hall, Gray Road, Sunderland SR2 8JB, UK (e-mail: joe.elliott@sunderland.ac.uk).

high levels of academic motivation, engagement and achievement in the Russian context.

Our research commenced in the mid-1990s as a result of what appeared to us to be striking differences in student achievement-related behaviour across these three milieux. Both primary and secondary school students in St Petersburg appeared to be considerably more motivated and hard-working than their peers in Kentucky and Sunderland and, not surprisingly, were performing at a higher level in many subjects. At this time, each milieu was being introduced to wide-reaching educational reforms geared to the raising of standards. We were intrigued to examine the extent to which these, largely school-based, initiatives might impact upon students when many important influences seemed to originate in their broader communities—a point noted by Coleman (1961) in the USA. Recognizing the importance of gaining an understanding of the many different factors that might impinge upon student behaviour (Bronfenbrenner, 1979), we sought to undertake a series of conceptual and empirical studies exploring different levels of the ecosystem.

Our first step was to observe lessons in many different types of school and speak informally with teachers, headteachers, local authority officers and academics about educational change and reform. Through our discussions, we sought to gain a greater understanding of broader socio-historical and socio-economic factors in St Petersburg and Kentucky that might impact upon student motivation. In particular, we examined the structure and organization of Russian schools and subsequently suggested that a combination of systemic factors, comprising a 'pedagogical nexus', helped to sustain high levels of motivation and achievement (Hufton & Elliott, 2000). In addition to embracing the current literature on achievement motivation, we also studied key texts that might help us consider the operation of broader cultural and social factors (e.g. Bronfenbrenner, 1971; Stevenson & Stigler, 1992). Our subsequent empirical work involved a combination of quantitative and qualitative methods—employing questionnaires, interviews, observations, academic testing, and teacher rating scales.

To obtain a broad picture in the first instance, we conducted surveys of a total of 6,000 students and 3,000 parents across the three milieux. In the student surveys, we explored attitudes to school, teachers and school subjects, asked about achievement-related behaviour, both at home and at school, and queried students about their wishes and expectations for the future. We sought students' academic self-perceptions, asked them what they believed their teachers and parents thought, and compared this information with independently derived teacher and parental evaluations. We quizzed students about the influence of peers upon their behaviour, and examined attributions for academic success and failure.

Having examined these data, we identified many issues that needed to be teased out more fully. Recognizing the inadequacies of quantitative approaches for such a task, we conducted in-depth semi-structured interviews with 144 secondary students (Hufton, Elliott, & Illushin, 2002a). Here, we sought to triangulate findings from our surveys, gain a richer understanding of the phenomena under investigation and explore the operation of impression management and social desirability confounds. A particular feature of our approach was to use non-native members of the team to conduct the interviews in each country. As common understandings could not be assumed in such situations, it proved possible for the foreign researcher to ask 'naive' questions that explored practices, attitudes and values, and receive from the student concerned a detailed answer, usually proffered with grace, patience and, often, no little bemusement.

Our parent survey (Elliott, Hufton, Illushin, & Willis, 2001b) explored very similar issues to those in the student surveys. As a result, we were able to examine the extent to which there was congruence between parent and child perceptions, and relate similarities and differences to home and school contrasts.

Although discussions with teachers had been ongoing since our first visits to each milieu, it was considered important to undertake a more systematic comparative investigation. Here, interviews appeared to be the most appropriate means of gaining access to issues of no little complexity. Our findings confirmed the value of the methodology, as the interview data provided information that would have been difficult to obtain via a questionnaire. In particular, these indicated that the apparent concurrence of teacher views across the three milieux masked important differences of meaning that were only revealed as these were further explored and contextualized (Hufton, Elliott, & Illushin, in press).

Some puzzling findings

As a result of these various studies, we have queried a number of puzzling findings that seemed to run counter to our expectations (Hufton, Elliott, & Illushin, 2002b). Our investigations clearly showed that children in St Petersburg were expected to work considerably more intensely in class, and even more so on their homework, than were the great majority of children in the two Western locations and, unsurprisingly, appeared to be generally performing at a higher level in many subjects. Indeed, in a basic test of mathematical computation that we gave to 3,000 9- and 10-year-olds, the St Petersburg group placed in the lowest of five ability groups by their teachers obtained a higher mean score than did the highest Sunderland and Kentucky groups (Elliott, Hufton, Illushin, & Laughlin, 2001a). Yet, despite such energetic performance, the Russian samples appeared to be less positive about their achievements and their workrates than their US and English peers, were more likely to believe that there was scope for improvement and tended to place greater emphasis upon natural talent in comparison with effort as a reason for academic success

The pressures placed upon Russian students to work hard on their studies, both in the classroom and at home, are considerable (Glowka, 1995; Muckle, 1988, 1990). Lessons are typically fast-paced (reflecting the influence upon pedagogy of the seventeenth century philosopher, Comenius) and intellectually demanding. As Alexander (2000) noted, work rates tend to be high, students are rarely distracted and little time is wasted on classroom routines or awaiting teacher attention: 'Task and activity dominated' (p. 416). In contrast, Alexander found much less engagement and high levels of distraction in US and English primary school classrooms. Individual lessons tended to be lengthy and at times meandering. Even the layouts of the classrooms reflected such dynamics. While the Russian classroom suggested that it was a place where hard work took place, in the US context, Alexander was left wondering whether they were places, '. . . for work, for play, for worship, or for rest and relaxation' (p. 185). In Kentucky high schools, we similarly observed comparatively lengthy lessons during which the cognitive pace (i.e. the speed at which new conceptual ground is covered) often lessened as the session proceeded. In many cases, students were permitted to undertake homework during the latter part of the session, this reflecting a practice that appears to be common in the USA (Martin *et al.*, 2000; Stevenson & Nerison-Low, 1998).

Homework demands in Russia are high (Elliott, Hufton, Hildreth, & Illushin, 1999; Elliott *et al.*, 2001a, 2001b); indeed, 9/10-year-olds in our Russian sample tended to work on homework for longer periods each evening than did 14/15-year-olds in the two Western samples, where these findings emerged from reports by both students and parents. Indeed, almost one-third of our St Petersburg adolescent sample reported that they usually spent 3 hr or more on homework per evening compared with 4.8% and 4.3% for Sunderland and Kentucky informants. A similar finding for US students is reported from a large-scale study in New York (Ban & Cummings, 1999).

Such demands upon Russian youth are not recent phenomena, however. One study of secondary-school students (Zhurkina, 1973) conducted between 1967 and 1969, for example, revealed that they spent an average of 32–33 hr per week at school and a further 18–20 hr doing homework. On Wednesdays and Thursdays, often particularly heavy days, students might have had as many as 6–7 hr of homework each evening. Nevertheless, despite having experienced such pressures themselves, and becoming increasingly cognizant of the intense pressure this places on many children, there appears to be little evidence that a significant proportion of parents or teachers are eager to see this workload reduced (Elliott *et al.*, 2001b; Hufton *et al.*, in press).

As we note elsewhere (Hufton *et al.*, 2002a), motivation (a cognitive variable) is not the same as engagement (actual behaviours involved in undertaking a given activity). This distinction has important methodological implications:

> Because motivation is a subjective experience, self-report instruments are needed to measure it directly. Observational measures of behaviour during task engagement are only indirect measures of motivation, and measures of ultimate task performance are not measures of motivation at all. (Brophy, 1999, p. 17)

However, we found that interview and survey responses of our US informants often provided a picture of higher academic motivation than their actual behaviours suggested. This raises an interesting question about how one reconciles dissonant findings from different sources across different cultures. We are reminded of several of our student informants (mainly American) who consistently expressed high levels of achievement motivation yet whose lifestyles, and understandings of what behaviours might reasonably be expected to reflect such a stance, appeared to contradict their self-reports. This seeming paradox is echoed in an ethnography of a US high school (Grant & Sleeter, 1996) where, in interview, the students stated that they believed in school and valued education, seeing it as a means of fulfilling their aspirations, yet, '... on a day to day basis, they invested minimal effort in it' (p. 222). In our own cross-cultural analyses of motivation, therefore, we have sought to consider motivation and engagement in combination. This was a further reason for supplementing self-report studies with measures of actual student behaviours, and seeking data from parent and teacher informants.

Why don't effort attributions result in high work rates?

Given the high levels of engagement that we observed in St Petersburg classrooms, and which accorded with the wider literature, we conducted a number of studies of attributional beliefs with the expectation that Russian respondents would emphasize effort rather than ability as the key explanatory reason for academic success. In contrast, and in line with the cross-cultural studies of Stevenson and his colleagues (e.g.

Stevenson & Stigler, 1992), we anticipated that US (and probably, English) students would offer a higher proportion of ability attributions. We were, therefore, surprised to obtain a consistent finding whereby a stronger emphasis upon effort was evident in Kentucky and Sunderland. In our surveys of students and parents, only St Petersburg adolescents ranked ability above effort (Elliott *et al.*, 1999), and for both younger students and parents, the primacy of effort was much less evident in the Russian context. These puzzling findings were explored in our follow-up interviews. Our findings from these were much in line with those derived from the survey data: as before, the Western children, particularly those from Kentucky, placed great emphasis upon the primacy of effort (Hufton *et al.*, 2002a). This is not a unique finding, however; an American emphasis upon effort has been highlighted by Bempechat and Drago-Severson (1999) who included examination of findings from the large-scale Third International Mathematics and Science Study (TIMSS) (Beaton *et al.*, 1996). This study of nations around the world showed a strong emphasis upon effort by English and US children that was not matched by several academically successful Pacific Rim countries.

Our reflections upon the accumulated data led us to propose several closely related reasons for the fact that greater emphasis upon effort by the Western groups did not appear to result in comparatively high work rates. Firstly, there appeared to be very different understandings about how intensive a work rate might need to be for it to equate to the descriptor 'hard-working'—as with subjective perceptions of motivation, not only are individuals in any context likely to use such terms in rather different ways, but also normative understandings are likely to vary greatly across cultures. Thus, in the same way that high motivation was widely reported but the related behaviours not easily observed, many of the Western informants told us how important it was to work hard in their studies yet then described personal lifestyles that hardly reflected such perceptions. In a similar vein, the Kentucky and Sunderland students were more likely than those in St Petersburg to believe that they were working as hard as they could and consider that there was less room for improvement. This seemed to contradict our own observations where the difference between the American and Russian contexts was the most revealing (cf. Alexander, 2000, for a similar observation). In St Petersburg classrooms, the very demanding curriculum and workload were such that all students had to work hard to keep up. The difficulty of getting one of the highest grades was such that it was widely believed that a student had not only to work hard but also have a particular talent. Here then, in a culture where hard work was expected and generally evidenced, ability might be perceived to be a more discriminating variable. In the Kentucky schools we observed, the academic demands and work rates tended to be lower, and it appeared that being seen by teachers to be working hard was important for the achievement of high grades. However, in many classes, some children were clearly opting out or delivering the minimum acceptable. As a result, in such a context, effort might be a more salient and discriminating factor.

It is important to stress, however, that we have no evidence to suggest that high levels of effort are not greatly valued in all cultures. Rather it is what is perceived as constituting effort and how all participants respond to its apparent presence or absence that differs. As student effort is expected by Russian teachers, it is not seen as something that should require praise (Hufton *et al.*, 2002b, in press), although a failure to engage sufficiently will often result in disapprobation. Neither is positive affirmation necessary to ensure compliance and engagement—a feature often found in English and US schools (Alexander, 2000). Similarly, Russian students do not appear to perceive their efforts as particularly laudable and, thus, effort appears not to have the moral superiority over ability that was frequently suggested by our Anglo-American student informants (Hufton *et al.*, 2002a).

A second reason why the Kentucky/Sunderland attributional emphasis upon effort did not appear to be realized in practice centred upon peer pressures. Goal theory is increasingly recognizing the importance of social goals (Urdan & Maehr, 1995) and, like Bronfenbrenner some three decades earlier (1971), we found peer influences in Russian classrooms to be considerably more pro-school and pro-learning than in the US and English contexts, where peers often reduced students' willingness to be seen to work hard (Elliott *et al.*, 1999, 2001a; Hufton *et al.*, 2002a). Bronfenbrenner and colleagues (Bronfenbrenner, 1967; Devereux, Bronfenbrenner, & Rodgers, 1965) found the negative influence of peers to be strong in England and the US, with children far more ready to follow the promptings of other children to engage in socially disapproved activities than to adhere to the moral strictures of their parents and other adults. In explaining such phenomena, Bronfenbrenner noted that where the peer group was highly autonomous, as is the case in many Western societies, it was more likely that it would exert an influence that is oppositional to prevailing adult values. In contrast, social systems such as those that prevailed in the former Soviet Union were more able to harness the powerful influence of the peer group to support and maintain existing adult values and objectives. The role of the peer group in the Soviet Union, he concluded, was not, as in the USA, left mainly to chance but rather was the 'result of explicit policy and practice' (p. 206) whereby the peer group was used as an agent of socialization geared to encouraging identification with societal values. Instilling in children the importance of group needs rather than one's own, the development of high moral qualities and obedience to adults were key elements of Soviet preschool education (Tudge, 1991). This process, *vospitanie* (upbringing), was perceived as a central element of the child's education whereby teachers exerted much influence over both child and family. The power of peers to undermine or support classroom learning in these countries has been confirmed more recently by a number of other comparative studies (Alexander, 2000; Glowka, 1995; Laihiala-Kankainen, 1998; Muckle, 1988, 1990).

A third reason for the seeming inconsistency between the stress upon effort and actual behaviour relates to the perceived value of the outcome. For any given sphere of activity, a belief that effort is essential for successful performance will have little impact upon behaviour where the outcome is perceived as comparatively unimportant. Thus the third factor that might explain the attributional paradox noted above is the differential value that is placed upon academic achievement and the cultivation of erudition. Whereas the all-round development of the social self has historically been an important feature of Russian society that prevails across the broad social spectrum (Muckle, 1988), in the USA and England, education has a predominantly instrumental focus—it is a means of access to high-quality employment. This perspective appears to be held across all socio-economic groupings, although its impact upon achievement-related behaviour may vary. Thus, in Anglo-American contexts, it may not be enough to see a link between educational outcomes and employment prospects; individuals need to believe that they can personally achieve a level of education that permits entry to attractive employment. Students from disadvantaged communities, where educational standards tend to be low, and job opportunities scarce, may feel unable to break free from a prevailing cycle of deprivation. In our interviews (Hufton *et al.*, 2002a), we noted the anxieties of disadvantaged students in Sunderland regarding the possibility of unemployment and contrasted these with young people in Kentucky whose concerns centred upon distaste for relatively easily attainable 'dead-end jobs' such as 'serving gas' and 'flipping burgers'. If, in such settings, it is believed that such undesirable outcomes cannot be avoided, however hard one tries in school, the instrumentally motivating link from education to work is broken, and there remains little reason to work hard on one's studies (Wilkinson, 1995).

In line with the value that Russians traditionally place upon scholarship as a means of self-development, we were not surprised that our survey of St Petersburg adolescents (Elliott *et al.*, 1999) indicated that 'being an educated person' was cited most often as the principal reason for working hard. Similarly, our interviews showed that, while for many Russian students, higher education was linked with prestigious employment, wealth was not the key motive. The following quotes (cited in Hufton *et al.*, 2002a, p. 281) exemplify the perspectives of many of our informants:

> I don't know how it is in England, but here a lot of educated people—teachers, doctors, scientists—do not have wealthy lives. This is upsetting to me. Some people observing this may think, 'What do I need education for?—I'll live better without it.' Well, for me now, education is obligatory. I wouldn't be able to live without it. I need a sort of spiritual thing to live on. The sort of life when you are rich and not educated—I think that this can't satisfy me.

> I think you still need education, well for yourself, to know something, to study history, to know your country better, to have some vision of the world.

> I personally think that money is not something to value. In this world it is more important to build your personality. I would think that you haven't reached your potential. The main things in life are family atmosphere and good friends.

> A man doesn't live for money only ... something else is also important. Well, spiritual values, a soul ... not only material things.

> (Being educated) ... is more than important. It may be the aim of life.

> It is good to talk with the educated person.

While similarly dismissing the suggestion that one should leave school early, no Sunderland, or Kentucky, 15-year-old spoke in these terms.

Adult role models similarly reflect different preoccupations in the USA, England and Russia. Historically, Soviet adults have tended to spend more time reading and studying than their American counterparts (Zuzanek, 1980). The perceived importance of learning for Soviet youth was heightened from the 1920s when both an interest in scientific and technological development and the prestige of learning mushroomed. Thus education was not perceived primarily as a means of social mobility but was perceived more as an obligation to others. As Kelly (1999) puts it, there was '... an overt and unremitting emphasis on cultivation as a public and collective duty, rather than as an individual and private quest' (p. 203). Such influences appear to have proven particularly influential for working class youth; Russian time-budget studies showing a strong emphasis upon reading as a form of self-education in analyses of young factory workers' leisure time (Ariamov, 1928; Frankfurt, 1926; Smirnov, 1929). Unlike many Western contexts, where the long-term economic and vocational benefits of being educated are highly salient, it would appear that Russian families have traditionally placed greater emphasis upon attaining the immediate goals of current educational performance. Even now, when there is great uncertainty about what will transpire in the future, many Russians seem to place more emphasis on learning in the here and now and trust that things will subsequently work out for the best.

Schooling influences

Shen and Pedulla (2000) found that, whereas self perceptions were positively associated with higher performance when studying students within individual countries, when cross-country analyses were conducted, an inverse correlation resulted. Furthermore, factors that may explain motivational and performance differences in children within a culture may not be as significant when differences between cultures are examined. Thus, the reasons why children in Pacific Rim or Eastern European Countries appear to work so hard may not be found from analysis of studies largely based in the USA and drawing upon Anglo-American theories. Similarly, meaningful understandings may not be derived purely from student accounts. Our tentative conclusions as to why levels of motivation and engagement appeared to be comparatively high in St Petersburg centred largely upon cultural traditions, values, historical practices, and the operation of a pedagogical nexus—a linkage of finely intertuned, interactive and mutually reinforcing influences, acting on, within and through the schooling process itself (Hufton & Elliott, 2000).

Bronfenbrenner (1979) stated that within a given culture or subculture, settings might be very much alike, although between cultures, these could be very different.

> It is as if within each society or subculture there existed a blueprint for the organisation of every type of setting. Furthermore, the blueprint can be changed, with the result that the structure of the settings in a society can become markedly altered and produce corresponding changes in behaviour and development. (p. 4)

It appears that the Russian blueprint has altered significantly for, despite echoing those of most other researchers, our findings are now challenged by more recent observations provided by Russian commentators, politicians and researchers. Concerns have been repeatedly expressed that the economic and social consequences resulting from the breakup of the Soviet Union, together with the influence of globalization (Arnett, 2002), have influenced an increasing number of teenagers to turn away from a collectivist orientation, hold a more instrumental view of education and adopt increasingly materialist values (Chuprov & Zubok, 1997; Williams, 1997). In turn, these have resulted in a lessening of the esteem in which education has been traditionally held and, in many cases, to a reduction in student motivation and achievement. Indeed, it has been suggested recently (Dolzhenko, 1998) that Russia is likely to be one the few major industrialized nations where levels of educational performance are in decline; a perception supported by findings from a recent comparative international study (OECD, 2001). In particular, there appears to be some evidence of a growing bifurcation of attitudes towards schooling and the gradual erosion of the broader consensus about the importance of academic success. In short, while many students continue to be highly motivated and work very long hours, an increasing minority are not only disenchanted with their schooling but physically dropping out. This does not appear to be a result of any less interesting classroom experiences, although we would not wish to suggest either that Soviet schooling was an intrinsically appealing experience for all students. Indeed, some describe this process as dehumanizing and 'directed at the destruction of school pupils' individuality' (Westbrook, 1994, p. 107).

Nevertheless, many Russians look back fondly upon their education during the Soviet period (Schweisfurth, 2000), and there appears to have been widespread acceptance that while not always 'fun', education had a meaningful and valuable purpose. Certainly, our findings strongly reflect such perceptions, although they may be analogous to the light from a far-distant star that, in reality, has long since been consumed. It is possible that our data, gathered in the 1990s, were garnered from students who had less exposure to, and thus had been less influenced by, Western, market-oriented social and economic forces than the present generation currently being educated in Russian schools.

In his five-nation study of primary school classrooms, Alexander (2000) noted that different understandings about the nature of freedom and authority were important influences upon classroom behaviour. Describing the tensions evident in England and America, where student autonomy and empowerment were highly valued, he noted that teachers often had to work hard to maintain order, Of the five countries studied, the 'sharpest contrasts' in this respect were between Russia and the USA:

> In the one context the substantive messages about the nature of knowledge, teaching and learning and about behavioural norms and expectations were unambiguous yet also—bar the occasional brief reminder—tacit; in the other context they were the subject of frequent reminders by the teacher and often intense encounters ranging from negotiation to confrontation. (2000, p. 318)

Alexander's cross-cultural observation that academic engagement appeared to be lower in countries where students had greater freedoms seems to run counter to the central tenets of motivation theories such as that of Deci and Ryan (1985). Many of these stress the importance of authenticity (i.e. activities should have meaning for students' everyday experience and future goals), challenge, choice over content and learning approaches, and relate to student skills, interests and abilities (Yair, 2000). It is argued that, where such factors operate, there is more likelihood of intrinsic motivation, a less passive orientation, increased feelings of control and a greater sense of personal accomplishment. This menu bears little resemblance to traditional Russian pedagogy, however.

Similar to Alexander (2000) we found that as late as 1997/98, Russian schools appeared to be largely resistant to broader social turbulence. We argued that these institutions had a key functional role of providing a locus where stability and continuity could be maintained (O'Brien, 2000). This might help to explain the fact that teachers continued to practise even when their wages became virtually worthless, or indeed, when they were not paid at all. However, schools necessarily reflect the societies in which they operate, and it would appear that changes in Russian schooling, structural, curricular and pedagogic, are increasingly challenging traditional practices and beliefs. As Russian society metamorphoses and traditional commitments to authority, collectivism and intellectualism decline, it would appear that there is now a major threat to that very secure classroom context that has traditionally resulted in high academic standards and shared social and moral understandings.

In a society experiencing major upheaval, the Russian school continues to be seen by many as an important means of upholding desirable moral and social values (Karakovsky, 1993). However, the strong ideological stance and emphasis upon *vospitanie*, resulted in an educational system with a:

> ... strong emphasis upon factual content, a reluctance to admit to controversy or uncertainty on any point, a consequent tendency to reduce aesthetic or ...

philosophical subjects to a catalogue of stereotyped statements, little consideration of the child as recipient of all this, a strongly formal atmosphere, and stress on classroom rituals ... The subject most of all, and the teacher in second place, are firmly in control of all that happens. (Muckle, 1990, p. 104)

The 1992 Law on Education of the Russian Federation downgraded the function of *vospitanie* and, in endeavouring to democratize education, initiated a series of reforms that gave greater freedoms to teachers and students. Such an emphasis closely reflected social and ideological shifts taking place in broader Russian society. Current motivational theory (e.g. Deci & Ryan, 1985) might lead one to anticipate that the shift towards greater personal autonomy, for example, through greater emphasis upon individualized, student-centred education and heightened teacher–student collaboration—'a shift from the pedagogy of command to the pedagogy of cooperation' (Nikandrov, cited in Alexander, 2000, p. 78)—would result in higher levels of student motivation. This does not appear to be the case, however, and the changes have caused a degree of disruption, confusion and teacher discontent mirrored by attempts to dilute or minimize the implementation of educational reform (Webber, 2000). This raises the interesting question as to whether educational democratization, running counter to the traditional Russian valuing of authoritarian systems (McFarland, Ageyev, & Djintcharadze, 1996), has actually resulted in conditions that have reduced student motivation— a phenomenon that appears to contradict Western theorizing.

Beyond the classroom

School life necessarily reflects those many broader social factors that impact upon the attitudes, orientations and behaviour of the current generation of Russian children. These include political and economic upheaval, changes in employment opportunities, widespread shifts in broader societal values, a weakening of the prestige of education and the professions, and a diminishing role for education as a means for social mobility. In addition, strong trends towards competitiveness and individualism have been reflected in the education system by a plethora of structural and pedagogic reforms, many of which have resulted in the development of socially divisive educational hierarchies and inequalities (Konstantinovskii & Khokhlushkina, 2000).

For Cherednichenko (2000) an important element in the disaffection of many young people is the increasing emphasis upon social differentiation by means of specialist schools and curricula, reflecting the marketization of education. If the 1980s was the era of many innovatory and experimental teaching approaches, the 1990s was a time of diversification and differentiation in the type and roles of schools (Sutherland, 1999). This resulted in a mushrooming of the number of well-resourced specialist schools that have increasingly drawn upon the most skilled teachers and selected the most able students. Other schools have had to cope in an educational system that experienced draconian budgetary cuts (Rakhmanin, 1997). The end result of this trend to specialization has been polarization. While increasing numbers of students are seeking to study subjects at institutes and universities, the courses they are selecting tend to be geared to accruing the greatest financial rewards (economics, finance, law, foreign languages), and those who have graduated in other subjects are turning their backs on their disciplines in a search for greater income (Rutkevich, 2000). At the other end of the educational scale, many students appear increasingly alienated (Andriushina, 2000), particularly those for whom learning is a struggle and who find themselves in unfashionable schools. Many students appear less oriented to their teachers (Bocharova & Lerner, 2000) and express concerns that school curricula have changed too little and fail to prepare young people for the new economic pressures that will mark their passage into adulthood (Iartsev, 2000). This disenchantment is exacerbated by continuing curriculum overload that leaves many students exhausted and offers little time for socialization and leisure (Filippov, 2001). Given the above, it is not unsurprising that school dropout rates have steadily increased since the end of the 1980s (Cherednichenko, 2000; Grigorenko, 1998), and up to one and a half million young people are now seen as neither working nor attending school (Likhanov, 1996). The end result is an increasing trend towards social exclusion that mirrors that more traditionally found in Western society.

Changing economic circumstances appear to be impacting significantly upon student motivation. The material position of young people in Russia appears not to be greatly influenced by how hard they work or by their educational level (Zubok, 1999). Rather, what matters is the nature of their employment, something that is often independent of performance at school or university, or perhaps even inversely related:

> Roughly speaking, the more education one has nowadays, the less money one earns.
> (Nikandrov, 1995, p. 54)

One might say, however, that here little has changed, as under the Soviet system, employment was centrally controlled and guaranteed, and opportunities for advancement and remuneration were often made available irrespective of the individual's level of education (Kopytov, 2000). Indeed, one might contend that this phenomenon may help to explain why education in Russia has long been valued as an end in itself. Differences in life standards were minimal—the old Soviet joke being that, under capitalism, wealth was unevenly distributed, whereas under socialism, poverty was evenly distributed—and even those who had wealth had to conceal this for fear of being persecuted for economic crimes (Nikandrov, 2000). What has now changed is a shift to large-scale inequality, a growth of individualism, and an unstable economic situation in which entrepreneurial skills can bring about immense wealth. Such factors have resulted in a shift from the traditional regard for learning as an intrinsically valuable end in itself, and a sign of a cultured person, to an emphasis upon education as a means to achieving individualistic goals of success and prosperity. Allied to this has been a changing perception of work from something that was widely perceived as being individually meaningful and socially valuable to an activity that is primarily a means of making money, legally or illegally (Kim, 2000; Ol'shanskii, Klimova, & Volzhskaia, 2000). A by-product of such shifts has been growing recognition, on the part of many young people, that economic success may not be achieved by following societal strictures on how this should be achieved, which in turn has for many resulted in a sense of anomie (Zubok, 1999).

Such stressors are compounded by massive problems of child ill-health and chronic fatigue (Baranov, 1998); factors further exacerbated by the oppressive educational workload (Filippov, 2000, 2001). In the opinion of many commentators, social dislocation has resulted in a large increase in psychological problems. The rejection of Soviet emphases upon country and collective, and the irrelevance for many young people of the beliefs of their forefathers, has left a high proportion of children and youth alienated from traditional values. The weakening of mechanisms of social regulation that largely operated through state and societal institutions has resulted in a vacuum whereby young people's value systems are increasingly gleaned from mass culture and mass media (Karpukhin, 2000). In addition, as peer groups become more autonomous, increasingly akin to those in Western societies, traditionally powerful pro-adult, pro-school peer influences (Bronfenbrenner, 1967) now appear to be declining.

Unlike England and the USA, relative economic deprivation in Russia appears traditionally to have had less bearing on differential educational achievement, although this now also appears to be changing. A further complication has been the radical shift in the social order; those at the socio-economic top of society were at the margins only a few years ago, whereas those who were recently at the socio-economic top are now often at the margins (Sternberg & Grigorenko, 2000). High levels of education may prove to have limited value for coping with societal change; for example, practical abilities have been recently found to be more predictive of positive psychological health than analytical intelligence (Grigorenko & Sternberg, 2001). Given such a volte-face, it is now difficult for many Russian parents to have confidence in the messages they would wish to pass on to their children, or for children to learn from their parents' example (Shurygina, 2000).

While the available evidence suggests that levels of achievement motivation on the part of many young Russians are declining, it is difficult, at present, to ascertain the relativity of such a shift. Russian commentators may bemoan an apparent change in young people's attitudes and behaviour, yet these may still be much closer to those of Soviet youth in the past than to their peers in contemporary England and the USA.

The need for more encompassing theory and methodology

To what extent can current psychological theories of, and approaches to, motivation capture the complexity of those issues that appear to have a bearing on the rapidly shifting Russian context? As the culture of the market place becomes increasingly established in Russian society and its educational consequence, stratification, leads to an increasingly alienated underclass that is less likely to accept the strictures of adult authority, or be influenced by pro-school peers, psychologists may be left wondering about the extent to which their conceptual and theoretical frameworks are capable of shedding meaningful light on key motivational influences. For those under severe economic and social duress, the satisfaction of basic needs may take precedence over the achievement goals and values that are the focus of many contemporary theorists (Murdock, 2000). Certainly, our examination of the Russian experience leads us to question the extent to which studies of students' subjective experience—attributions, performance goals, self-efficacy, intrinsic motivation and suchlike—in isolation, or in combination, can capture the essence of why students in some cultures, at particular times (cf. Bronfenbrenner, 1995) appear to be more willing to invest large reserves of energy in their schooling than others.

In a detailed review of the achievement motivation literature, Murphy and Alexander (2000) note that work has typically been undertaken by US researchers studying US students, and most of this is underpinned by Western perspectives. They question whether the conclusions from this body of work can be generalized to other cultures and recommend that similar studies should be undertaken in other cultures. We similarly query the extent to which factors that help to explain motivational differences between US students within one or more schools (which form the great majority of cited studies in this field), and which reflect US cultural understandings and values, are necessarily those that are most significant for all societies. Indeed, in the light of our comparative work, we wonder whether such studies provide a full picture even of the US context. It is conceivable that investigations that focus upon differences in student accounts within any given cultural context may result in underestimation of, or indeed a failure to recognize, powerful motivational forces that operate not only across, but also within, any given cultures.

We also reject Murphy and Alexander's implicit suggestion that the use of traditional methodologies will suffice for cross-cultural examination. It is not, in our opinion, sufficient merely to replicate existing studies in other countries to discover whether similar findings pertain; rather, in order to gain a greater understanding of the interplay of influences upon development and motivation, investigations need to become considerably more sophisticated and wide-ranging.

While some researchers in the field of motivation are showing an increasing interest in the contribution of contextual and cultural factors (Jacobs & Osgood, 2002; Maehr & Pintrich, 1995; Salili, Chiu, & Hong, 2001; Urdan, 1999; Volet & Jarvela, 2001), the discipline's experimental and psychometric roots continue to be highly influential (Jarvela, 2001). Where socio-structural and cultural factors are explored, these tend to be in relation to differences between cultural groupings with respect to one or more specified psychological constructs (e.g. Chirkov & Ryan, 2001) rather than through an examination of the complex, multi-systemic interaction of factors that might result in a greater or lesser orientation to learning. Furthermore, in many investigations, the focus tends to be upon the study of individual differences (Maehr & Yamaguchi, 2001) involving etic rather than emic data (Elliott & Bempechat, 2002). The importance of the emic in cultural psychology, and the value of combining emic and etic data in cross-cultural studies, is now recognized (Triandis, 2001; Triandis & Suh, 2002) yet, somewhat surprisingly, such understandings are rarely reflected in the achievement motivation papers that one typically finds in the most prestigious international journals.

As noted earlier, our cross-cultural motivation researches have been greatly influenced by Bronfenbrenner's (1979) approach to human development that likens aspects of the ecological environment to a set of Russian matryushka dolls in which each nestles inside another. At the innermost level, the microsystem, lies the immediate settings in which an individual functions. Next, at the level of the mesosystem, one considers how these different settings, the school, the home, the playground, the shopping mall, interconnect. Exosystems, the third level, consist of some settings in which the individual is not even present, for example, the development of the young child may be affected by events that occur in the parents' workplace, such as a promotion or pay increase. At the supraordinate level, the macrosystem refers to the comprehensive network of relational systems that operates within a culture. This includes such elements as educational and vocational opportunities, socio-political and socio-economic factors and the various roles and responsibilities accorded by society to individuals on the basis of such variables as age, ethnicity and gender. The macrosystem may now be increasingly open to global influences (Le Tendre, Baker, Akiba, Goesling, & Wiseman, 2001). While the past decade has seen an increase in research examining how peers, parents and teachers influence learning and achievement (although peer influences upon motivation have, until recently, been relatively neglected; Ryan, 2000) there is still a relative dearth of studies examining how motivation, engagement and learning occur within macrolevel states of affairs (Murdock, 2000). Of course, this present position largely reflects the dominant paradigm within educational psychology which, while beginning to draw increasingly upon methodological approaches from anthropology and sociology (Volet, 2001), too seldom contributes to broader multidisciplinary investigations that offer the promise of providing richer and more comprehensive understandings of social phenomena.

Conclusions

This paper does not seek to present empirical findings that can be generalized across cultures. Rather, by presenting a relatively detailed account of a milieu experiencing a rate of change that, indeed, might be considered to be far from typical, we seek to highlight the complex interplay of historical, cultural, social, economic and pedagogical factors that bear upon student development and motivation. The Russian illustration not only shows the important influence of long-standing traditions and values upon overall patterns of motivation but also demonstrates the impact upon development and motivation of a series of changes operating at various levels within the ecosystem. Such an illustration, we believe, illustrates the paucity of accounts that examine achievement motivation in terms of isolated factors such as pedagogic change or managerial styles.

In providing this account, we wish to highlight the inadequacy of ethnocentric theory and enquiry and the sterility of dominant methodologies where these are employed in isolation. To address such weaknesses, we call for new multimethod, multilevel approaches to the study of achievement motivation that can provide richer and more authentic understandings of this most fundamental and important educational issue.

References

Alexander, R. (2000). *Culture and pedagogy: International comparisons in primary education.* Oxford: Blackwell.

Andriushina, E. V. (2000). The family and the adolescent's health. *Russian Education and Society*, 42(4), 61-87.

Ariamov, (1928). *Working class youth.* Moscow.

Arnett, J. J. (2002). The psychology of globalization. *American Psychologist*, 57, 774-783.

Ban, T., & Cummings, W. K. (1999). Moral orientations of schoolchildren in the United States and Japan. *Comparative Education Review*, 43, 64-85.

Baranov, A. (1998). A real threat to the nation's future. *Russian Education and Society*, 40(1), 6-16.

Beaton, A. E., Mullis, I. V., Martin, M. O., Gonzalez, E. J., Kelly, D. L., & Smith, T. A. (1996). Mathematics achievement in the middle school years: I.E.A.'s third international mathematics and science study (TIMSS). Boston: Boston College.

Bempechat, J., & Drago-Severson, E. (1999). Cross-national differences in academic achievement: Beyond etic conceptions of children's understandings. *Review of Educational Research*, 69, 287-314.

Bocharova, O., & Lerner, A. (2000). Characteristics of the way of life of adolescents. *Russian Education and Society*, 42(6), 37-48.

Bronfenbrenner, U. (1967). Response to pressure from peers versus adults among Soviet and American school children. *International Journal of Psychology*, 2(3), 199-207.

Bronfenbrenner, U. (1971). *The two worlds of childhood.* London: Allen & Unwin.

Bronfenbrenner, U. (1979). *The ecology of human development.* Cambridge, MA: Harvard University Press.

Bronfenbrenner, U. (1995). Development ecology through space and time: A future perspective.

In P. Moen, G. Elder, & K. Luscher (Eds.), *Examining lives in context: Perspectives on the ecology of human development*. Washington, DC: American Psychological Association.

Brophy, J. (1999). Research on motivation in education: past, present, and future. In T. C. Urdan (Ed.), *Advances in motivation and achievement. Vol. 11, The role of context* (1-44). Greenwich, CT, JAI Press.

Bucur, M., & Eklof, B. (1999). Russia and Eastern Europe. In R. F. Arnove & C. A. Torres (Eds.), *Comparative education: The dialectic of the global and the local*. Lanham, MD: Rowman & Littlefield.

Canning, M., Moock, P., & Heleniak, T. (1999). *Reforming education in the regions of Russia. World Bank technical paper no. 457*. Washington DC: The World Bank.

Cherednichenko, G. A. (2000). School reform in the 1990s. *Russian Education and Society*, *42*(11), 6-32.

Chirkov, V. I., & Ryan, R. M. (2001). Parent and teacher autonomy support in Russian and U.S. adolescents: Common effects on well-being and academic motivation. *Journal of Cross-Cultural Psychology*, *32*, 618-635.

Chuprov, V., & Zubok, I. (1997). Social conflict in the sphere of the education of youth. *Education in Russia, the Independent States and Eastern Europe*, *15*(2), 47-58.

Coleman, J. (1961). *Adolescent society: The social life of the teenager and its impact on education*. New York: Free Press.

Deci, E. L., & Ryan, R. M. (1985). *Intrinsic motivation and self-determination in human behavior*. New York: Plenum.

Devereux, E. C., Bronfenbrenner, U., & Rodgers, R. R. (1965). *Child-rearing in England and the United States: A cross-national comparison*. Unpublished manuscript.

Dolzhenko, L. (1998). The college student today: A social portrait and attitudes toward schooling. *Russian Education and Society*, *40*(11), 6-15.

Elliott, J. G., & Bempechat, J. (2002). The culture and contexts of achievement motivation. In J. Bempechat & J. G. Elliott (Eds.), *Achievement motivation in culture and context: Understanding children's learning experiences. New directions in child development* (Vol. 96). San Francisco: Jossey Bass.

Elliott, J., Hufton, N., Hildreth, A., & Illushin, L. (1999). Factors influencing educational motivation: A study of attitudes, expectations and behaviour of children in Sunderland, Kentucky and St Petersburg. *British Educational Research Journal*, *25*(1), 75-94.

Elliott, J. G., Hufton, N., Illushin, L., & Lauchlan, F. (2001a). Motivation in the junior years: International perspectives on children's attitudes, expectations and behaviour and their relationship to educational achievement. *Oxford Review of Education*, *27*, 37-68.

Elliott, J. G., Hufton, N., Illushin, L., & Willis, W. (2001b). 'The kids are doing all right': International differences in parental satisfaction, expectation and attribution. *Cambridge Journal of Education*, *31*, 179-204.

Filippov, V. (2000). On the results of the past year and the tasks of the current year. *Russian Education and Society*, *42*, 87-100.

Filippov, V. (2001). Education in Russia: Current state, problems and prospects. *Russian Education and Society*, *43*, 5-27.

Frankfurt, L. (1926). *Working-class youth and the book*. Moscow-Leningrad.

Glowka, D. (1995). Schulen und unterricht im vergleich: Rusland/Deutschland (Schools and teaching in comparison: Russia and Germany). New York: Waxmann.

Grant, C. A., & Sleeter, C. E. (1996). *After the school bell rings* (2nd ed.). London: Falmer.

Grigorenko, E. L. (1998). Russian 'defectology': Anticipating perestroika in the field. *Journal of Learning Disabilities*, *31*(2), 193-207.

Grigorenko, E. L., & Sternberg, R. J. (2001). Analytical, creative and practical intelligence as predictors of self-reported adaptive functioning: A case study in Russia. *Intelligence*, *29*, 57-73.

Hufton, N., & Elliott, J. G. (2000). Motivation to learn: The pedagogical nexus in the Russian school: Some implications for transnational research and policy borrowing. *Educational Studies, 26*, 115-136.

Hufton, N., Elliott, J. G., & Illushin, L. (2002a). Educational motivation and engagement: Qualitative accounts from three countries. *British Educational Research Journal, 28*, 267-291.

Hufton, N., Elliott, J. G., & Illushin, L. (2002b). Achievement motivation across cultures: Some puzzles and their implication for future research. In J. Bempechat & J. G. Elliott (Eds.), *Achievement motivation in culture and context: Understanding children's learning experiences. New directions in child development* (Vol. 96). San Francisco: Jossey Bass.

Hufton, N., Elliott, J. G., & Illushin, L. (in press). Teachers' beliefs about student motivation: similarities and differences across cultures. *Comparative Education.*

Iartsev, D. V. (2000). Characteristics of the socialisation of today's adolescent. *Russian Education and Society, 42*(11), 67-75.

Jacobs, J. E., & Osgood, D. W. (2002). The use of multi-level modeling to study individual change and context effects in achievement motivation. In P. R. Pintrich & M. L. Maehr (Eds.), *Advances in motivation and achievement. Vol. 12: New directions in measures and methods* (pp. 277-318). Greenwich, CT: JAI Press.

Jarvela, S. (2001). Shifting research on motivation and cognition to an integrated approach on learning and motivation in context. In S. Volet & S. Jarvela (Eds.). *Motivation in learning contexts: Theoretical advances and methodological implications* (pp. 3-14). London: Pergamon.

Karakovsky, V. A. (1993). The school in Russia today and tomorrow. *Compare, 23*(3), 277-288.

Karpukhin, O. I. (2000). The young people of Russia: Characteristics of their socialisation and self-determination. *Russian Education and Society, 42*(11), 47-57.

Kelly, C. (1999). Kul'turnost' in the Soviet Union: Ideal and reality. In G. Hosking & R. Service (Eds.), *Reinterpreting Russia* (pp. 198-213) London: Arnold.

Kim, N. (2000). Education given, education received. *Russian Education and Society, 42*(2), 59-64.

Konstantinovskii, D. L., & Khokhlushkina, F. A. (2000). The formation of the social behaviour of young people in the sphere of education. *Russian Education and Society, 42*(2), 26-58.

Kopytov, A. D. (2000). Problems of young people's employment: The regional approach. *Russian Education and Society, 42*(7), 15-28.

Laihiala-Kankainen, S. (1998). *Russian pupils in Finnish schools—problems created by differences in pedagogical cultures.* Paper presented at the European Conference on Educational Research, Slovenia.

LeTendre, G. K., Baker, D. P., Akiba, M., Goesling, B., & Wiseman, A. (2001). Teachers' work, institutional isomorphism and cultural variation in the U.S., Germany and Japan. *Educational Researcher, 30*(6), 3-16.

Likhanov, A. (1996). The position of children in Russia. *Nezavisimaia Gazeta.*

Maehr, M. L., & Pintrich, P. R. (Eds.), (1995). *Advances in motivation and achievement Vol. 9, Culture, motivation and achievement.* Greenwich, CT: JAI Press.

Maehr, M. L., & Yamaguchi, R. (2001). Cultural diversity, student motivation and achievement. In F. Salili, C. Chiu, & Y. Hong (Eds.), *Student motivation: The culture and context of learning* (pp. 123-148). New York: Plenum.

Martin, M. O., Mulliss, I. V., Gonzalez, E., Gregory, K. D., Smith, T. A., Chrostowski, S. J., Garden, R. A., & O'Connor, K. M. (2000). *TIMSS 1999: International science report.* Boston: International Study Centre, Boston College.

McFarland, S. G. Ageyev, V. S., & Djintcharadze, N. (1996). Russian authoritarianism two years after communism. *Personality and Social Psychology Bulletin, 22*, 210-217.

Muckle, J. (1988). *A guide to the Soviet curriculum.* London: Croom Helm.

Muckle, J. (1990). *Portrait of a Soviet school under glasnost.* London: Macmillan.

Murdock, T. (2000) Incorporating economic context into educational psychology: Methodological and conceptual challenges. *Educational Psychologist*, *35*, 113-124.

Murphy, P. K., & Alexander, P. A. (2000). A motivated exploration of motivation terminology. *Contemporary Educational Psychology*, *25*, 3-53.

Nikandrov, N. D. (1995). Russian education after perestroika: The search for new values. *International Review of Education*, *41*(1-2), 47-57.

Nikandrov, N. D. (2000). Education in modern Russia: Is it modern? In K. Mazurek, M. A. Winzer, & C. Majorek (Eds.), *Education in a global society: A comparative perspective* (pp. 209-223). Boston: Allyn & Bacon.

O'Brien, D. (2000). *From Moscow, living and teaching among Russians in the 1990s.* Nottingham: Bramcote Press.

Ol'shanskii, V. B., Klimova, S. G., & Volzhkaia, N. (2000). School students in a changing society (1982-1997). *Russian Education and Society*, *42*, 44-40.

Organization for Economic Cooperation and Development (OECD) (1998). *Reviews of national policies for education: Russian Federation.* Paris: OECD.

Organization for Economic Cooperation and Development (OECD) (2001). *Knowledge and skills for life: First results from PISA 2000.* Paris: OECD.

Pichugina, G. V., & Guryanova, M. P. (1999). The labour training of rural students: Data and facts. *Shkola I Proizvodstvo*, *5*, 10-12.

Rakhmanin, V. (1997). Education as a factor of humanistic security and social development. *Russian Education and Society*, *39*(11), 57-70. (Original source: Obrazovanie kak faktor gumanisticheskoi bezopasnosti I sotsial'nogo razvitiia. *Alma Mater*, 1997, *2*, 3-7).

Rutkevich, M. (2000). Change in the social role of the general education school in Russia. *Russian Education and Society*, *42*(2), 5-25.

Ryan, A. M. (2000). Peer groups as a context for the socialisation of adolescents' motivation, engagement and achievement in school. *Educational Psychologist*, *35*, 101-111.

Salili, F., Chiu, C., & Hong, Y. (2001). *Student motivation: The culture and context of learning.* New York: Plenum.

Schweisfurth, M. (2000). Teachers and democratic change in Russia and South Africa. *Education in Russia, the Independent States and Eastern Europe*, *18*(1), 2-8.

Shen, C., & Pedulla, J. J. (2000). The relationship between students' achievement and their self-perception of competence and rigour of mathematics and science: A cross-national analysis. *Assessment in Education*, *7*, 237-253.

Shurygina, I. I. (2000). The life strategies of adolescents. *Russian Education and Society*, *42*(9), 5-24.

Smirnov, V. I. (1929). *The psychology of adolescence.* Moscow-Leningrad.

Steinberg, L. (1996). *Beyond the classroom: Why school reform has failed and what parents need to do.* New York, Touchstone Books.

Sternberg, R. J., & Grigorenko, E. L. (2000). Theme park psychology: A case study regarding human intelligence and its implications for Education. *Educational Psychology Review*, *12*(2), 247-268.

Stevenson, H. W., & Nerison-Low, R. (1998) *To sum it up: Case studies of education in Germany, Japan, and the United States.* Washington, DC: National Institute on Student Achievement, Curriculum and Assessment: US Department of Education.

Stevenson, H. W., & Stigler, J. W. (1992). *The learning gap: Why our schools are failing and what we can learn from Japanese and Chinese education.* New York: Summit Books.

Sutherland, J. (1999). *Schooling in the new Russia: Innovation and change, 1984-95.* London: Macmillan.

Triandis, H. C. (2001). Individualism and collectivism: Past, present and future. In D. Matsumoto (Ed.), *The handbook of culture and psychology.* Oxford: Oxford University Press.

Triandis, H. C., & Suh, E. M. (2002). Cultural influences in personality. *Annual Review of Psychology*, *53*, 133-160.

Tudge, J. R. H. (1991). Education of young children in the Soviet Union: Current practice in historical perspective. *The Elementary School Journal, 92,* 121–133.

Urdan, T. C. (1999). The role of context. In T. C. Urdan (Ed.), *Advances in motivation and achievement* (Vol. 11, pp. 1–44). Greenwich, CT: JAI Press.

Urdan, T. C., & Maehr, M. L. (1995). Beyond a two-goal theory of motivation: A case for social goals. *Review of Educational Research, 65,* 213–244.

Van Hoorn, J. L., Komlosi, A., Suchar, E., & Samelson, D. A. (2000). *Adolescent development and rapid social change: Perspectives from Eastern Europe.* New York: State University of New York Press.

Volet, S. (2001). Emerging trends in recent research on motivation in learning contexts. In S. Volet & S. Jarvela (Eds.), *Motivation in learning contexts: Theoretical advances and methodological implications* (pp. 319–334). London: Pergamon.

Volet, S., & Jarvela, S. (Eds.) (2001) *Motivation in learning contexts: Theoretical advances and methodological implications.* London: Pergamon.

Webber, S. L. (2000). *School, reform and society in the new Russia.* London: Macmillan

Westbrook, M. (1994). St Petersburg's independent schools. In A. Jones (Ed.), *Education and society in the new Russia* (pp. 103–117). Armonk, NY: M. E. Sharpe

Wilkinson, C. (1995) *The drop out society: Young people on the margin.* Leicester: Youth Work Press.

Williams, C. (1997) Convergence or divergence? A comparative analysis of youth in Russia and Britain. *Education in Russia, the Independent States and Eastern Europe, 15*(1), 12–20.

Yair, G. (2000). Reforming motivation: How the structure of instruction affects students' learning experiences. *British Educational Research Journal, 26,* 191–210.

Zhurkina, A. Y. (1973). *Time-budgets of high school students: Sociological problems of education.* Moscow: Pedagogika.

Zubok, I. A. (1999). Exclusion in the study of problems of young people. *Russian Education and Society, 41*(9), 39–53.

Zuzanek, J. (1980). *Work and leisure in the Soviet Union.* New York: Praeger.

Development and Motivation, 173–189
BJEP Monograph Series II, 2
© 2003 The British Psychological Society

www.bps.org.uk

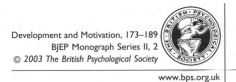

Towards a model that integrates motivation, affect and learning

Monique Boekaerts*

Centre for the Study of Education and Instruction, Leiden University,
The Netherlands

In the last decade, we have witnessed an explosion of models of self-regulated learning. These models explain why students are willing to invest resources to accomplish curricular goals and how they steer and direct the learning process in order to reach these goals. However, most of these models struggle with the inclusion of affect. Although most researchers agree that emotions and moods influence the learning process, they have difficulty describing how affect inhibits or facilitates the self-regulation process. One of the reasons why the study of affect is underdeveloped in educational psychology is that the research has focused on learning outcome, for example on reading comprehension or mathematics achievement, and that affect has been treated as a by-product of the cognitive processing system. In my own research, I have focused on motivation and affect as outcome variables in their own right. My base position is that we need two parallel processing pathways to explain task engagement in the classroom. One of the basic tenets of my Model of Adaptive Learning (Boekaerts, 1992, 1995; Boekaerts & Niemivirta, 2000) is that students have two priorities. On the one hand, they want to reach the learning goals in order to be successful at school and beyond. On the other hand, they want to keep their sense of well-being within reasonable bounds. These two priorities may be in harmony or in disharmony in the classroom, and most students have found their own idiosyncratic way of straddling the divide between their need for mastery and achievement and their need for happiness and satisfaction. The implications for the study of motivation and development are that we need to gain insight into the personal goals that are salient for a student in a specific developmental time window (e.g. adolescence) and study how these salient personal goals influence their perception of the learning opportunities.

We have only just begun to systematically study students' personal goals and link them to their actual behaviour in the classroom. Preliminary results suggest that

* Requests for reprints should be addressed to Monique Boekaerts, Centre for the Study of Education and Instruction, Leiden University, Wassenaarseweg 52, 2333 AK Leiden, The Netherlands (e-mail: boekaert@fsw.leidenuniv.nl).

students' salient personal goals are closely linked to (1) the meaning-generating process (cold cognition pathway) and (2) emotional evaluations of learning opportunities (hot cognition pathway). Activity in both these pathways forms the interface between learning opportunities and student performance. It is easy to imagine that the meaning-generating process as well as the emotional evaluations of learning opportunities change with age, mainly because the focus of students' salient personal goals also shifts when a new developmental time window becomes operative (Boekaerts, 2003a). However, connecting motivation to development still requires large inferential leaps, because our insight into these issues is still fragmentary. At the moment, our research group is beginning to unravel the effect of goal frustration and goal facilitation on learning and motivation in school, and I will offer some suggestions and speculations about the impact that affective states have on student development.

In search of two parallel processing pathways

It is not my intention to review my work on motivation and affective states here. Instead, I present ideas that I think are important in conceptualizing motivation. This chapter is organized in terms of a set of conceptual themes that have been central in my thinking about the effect of motivation and affective states on student thinking about learning and performance.

In 1992, I introduced the first version of my own self-regulation model, the Model of Adaptive Learning (Boekaerts, 1992). My main position was, and still is, that students learn in multiple, overlapping contexts and that each of these contexts has a favourable or unfavourable effect on the learning process as well as on interactions with teacher and peers. These contexts include the domain to which the learning task belongs, the instructional context, the social context, and the cultural context. I realized that, whilst many of these contexts are hidden, they are powerfully present in the students' meaning-generating process. In this chapter, I do not focus explicitly on students' perception and interpretation of the rules and regulations that apply in these multiple, overlapping contexts. Rather, I refer to the way these contexts are reflected in the students' appraisals and affective states that influence task engagement and performance assessment.

Motivation is situated

My model of the Adaptive Learning Process has evolved over the years (see Boekaerts, 1995, 1996; Boekaerts & Niemivirta, 2000). It was guided by conceptualizations of motivation that assume variability in motivation across learning situations and time. In particular, I was influenced by theories and models from mainstream psychology, such as the work of Frijda (1988), Kuhl (1984), Lazarus and Folkman (1984) and Leventhal (1980). In accordance with leading motivation researchers in educational psychology, I assumed that students' general motivational beliefs and their domain-specific motivational beliefs form the basis for their engagement in the classroom. However, contrary to assumptions made at the time, I proposed that motivation is situated (situation-specific motivation) and thus empirically distinct from domain-specific motivation. I maintained that domain-specific theories of motivation tell us something about students' tendency to approach domain-specific tasks but that they are situationally blind. Indeed, domain-specific theories, such as Achievement Goal Theory,

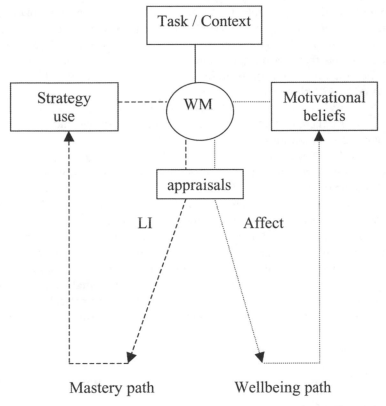

Figure 1. Model of Adaptive Learning, consisting of the appraisal part (top half) and the action part (bottom half). Two parallel processing pathways are depicted: the cold cognition pathway (dashed line), representing the mastery path, and the hot cognition pathway (dotted line), symbolizing the well-being path. WM = working memory; LI = learning intention theory.

do not take account of the content of a learning task and of the way students assign meaning to the task and the context in which it is embedded. By contrast, situational motivation or learning intention is generated in the actual learning situation and is an aspect of the mental representation of the learning task that students make while interacting with the content of a curricular task and its social and instructional context.

My model of the Adaptive Learning Process is schematically represented in Fig. 1. It consists of two main parts: the appraisal part (top part of the model) and the action part (bottom part of the model). As can be seen from this figure, the appraisals take up a central position in the model. Students generate meaning (appraise the situation) on the basis of three sources of information: (1) the task, embedded in the instructional and social context, (2) their domain-specific strategy use and (3) their domain-specific motivational beliefs. The model assumes that there is an empirical distinction between domain-specific motivational beliefs and situation-specific motivation (learning intention) and that the appraisals mediate the effect of domain-specific beliefs on learning intention and affect experienced in the situation.

As regards the action part of the model, it was assumed that students have two priorities. The first is to increase their resources, including their strategy use in a domain. The second priority is to keep their sense of well-being within reasonable bounds. These priorities are represented in the Model of Adaptive Learning by two dynamic, parallel pathways, namely the mastery path, drawn in blue (broken lines) thus symbolizing cold cognition, and the well-being path, drawn in red (dotted lines) to symbolize hot cognition. It was hypothesized that the cold processing path originates in an appraisal process that has no consequences for well-being and leads to a learning intention. The hot processing path originates in situation-specific affect and initiates concern-related monitoring.

Since 1992, my co-workers and I have developed and validated the On-line Motivation Questionnaire (OMQ) to register students' appraisals and emotion states, as well as their learning intention, reported effort, result assessment and attribution processes (for a description, see Boekaerts, 2002a). The OMQ is a generic instrument that can be adapted to register students' thoughts and feelings about tasks and courses in various domains of study. This instrument was used in several longitudinal studies in primary education, junior high school, high school, vocational school and higher education. We investigated the effect of students' appraisals on their learning intention and affective states in several domains, including mathematics, history, foreign language learning, native language learning, vocational subjects and, most recently, educational psychology. Evidence to date indicates that students' appraisals explain more variance in learning intention and reported effort than either domain-specific or general measures of student motivation (cf. Boekaerts, 1999b). The appraisals also mediate the effect of domain-specific motivational beliefs on learning intention (Boekaerts, 1999b; Seegers & Boekaerts, 1993). Our results yield evidence that students are prepared to invest effort in a curricular task, provided that the meaning-generating process is successful. This implies either that they value the task (task attraction or task relevance) or that they enjoy being self-efficacious (subjective competence combined with task attraction).

Contrary to our prediction, the appraisals only partially mediate the effect of domain-specific motivational beliefs on reported emotion states (Boekaerts, 1999b). We defined emotion state as a combination of positive and negative emotions in response to the learning task that students report, either when they are first confronted with the task (emotion state 1) or after they have finished the task (emotion state 2). Since we aggregated positive and negative emotions, our measure of emotion states ranged from very negative (feeling tense, worried, irritated, ill at ease) to very positive (feeling happy, at ease, content). Interestingly, a direct effect of fear of failure and avoidance ego-orientation had to be tolerated on emotion state 1 in our studies with junior high school students and high school students but not with primary school students. This finding indicates that a history of failure within a particular domain or a mindset characterized by avoidance ego-orientation (e.g. wanting to hide mistakes) in a domain predisposes students to experience negative emotions in situations that are linked to that domain. However, we observed that this predisposition does not automatically lead to low learning intention. Indeed, we found that learning intention and affect, measured before the students started on the task, were not statistically associated, after controlling for their appraisals. In other words, an emotion state generated before starting on a learning task does not have a direct impact on the students' intended actions, and this means that students who report negative emotions (e.g. feeling irritated, feeling tense) may nevertheless agree to initiate a learning task. Conversely, students may express positive emotions at task onset (e.g. feeling happy, excited) but choose not to invest effort into the task.

These results suggest that there are indeed two separate, parallel processing pathways: the cold and hot cognition pathways. Activity in the cold cognition pathway consists of multiple meaning-generating processes that are the building blocks of learning comprehension and problem solving. Domain-specific information stored in long-term memory is activated by relevant cues in the task or the instruction that accompanies the task, and this information forms the basis of the mental representation that students make of the learning opportunity. It steers and directs the meaning-generating process and determines the degree of effort that the students are willing to invest for the benefit of increasing their resources (improve their strategy use in a domain). In contrast, activity in the hot cognition pathway is triggered by emotions and moods during the actual learning episode. Students engage in non-stop evaluative processes that explore the task and its context carefully for cues that are linked up with previously experienced affective states. They pick up cues in the instructional and social environment that have *consequences for well-being* (e.g. fellow students are not putting in effort, the teacher is not willing to provide support). This evaluative information is treated as a warning signal and influences decision making (e.g. decision to continue or discontinue the task = short-term effect) but also impacts on the value attached to the type of task (long-term effects).

Studying the dynamic and interactive role of emotions and meaning-generating processes

Emotions are sources of information

Confirmation of the hypothesis that cold and hot information pathways are empirically distinct prompted us to set up two separate research lines. Our volition and motivation studies focused on the students' willingness to invest effort (motivation control) and their persistence in goal pursuit (volition control). There is insufficient space here to describe the results of these studies. The interested reader is referred to Boekaerts (1997, 2002a) and to Vermeer, Boekaerts, and Seegers (2000). Our coping studies focused on how students deal with stressful situations and negative affect (emotion control) experienced in academic and social situations (Boekaerts, 1993, 1996, 1999a, 2002b; Boekaerts & Seegers, 1994; Röder, Kroonenberg, & Boekaerts, 2003). These studies led to major insights into students' engagement and disengagement patterns. We differentiated between adaptive and maladaptive initiation, continuation and discontinuation strategies. 'Mindful effort' or problem-solving behaviour and 'mindful disengagement' were identified as adaptive processing strategies and contrasted with maladaptive processing strategies, such as 'mindless or undirected effort' and 'avoidance behaviour' (see Boekaerts, 1999a, 2002b).

At the end of the last millennium, however, we realized that by studying the cognitive, motivational, volitional and emotional regulatory processing systems separately, we had failed to take sufficient account of the dynamic and interactive role that affective states play in classroom learning. Indeed, it is easy to imagine that students who are engaged in meaningful learning but who are plagued by emotional turmoil during task performance interpret increases in the level of arousal as a signal that 'the situation is more problematic than they had originally thought'. Frijda (1988) referred to such situations as 'annoyers' because students think that these situations may cause damage, loss or harm. Likewise, students who expect a difficult task with many obstacles, but experience feelings of joy, relief or pride while doing the task, tend to reset their internal standard, often reflected in coasting behaviour (see Carver &

Scheier, 2000). What I am saying is that emotions experienced during goal pursuit are sources of information that students interpret and use. It is strange that researchers involved in research on learning and instruction have largely neglected this source of information. For their part, researchers on motivation have paid little attention to the reciprocal relationship between experienced affective states and learning intention, and their joint effect on learning acquisition and problem solving. This implies that we know very little about the impact of affective states on learning and motivation processes and about the way in which different instructional settings shape children's emotional experiences.

Emotions are energizers and means of communication

Frijda (1988) described emotions as action-readiness tendencies that occupy centre stage in human functioning and social life. Emotions provide energy and impact on attention, recall, event interpretation, decision making and problem solving. Once activated, emotions tend to override goals and actions, even considerations of appropriateness or long-term consequences. They tend to persist in some form or other (e.g. direct urge, mood, feeling), taking on a life of their own and affecting all ongoing activities. Frijda and Mesquita (1995) and Moffat and Frijda (2000) described emotions as complex, structured phenomena that are part of the very process of interacting with the environment. Frijda and his colleagues explained that each emotion process takes the form of a sequence of steps that is initiated with a primary appraisal of the event or situation as relevant or irrelevant to one or more concerns. Either way, a warning signal interrupts all cognitive processing to make sure that the event that caused the interruption is evaluated and that one's coping potential is considered in relation to the potential threat. If this potential is low, more warning signals are emitted, because more attention is needed to deal with the event.

Oatley and Johnson-Laird (1996) viewed emotions basically as a means of internal and external communication. These researchers described the emotional experience as consisting of two types of evaluation processes. These processes produce signals that set the brain into distinct modes that are linked to goals and priorities and which steer behaviour toward mode-appropriate classes of actions. The first evaluation process consists of perceptual processes that occur unconsciously and trigger a distinct, non-propositional signal that propagates through the multiple processing systems of cognitive architecture to produce the basic emotion. Its function is to make the event or situation that caused it salient in the mind of the student. A second, much slower, evaluation process produces the phenomenological experience of the emotion, provides propositional information of the type of emotion (a distinctive positive or negative experience, such as feeling anger, happiness or sadness) and the reason that caused it. Oatley and Johnson-Laird argued that the two emotion signals are usually tied together in the person's mind. Individuals are usually aware that they are having an emotional experience, and they can describe the affective characteristics of the experience. However, the two distinct signals may also be dissociated. Some individuals may sometimes report being unaware of the non-propositional emotion signal that triggered the phenomenological experience. Likewise, some individuals may experience emotional turbulence in their system, while feeling unable to label it and without realizing what caused it.

Klinger's theory of emotion also assumes two stages in the emotional response. Klinger (1996) maintained that some emotional responses are innately linked to specific stimuli and are readily conditioned, while other emotional responses are triggered by a 'current concern' (i.e. an internal state associated with goal pursuit). Klinger summarized behavioural and electrophysiological evidence that suggests that early emotional responses begin within 300 ms after exposure to the relevant stimulus. This is early enough to be considered 'non-conscious' processing. Klinger further documented that this non-conscious processing occurs in parallel with early, global perceptual and cognitive analysis and that it is highly likely that these two processing systems exert reciprocal influences at several levels of processing. He proposed that the intensity of the early emotional reaction to a stimulus affects the probability that the stimulus will continue to be processed cognitively:

> ...the results of continued cognitive processing in turn clearly modulate the intensity and character of the merging emotional response. Should the emotional response pass some as yet unknown kind of threshold, it presumably begins to recruit other, slower subsystems, such as autonomic and endocrine responses; non-volitional motor responses, such as facial and postural expressions; conscious affect; conscious cognitive processing; and ultimately action. By that time it has emerged as a full-scale emotional response. (pp. 184–185)

Following the reasoning of Frijda and colleagues, of Klinger, and of Oatley and Johnson-Laird, we view a full-scale emotional response as consisting of two main parts (see Fig. 2). The first part is the 'early non-conscious reaction to a stimulus or event'. Sensors that are attached to salient personal goals (component 3) and to a database of innate and conditioned emotional triggers (component 2) monitor the input (component 1) for danger signals. A signal is sent to the brain (component 4) when a perceptual pattern fits a stored danger signal. This warning signal leads to physiological changes (component 5) and brings students to a state of alertness and readiness to actively explore the environment for cues that inform them whether the situation is problematic or benign. The second part of the emotional response refers to the conscious part of the emotional experience. Physiological changes that the student is aware of, as well as other relevant cues in the external and internal environment, are interpreted and labelled (component 6), thus determining the current affective state (component 7) (which is basically positive or negative) and mode-appropriate action (component 8).

Emotions affect students' functioning in the classroom

It should be obvious by now that I am interested in the structure of the emotional response. The questions that lie behind this interest are both abstract and concrete. In the previous sections I have addressed rather abstract questions, such as: 'Which constructs are most useful in thinking about and describing affective states'. I will now turn to a more practical aspect, namely: How do multiple positive and negative emotions influence students' functioning in the classroom?

Students' academic emotions have not been studied extensively, with the exception of test anxiety. Other positive and negative emotions have been largely ignored. In recent years, a group of researchers mostly based in Germany set out to study the effect of academic emotions on motivation, learning and achievement. Pekrun, Goetz, Titz, and Perry (2002) set up a research programme to demonstrate that academic emotions serve the function of preparing and sustaining reactions to important events and states. These researchers hypothesized that emotions provide motivational and physiological

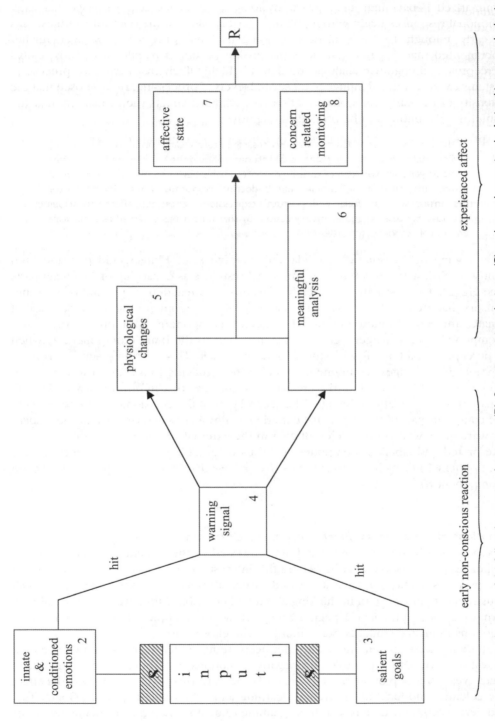

Figure 2. Schematic depiction of the full-scale emotional response (**R**). Sensors monitor the input (**S**) to detect danger signals. A signal is sent to the brain when a hit is made. This warning signal produces physiological change and initiates meaningful analysis leading to a specific affective state and concern-related monitoring.

energy by triggering action-related wishes, goals and intentions, thus directing students' attention and modulating their thinking. Pekrun *et al.* (2002) went beyond the traditional valence dimension of emotion (positive and negative mood), bringing another traditional dimension of emotion to bear on the classification of academic emotions. They argued that emotions may be activating or deactivating cognitive and physiological processes. Using these two dimensions allowed them to differentiate between four groups of academic emotions, namely positive activating emotions (e.g. enjoyment of learning, hope for success, pride), positive de-activating emotions (e.g. relaxation after success, relief), activating negative emotions (e.g. irritation, shame, anxiety), and de-activating negative emotions (e.g. hopelessness, boredom). Pekrun *et al.* predicted and found that these four categories of emotions differentially affected motivation, the use of learning strategies and achievement. Cross-sectional, longitudinal and diary studies showed that students experience a great variety of self-referenced, task-related and social emotions in academic settings. More specifically, all positive academic emotions (except relief) predicted high achievement, and all negative emotions were linked to low achievement. In line with theoretical expectations, much higher negative correlations were found between the de-activating emotions (hopelessness and boredom) and measures of motivation and achievement, compared with the activating negative emotions of anxiety, anger and shame.

Recently, several researchers have argued (for review, see Fredrickson, 2001) that some individuals experience both positive and negative emotions in relation to an event or situation, whereas others only report negative emotions. Fredrickson summarized the literature and concluded that positive emotions experienced in close connection to negative emotions may undo the detrimental effect that the latter have on performance. She argued that all students experience some increase in their level of arousal when they have to perform in public. However, the performance of those students who interpret and label any arousal felt as negative (e.g. ill at ease, nervousness, anxiety, worry) will be more impeded than the performance of students who label the increased level of arousal in terms of both negative and positive emotions (e.g. pleasure in being selected to do the job, hopefulness, excitement, anticipated pride).

Clearly, we can gain more insight into students' affective states and the way these states impact on their academic functioning by studying the reciprocal influence that positive and negative emotions have on the mental representation that students make of a learning opportunity. The main question is then: 'How do positive and negative emotions interact to determine students' psychological well-being in the classroom?'

Interpreting multiple feeling-related cues

Schiefele (1996) argued that students store their positive and negative experiences as positive or negative feeling-related valences. In line with Schiefele's theorizing, we conceptualized feeling-related valences as affective states experienced in relation to a class of learning situations in a particular domain (e.g. doing individual work in the mathematics class). These experiences become part of the students' cognitive-emotional representation system. When these students are confronted with similar learning opportunities, they activate the stored affective state, and this information becomes part of the mental representation that they form about the current learning activity. In other words, activated affective states sensitize students to cues in the learning environment. These states serve to monitor and protect the students' goals and ensure fast action. For example, students who have observed on many occasions that their actions do not lead to satisfactory outcomes in the mathematics domain have encoded situations that invite them to demonstrate their mathematical problem-solving skills as dominantly negative. This implies that negative expectations and feeling states (feeling tense, ill at ease, anxious and unpleasant) have been tagged to mathematical problem-solving and to all individual work in the mathematics classroom, resulting in habitualized responses, such as avoidance behaviour or mindless action.

In the last decade, many researchers have shown that allowing students to share their ideas and solution steps with their fellow learners and inviting them to combine efforts to find a mathematical solution to a problem result in positive affective states (e.g. feeling at ease, happy, satisfied that they are a valued member of the group and that others are prepared to help them). These positive feelings are also tagged to mathematical problem situations and may gradually change students' beliefs about mathematics learning. I am not saying that students who have experienced a positive mode while solving mathematics problems in small groups are now free from maths anxiety. They are not. Chances are that they still experience anxiety, but this negative emotion now seems to be less debilitating. My hypothesis is that during maths lessons set up according to the principles of social constructivism, warning signals are still sent to the brain and create physiological changes. However, the way that students interpret these changes has altered, because the maths-learning environment now consists of multiple contextual cues that students process simultaneously. Some of these cues are linked to salient academic goals, whereas other cues are linked to salient socio-emotional goals. It is highly likely that these different cues elicit distinct, even opposite, emotions that together create a feeling state that is less negative.

Measuring positive and negative affective states

In our attempt to examine the effect of emotions on learning intention and strategy use, we have used the On-line Motivation Questionnaire (OMQ) as a research tool. Emotions are measured at two measurement points during the learning episode; namely, when the students are introduced to the task (emotion state 1) and again after they have completed the task (emotion state 2). The subscale of the OMQ that measures emotions consists of several 4-point Likert scales that register the intensity of academic emotions felt (e.g. feeling at ease, nervous, happy, worried, irritated, fed up, concerned). The scale is constructed in such a way that the intensity of both positive and negative emotions is measured, and then aggregated. Hence, the magnitude of students' positive and negative emotions is translated into a single score that is located somewhere between the positive and negative pole of the dimension.

Results with these data sets revealed that students who report intense positive (negative) emotions in relation to a maths assignment tend to report a similar emotion state a few weeks later in relation to a similar task. Test–retest correlations were in the range .53–.86. The association between students' appraisals of the task and the intensity of their reported emotions was modest to moderate. The highest correlations were found between intensity of emotions (emotion state 1) and task attraction (.52–.63). This implies that (dis)liking a maths task shares between 25% and 36% of the variance with emotional state. It is noteworthy that students' assessment of their performance was also associated with their emotion state. Correlations ranged from .45 to .58. This result suggests that the higher the magnitude of positive emotions experienced when a homework task is finished, the more favourably students judge their performance on the task, and vice versa; the higher the magnitude of negative emotions, the more unfavourably they assess their performance.

Data from a variety of sources fit this picture. Mood researchers have found that positive mood is associated with increased attention to the positive features of a situation or event, and the reverse is true for negative mood. Also, being in a good mood increases the likelihood that good events will happen, and being in a bad mood makes bad events more likely (Forgas & Bower, 1987). Forgas and Bower (1987) found that individuals who had been put in a happy or sad mood spent more time reading mood-consistent information about specific targets, and their recall of mood-inconsistent information was inferior to mood-consistent information. An interesting experiment conducted by Martin, Ward, Achee, and Wyer (1993) neatly demonstrated that induced mood states push students' behaviour in a specific direction. These researchers placed students in either a positive or negative mood state by having them watch positive and negative video clips. Then they gave them an ambiguous task. The students had to answer specific questions while doing the task. Martin *et al*. (1993) varied the instructional conditions and examined how long students persisted with the task under the various conditions. One group of students was asked to answer the question: 'Have I processed enough to make a decision? If the answer is yes, then stop. If the answer is no, then continue'. A second group had to answer the question: 'Am I still enjoying the task? If the answer is yes, then continue. If the answer is no, then stop'. These researchers found that mood interacted with type of instruction. Students who had been answering the question, 'Have I processed enough to make a decision?' stopped sooner if a good mood had been induced. Students who had been put in a bad mood stopped sooner than those in a good mood, when they had been asked to answer the question: 'Am I still enjoying the task?' The dependent variable was the amount of time the students spent on the tasks and the number of behaviours they considered before making a decision. These results demonstrate that there is a close association between a good mood and saying 'Yes' and between a bad mood and saying 'No'. This seems to suggest that a positive affective state is linked to compliance with, or agreement with, the instructions (harmony model) and that negative affective state is closely associated with disagreement, adversity and conflict (disharmony model).

The literature review on mood, in particular the favourable effect of positive affect on information processing, as well as the information gathered from our students, convinced us that it is not sufficient to aggregate positive and negative emotions and pretend that they are opposites on a bipolar scale. As Moffat and Frijda (2000) maintained, concerns are matched continuously and in parallel. Close matches and concerns that are highly relevant to the person will produce a stronger warning signal, meaning that the emotion will be felt more intensely. These researchers pointed out that emotions should be given a size (intensity) and a sign (positive or negative valence). Following their suggestion, we wanted to test the hypothesis that intensity of feeling state, and positive and negative emotions have separate effects on cognitive processing. Boekaerts reanalysed one of the data sets collected with the OMQ in relation to maths homework. Using PRINCALS analyses to examine the structure of the reported emotions after the students had finished their maths homework, she identified two separate components, namely an intensity component and a bipolar valence component. Students could now be given three separate scores; namely an intensity score (magnitude of felt arousal), an indication of positive affect and one of negative affect. Intensity of emotions was strongly correlated with negative affective state (.54) but only modestly with positive affective state (.12). The association between positive and negative affect was $-.44$. Boekaerts predicted and found that students' answer to the question, 'Did you do well on this homework task?' was closely linked to their perception of the characteristics of their affective state. Students who judged that they had the necessary resources to meet task demands (appraisal) tended to assess their maths homework performance as successful. However, characteristics of their affective state (emotional evaluations of the consequences for well-being) mediated this effect. Confidence in one's own capacity to do the task that coincided with positive affect during task performance (e.g. feeling at ease, happy, content) increased the likelihood that performance was assessed as being 'successful'. Confidence that coincided with negative affect (feeling irritated, nervous, worried, or fed up) did not directly decrease the likelihood that performance was assessed as successful, but confidence associated with high intensity of emotions (felt arousal) did.

Emotions make students aware of goal pursuit

As mentioned previously, Klinger (1996) argued that individuals who become committed to pursuing a goal represent that event in an internal state that he coined 'current concern'. One of the functions of a current concern is to elicit emotional reactivity to cues that are associated with the goal pursuit. Klinger summarized substantial evidence to support the notion that what individuals are aware of, observe, remember and think about is ultimately governed by their current concerns. The relationship between people's current concerns (or goal commitments) and cognitive processing seems to be mediated by the emotional responses evoked by concern-related cues. Oatley and Johnson-Laird (1996) also stated that emotions usually imply the existence of a situation or event that is relevant to a salient conscious or unconscious goal. The emotion signal within the brain interrupts the ongoing activity and urges the individual to engage in mode-appropriate classes of action.

Observations and interviews in vocational school and higher education informed us that emotions are most likely to arise when students meet obstacles or problems that they had not anticipated on their way to the goal. Students also get upset when they become aware of regress (progress) instead of the expected progress (regress) with respect to a salient goal (Carver & Scheier, 2000). Interestingly, we noted that some students reacted to the same feedback, obstacles or conflict with intense emotions, whereas others reported only mild emotions, and still others experienced no conscious emotions. In line with Frijda's theorizing, students told us that mild emotions are often not noticed until somebody draws attention to the environmental cue that caused it (e.g. 'If I were you I would refuse to help him now, he has never offered you any support in the past'). By contrast, intense emotions tend to stop all ongoing behaviour, taking on a life of their own.

In order to gain some insight into students' conceptualization of their emotions in relation to their goals, we set up a pilot study. We asked four students to register their emotions on-line on a pre-coded sheet. Their maths teacher then told these students that they had to work together on a maths assignment. We observed them from a distance without their being aware that we were closely monitoring their behaviour during that lesson. In a stimulated recall session that followed immediately after they had presented their solution in public, we asked the four students to reflect on the learning episode, individually. Using the emotions that they had recorded as a cue, they described their thoughts and feelings and linked these cognitions to the task and its context. We also prompted them to elaborate on their explanation when appropriate.

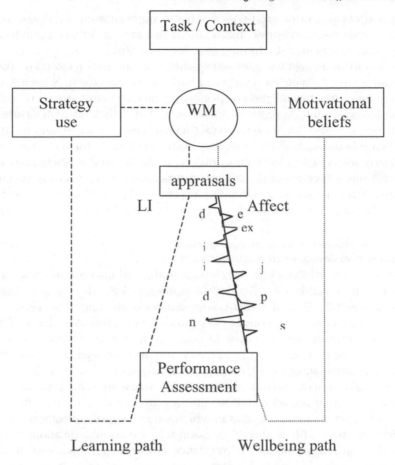

Figure 3. Affective path described by a student after a group learning experience. He reported several successive emotions: disappointed (*d*), at ease (*e*), excited (*ex*), irritated (*i*), joy (*j*), disappointed (*d*), proud (*p*), nervous (*n*) and satisfied (*s*). WM = working memory; LI = learning intention.

In Fig. 3, the affective path that one of the students described is visually represented. This student explained that he felt disappointed (*d*) that he had to work together on a maths assignment with Els, because he considered her a nerd. Later, he felt at ease (*e*) because Bart was also in his group. He felt excited (*ex*) when the group accepted his suggestion to organize the task differently. A few minutes later, he was irritated (*i*) because Els made several irrelevant comments that threatened to slow down the problem-solving process. He experienced joy (*j*) when he noted that his group was progressing much faster than the other groups and disappointment (*d*) when there was no room on the flip-over sheet to write down one of his suggestions. The student reported that he had felt increased arousal when he heard that he had to present the group solution in public, feeling at the same time proud (*p*) and nervous (*n*). He finished the learning episode feeling satisfied (*s*) about a job the teacher declared 'well done'.

As can be viewed from this example, students have certain expectations about a group learning situation, about their own actions in that situation, the reaction of group members to their actions, the rate of progress and the quality of the product they are presenting. Expectations that are fulfilled seem to be associated with positive feeling states, such as enjoyment and pride. Expectations that are not fulfilled seem to raise the level of arousal and are identified as negative feeling states.

The results of this and similar interviews made us aware of the close link that exists between experienced emotions and a student's personal goals. Students seem to experience emotional turmoil when personal goals are obstructed or frustrated. Interestingly, several students reported spontaneously that they felt ill at ease with their French teacher because he always forces them to use a deep learning processing strategy, even when they told him that they were pressed for time, or that they were not particularly interested in the subject matter. Being allowed to share resources and interests with one's friends usually triggers positive emotions. There is accumulating evidence that particular learning conditions are encoded as 'facilitating' personal goals, while other learning conditions are largely encoded as 'frustrating' personal goals.

Personal goals give meaning to a student's life

Although researchers involved in research on learning and instruction are aware of the fact that socio-emotional goals and academic goals may be in harmony or in conflict, educational researchers have not adequately addressed this important issue. Granted, they have studied students' goal orientations, and it has been shown that students may be ego-oriented in relation to one content domain and mastery-oriented in relation to another domain (see Dweck, 2003), but little is known about what students actually do when their goal orientation is in conflict with the context within which they learn. Some studies have described students' frustration when they have to cross borders between the multiple contexts within which they are growing up (e.g. Phelan, Yu, & Davidson, 1994), yet systematic studies in which students' goal frustration is the object of scientific scrutiny are still lacking. The reason why we know little about the effect of goal frustration on motivation and performance is that educational researchers have focused mainly on the 'what' and 'how' of academic goal pursuit and have largely ignored the 'what', 'how' and 'why' of socio-emotional goals in relation to academic goals. I have repeatedly drawn researchers' attention to the large gaps in our knowledge on the coordination of salient academic and social goals (e.g. seeking approval from friends and getting good grades). Ford (1992) pointed out that the content of students' *personal* goals is highly informative when it comes to explaining and predicting their actions in the classroom. These personal goals give meaning to a student's life and initiate non-stop evaluation processes that monitor the input to detect cues that signal progress toward desirable end-states and distance from undesirable end-states. Clearly, there are at present different goal models—some dealing with academic goals, others dealing with socio-emotional goals. There are also some models that deal with both socio-emotional goals and academic goals in the same model (e.g. Dowson & McInerney, 2001; Urdan & Maehr, 1995), but even in the latter models, socio-emotional goals tend to be conceptualized 'in the service' of academic goals.

In line with Heckhausen and Farruggia's (2003) life span theory of control, I have argued (Boekaerts, 2003a) that adolescents' personal goals may change in focus when a new developmental time window becomes operative. At the same time, their primary control processes (trying to change the environment directly) as well as their secondary control processes (internal processes to optimize motivational resources for primary control) may undergo radical changes. Due to space limitations, it is not possible to give a full account of the way the goal system is structured. The interested reader is referred to Carver and Scheier (2000) and Boekaerts (2002c, 2003a, 2003b). Just to illustrate that salient goals change with development, consider the following example.

A higher-order goal that most students have at the apex of their goal hierarchy is, 'I want to be successful'. The translation of this rather abstract goal into distinct personal goals, or action programmes pursued in daily life, changes a great deal as students move up the educational system. In primary education, many students translate this higher-order goal into distinct personal goals, such as 'I want to get good grades' and 'I want my teacher to like me', and link them to scripts that reflect effort and compliance to what parents and teachers expect of them. This implies that these students use primary control processes to maximize motivational investment in these important goals. In adolescence, students still value good grades, but some of them want to hide effort as a means of getting them. Achieving academic success now competes with many non-academic goals, such as 'I want to be a successful sportsman', 'I want to be a valued romantic partner', or 'I want to be a member of the consumer society'.

It is important to realize that students who have had a history of failure in a specific school subject (e.g. mathematics) encoded many learning situations related to that domain as harmful to their psychological well-being. As previously explained, this stored information, as well as the affective states it generates, impacts on the way they perceive learning opportunities in that domain. Mathematics is an important part of the curriculum in all cultures, and students cannot avoid it. In order to realize their 'I want to be successful' higher-order goal, they have to find a way to reduce the threat signals. What I am arguing is that students have developed different forms of compensatory secondary control (term borrowed from J. Heckhausen), aimed at buffering the negative emotional and motivational consequences of failure and loss. Many changes in personal goals that are noted as students grow up reflect the fact that they give up those goals that they find too difficult to achieve, too boring, too cumbersome or requiring the investment of too many resources. New personal goals that hold a higher potential of controllability for them are allied to their 'I want to be successful' higher-order goal. In line with my model of the model of the Adaptive Learning Process, the hypothesis is that, as students grow up, they learn to keep their two basic priorities in balance. They develop adaptive and maladaptive patterns of goal engagement and disengagement that fit their dominant appraisals (cold cognition pathway) and affective states (hot cognition pathway). I would like to speculate that the dominant affective states that students experience in relation to distinct learning opportunities in different domains directly influence the switches that occur in their salient personal goals across the life span. More research is needed to study the important relations between students' personal goals and affective states linked to these goals. In Leiden, we are currently engaged in a research programme that addresses these crucial relationships.

References

Boekaerts, M. (1992). The adaptable learning process: Initiating and maintaining behavioural change. *Journal of Applied Psychology: An International Review*, *41*, 377–397.

Boekaerts, M. (1993). Being concerned with well-being and with learning. *Educational Psychologist*, *28*(2), 149–167.

Boekaerts, M. (1995). The interface between intelligence and personality as determinants of classroom learning. In D. H. Saklofske & M. Zeidner (Eds.), *Handbook of personality and intelligence* (pp. 161–183). New York: Plenum.

Boekaerts, M. (1996). Personality and the psychology of learning. *European Journal of Personality, 10*(5), 377-404.

Boekaerts, M. (1997). Capacity, inclination, and sensitivity for mathematics. *Anxiety, Stress, and Coping, 10*, 5-33.

Boekaerts, M. (1999a). Coping in context: Goal frustration and goal ambivalence in relation to academic and interpersonal goals. In E. Frydenberg (Ed.), *Learning to cope: Developing as a person in complex societies* (pp. 175-197). Oxford: Oxford University Press.

Boekaerts, M. (1999b). Motivated learning: The study of student * situation transactional units. *European Journal of Psychology of Education, 14*(4), 41-55.

Boekaerts, M. (2002a). The online motivation questionnaire: A self-report instrument to assess students' context sensitivity. In P. R. Pintrich & M. L. Maehr (Eds.), *Advances in motivation and achievement. Volume 12: New directions in measures and methods* (pp. 77-120). New York: JAI.

Boekaerts, M. (2002b). Meeting challenges in a classroom context. In E. Frydenberg (Ed.), *Beyond coping: Meeting goals, visions and challenges* (pp. 129-147). Oxford: Oxford University Press.

Boekaerts, M. (2003a). Adolescence in Dutch culture: A self-regulation perspective. In F. Pajares & T. Urdan (Eds.), *Adolescence and Education. Volume III: International perspectives on adolescence and education*. Greenwich, CT: Information Age Publishing.

Boekaerts, M. (2003b). How do students from different cultures motivate themselves for academic learning? In F. Salili & R. Hoosain (Eds.), *Research on multicultural education and international perspectives. Volume 3: Teaching, learning and motivation in a multicultural setting* (pp. 13-31). Greenwich CT: Information Age Publishing.

Boekaerts, M., & Niemivirta, M. (2000). Self-regulated learning: Finding a balance between learning goals and ego-protective goals. In M. Boekaerts, P. R. Pintrich, & M. Zeidner (Eds.), *Handbook of self-regulation* (pp. 417-450). San Diego, CA: Academic Press.

Boekaerts, M., Otten, R., & Voeten, M. J. M. (2003). Exam performance: Are student's causal ascriptions school-subject specific? *Anxiety, Stress and Coping, 16.*

Boekaerts, M. & Seegers, G. (1994). Stress, coping, en prestatie-(motivatie) (Stress, coping, and achievement motivation). *Tijdschrift voor Onderwijsresearch, 19*(4), 356-365.

Carver, C. S., & Scheier, M. (2000). On the structure of behavioral self-regulation. In M. Boekaerts, P. R. Pintrich, & M. Zeidner (Eds.), *Handbook of self-regulation* (pp. 41-84). San Diego, CA: Academic Press.

Dowson, M., & McInerney, M. (2001). Psychological parameters of students' social and work avoidance goals: A qualitative investigation. *Journal of Educational Psychology, 93*(1), 35-42.

Dweck, C. S. (2003). Ability conceptions, motivation and development. *British Journal of Educational Psychology Monograph Series II, Part 2* (Development and Motivation), 13-27.

Ford, M. E. (1992). *Motivating humans: Goals, emotions, and personal agency beliefs*. London: Sage.

Forgas, J. P., & Bower, G. H. (1987). Mood effects on person perception judgements. *Journal of Personality and Social Psychology, 53*, 53-60.

Fredrickson, B. L. (2001) The role of positive emotions in positive psychology. *American Psychologist, 56*(3), 218-226.

Frijda, N. H. (1988). The laws of emotion. *American Psychologist, 43*, 349-358.

Frijda, N. H., & Mesquita, B. (1995). The social roles and functions of emotions. In S. Kitayama & H. R. Markus (Eds.), *Emotion and culture* (p. 51-88). Washington, DC: American Psychological Association.

Heckhausen, J., & Farruggia, S. P. (2003). Developmental regulation across the life span: A control-theory approach and implications for secondary education. *British Journal of Educational Psychology Monograph, Series II, Part 2* (Development and Motivation), 85-102.

Klinger, E. (1996). Emotional influences on cognitive processing, with implications for theories of both. In P. M. Gollwitzer & J. A. Bargh (Eds.), *The psychology of action*. New York: Guilford.

Kuhl, J. (1984). Volitional aspects of achievement motivation and learned helplessness: Toward a comprehensive theory of action control. In B. A. Maher & W. B. Maher (Eds.), *Progress in experimental personality research* (pp. 99–171). New York: Academic Press.

Lazarus, R. S., & Folkman, S. (1984). *Stress, appraisal and coping*. New York: Springer.

Leventhal, H. (1980). Towards a comprehensive theory of emotion. In L. Berkowitz (Ed.), *Advances in experimental social psychology* (Vol. 3, pp. 140–208). New York: Academic Press.

Martin, L. L., Ward, D. W., Achee, J. W., & Wyer, R. S. (1993). Mood as input: People have to interpret the motivational implications of their mood. *Journal of Personality and Social Psychology, 64*, 317–326.

Moffat, D. C., & Frijda, N. H. (2000). Functional models of emotion. In G. Hatano, N. Okada, & H. Tanabé (Eds.), *Affective minds* (pp. 59–68). Amsterdam: Elsevier.

Oatley, K., & Johnson-Laird, P. N. (1996). The communicative theory of emotions: Empirical tests, mental models, and implications for social interaction. In L. L. Martin & A. Tesser (Eds.), *Striving and feeling*. Mahwah, NJ: Erlbaum.

Pekrun, R., Goetz, Th., Titz, W., & Perry, R. P. (2002). Academic emotions in students' self-regulated learning and achievement: A program of qualitative and quantitative research. *Educational Psychologist, 37*(2), 91–105.

Phelan, P., Yu, H. C., & Davidson, A. L. (1994). Navigating the psychological pressures of adolescence: The voices and experiences of high school youth. *American Educational Research Journal, 31*(2), 415–447.

Röder, I., Kroonenberg, P. M., & Boekaerts, M. (2003). Psychosocial functioning and stress processing of children with asthma in the school context: Differences, and similarities with children without asthma.

Schiefele, U. (1996). Topic interest, text representation, and quality of experience. *Contemporary Educational Psychology, 21*, 3–18.

Seegers, G., & Boekaerts, M. (1993). Task motivation and mathematics achievement in actual task situations. *Learning and Instruction, 3*, 133–150.

Urdan, T. C., & Maehr, M. L. (1995). *Beyond a two-goal theory of motivation and achievement: A case for social goals, 65*(3), 213–243.

Vermeer, H. J., Boekaerts, M., & Seegers, G. (2000). Motivational and gender differences: Sixth-grade students' mathematical problem-solving behavior. *Journal of Educational Psychology, 92*(2), 308–315.

Development and Motivation, 191–207
BJEP Monograph Series II, 2
© 2003 The British Psychological Society

www.bps.org.uk

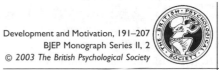

Conclusion

Colin Rogers* and Leslie Smith

Lancaster University, UK

The conference that led to the publication of this volume was highly enjoyable, intellectually rewarding, stimulating and, for the organizers at least, reassuringly successful. A common conclusion from participants was that the selection of papers had been exceptionally well planned, leading to a number of closely interrelated and mutually supporting sessions. The edited volume that this article concludes has not, and probably could not, fully capture that excitement and sense of progress and dynamism that was such a clear feature of the conference itself. However, we remain convinced that a sufficient proportion of that energy and flow of ideas has been captured in the printed text to enable the reader to share with us the belief that a conference designed to bring about the coming together of motivation and development was a clearly worthwhile enterprise.

In this Conclusion, we offer our interpretation of what seem to us to be interesting principles with a potential contribution to a joint account of development and motivation in education. These are:

- motivation and development;
- developmental pathways for motivated learning;
- research methods;
- education;
- self- and other inherent representations;
- ways ahead.

No claim is made by us that these are the sole principles worthy of attention, still less that our interpretations and evaluations are binding. Nevertheless, as we see things, the chapters in this volume have generated good ideas and evidence which could be contributory to resolving the main omission which was our starting point in the Introduction.

*Requests for reprints should be addressed to Colin Rogers, Department of Educational Research, Cartmel College, Lancaster University, Lancaster LAI 4YL, UK (e-mail: c.rogers@lancaster.ac.uk)

Motivation and development

The common position taken in each of the articles in this volume is that motivation and cognition are different aspects of the same mental process undergoing development. This position provides a solution to the problem about mental unity or plurality formulated by Aristotle (see Introduction). This is a significant advance just because the starting point for this volume was that motivation was to be found in one area of research dealing with one 'part' of the mind, and cognitive development in another area of research dealing with another 'part'. This position has the further merit of being open to theoretical and empirical extension. Moreover, its educational applicability is also noticed. Even so, the arguments for this common position turned out to be different. Three particular arguments are now taken up in this section.

In his discussion of the mind and development, Bickhard (pages 41–56) set out his claim that there is an inherent link between motivation and cognition. His starting point is that, with regard to human cognition, 'inertness that must be "energized" is not an option'. This is an arresting claim with far-reaching consequences. Central to his argument is the rejection of substance models of the mind and the adoption in their place of process models. At a stroke, this argument rules out representational models of the mind committed to any version of encoding or copying reality in virtue of inherent inertness. His preferred account is a process model based on action and interactive representation whereby organisms which are far-from-equilibrium systems must maintain their status. This is where motivation is required in action selection through norms operative in the organism's actions on the environment. This position has three key features. First, interactive representation has internal properties at work 'within' the interaction, and not merely external properties operating 'out there' on the agent. Second, this internality is normative and modal, rather than causal and contingent. Third, although this process model draws out the Newtonian conclusion that it is change rather than stability that needs to be assumed, the development of stabilized systems of action is also required. Stability will follow from effective adaptation to those aspects of the environment deemed to be of interest or which have come to provide a reference point for making judgments about the effectiveness of a current way of representing and operating the relevant aspects of the environment. Lack of adaptiveness is more likely to provoke instability. The focal point of the circular action is therefore crucial to any agent's development.

It is worth pointing out that Bickhard's account has the signal advantage of answering the key question posed in a masterful review of research on cognitive development by Flavell, Miller, and Miller (1993, pp. 47–48; our emphasis. See also Flavell, 1999): 'we have said nothing, however, about why the sensorimotor or any subsequent cognitive system should ever operate in the first place, nor about the circumstances under which it would be most likely to operate with maximum intensity and persistence. *What needs to be added* is an account of cognitive motivation—that is, of the factors and forces that activate or intensify human cognitive processing.'

A comparable commitment to motivation and cognition under development as twin aspects of the same process is due to Krapp (pages 57–84). His argument starts from the principle that interest is central to human development. This is a surprisingly neglected area in motivation research, surprising in that the development of personal interest is seen by many as key to the effective development of adaptive motivational strategies. His advance over this common-sense admission is to set out proposals for an adequate model of interest, such as person–object interaction (POI). Under POI, interests can be either situational or individual. The theoretical background to Krapp's work leads to his discussion of personal interests as specific and relatively stable person–object relationships. These stable relationships are both energizing in that the individual will seek out new information and ideas related to the interest, and also directing (in that they are more likely to seek out, and engage with, things which are of interest than things which are not). A related feature of POI is that the actual interests of a person are epistemic and motivating in representing the dynamic components to be realized in instructional settings. Stable interests contribute to an individual's personality, emotional state and evaluative system. Past interests have cognitive implications by virtue of their storage in the memory system and in underpinning knowledge structures and skills. This means that there is a link between an individual's representational and action system. A central feature of POI is its focus on the internal content of a person's interests which influence the structure of interests which develop during the life span.

Again, the common position was central to a third perspective, principally concerned with research in the moral domain but generalizing to other domains. In Turiel's account (pages 29–40), two different stances are taken in research about the relation between judgment and action. Under one stance, their linkage is extrinsic, leading to questions about individuals' moral consistency. Under the other, their linkage is intrinsic but subject to contextual constraints and opportunities, generative of alternative social judgments. Turiel interprets a body of evidence as showing that the demarcation of morality–sociality is made during early childhood and is being continually redrawn throughout later life in the light of new moral problems and new social contexts. Under this account, the key question is not whether people act on their moral judgments, but rather which judgments they make in different social contexts. Both motivational and developmental considerations will always be implicated, but in different ways depending on how the demarcation is applied by individuals in their struggle with priorities. There are twin paradigms here: one in which a social rather than moral judgment is made, the other where the judgment is moral rather than social. This pair does not map on to the conformity–confrontation distinction, but nor are these excluded. Adapting Turiel's superb example of Martin Luther King, conformity was manifest in his commitment to prevailing social mores, and confrontation in his challenge to racism and bigotry.

An interesting feature of these three arguments is their reference to the normative mind in action. This reference is important on two counts. First, it is in line with the widely accepted view that norms and values are paradigmatic of individuals in society. But in research on cognitive development generally, this has tended to be left out of account. Second, the interpretation of normativity for psychological use is problematic in several ways (see Smith, 2003). There are different types of normativity. One is the normativity of action selection by the bacterium or by the frog in its tongue-flicking (see Bickhard, pages 41–56) where this is internal to the activities for successful survival by the organism. Another is the normativity of individuals (see Krapp, pages 57–84) or societies (see Elliott & Hufton, pages 155–172), which includes valid normativity but also pseudo-normativity. Pareto's (1963, para. 972) remark is well taken that the human 'demand for logic is satisfied by pseudo-logic as well as by rigorous logic. At bottom what people want is to think—it matters little whether the thinking be sound or fallacious.' Demarcating this distinction is a delicate matter. Third, individual and social activities are well known to be multiple, but they also stand in a many–many relationship to multiple norms. Reverting back to children's demarcation of morality-sociality in Turiel's article, an example due to Williams (1996) is apposite about the boy torturing the cat, a clear case of cruelty, a case as morally outrageous as morally and objectively wrong, provided it was interpreted as cruelty. But was it? What if the boy saw his action as fun? Lurking here are the individual beliefs of any individual as well as the cultural context of any action. This example is not intended to settle questions about moral development; rather that one and the same action can be interpreted in different ways in the light of individual and social differences. Developmental differences enter here as well. Crucially, there are many norms available to individuals and societies, not all of which can be accepted at any one time, or even at all.

Developmental pathways for motivated learning

Emerging from a number of the articles included in this volume is the potentially important notion of developmentally different but equal pathways for motivated learning. As set out by Dweck (pages 13–27), in a consideration of developmental aspects of motivational processes, there are three main issues to be considered. First, that development is not unidirectional in nature. That is, one cannot assume that all development follows along the same royal road to the same destination. Second, analogous concepts arise at different times and, third, the formation of a concept and the start of any motivational impact of the possession of that concept are not necessarily the same. Given Dweck's concern with developmental aspects of motivation, and the early stages of those developmental processes, it is not surprising to see that she has, at times, adopted some of the more experimental methods popular with developmentalists. Dweck argues that motivationally relevant concepts have to become part of a relatively stable self-identity before they will begin to have a bearing on the motivational orientations of the individual person. That is, holding entity-like conceptions (for example concerning the meaning of what it is to be a 'good' person) will not necessarily have an impact upon aspects of motivation until these conceptions begin to determine the nature of the person's self-identity. Inherent in this proposition is the assumption that the beliefs acquired must come to matter to the individual in question.

In the striking examples cited by Fischer and Connell (pages 103–123) in their account of the development of differently valenced self-identities, we can again see the workings of developmentally different (very different) but still equal outcomes. The equality of course is clearly in this case quite unrelated to any notion of the equality of the personal impact of the outcome. It seems abundantly clear that the negatively valenced self-identities of those who had suffered early instances of abuse are far from equal in terms of the impact that they are likely to have upon the individual in question. Fischer and Connell again give us further insights into the nature of this aspect of the process when they say: 'Development is not the execution of a programme … it is a dynamically equilibrated, self-organizing process that is both driven internally toward higher levels of complexity and simultaneously supported and shaped powerfully by the contexts to which it has adapted over evolutionary time and to which it is constantly adapting in real time.' To be developmentally equal, then, a particular outcome has to have a broadly similar degree of complexity as the alternative (otherwise the press towards greater complexity would continue to a greater extent in one case than the other, and developmental equality could not be said to exist). In addition, it would also have to have a closely matched degree of adaptivity in relation to the relevant contexts.

A comparable commitment to the equality of alternative developmental pathways is invoked in Sokol and Chandler's (pages 125-136) argument under which humans are planning agents, and so are constituted by capacities to form and execute plans. This means that intentions—not desires—are fundamental. This view has implications for the revision of belief–desire psychology. The development and use of an interpretive theory of mind is necessary for and effective in securing the intention–desires distinction by children. In turn, this means that human mentality is active and interpretive, not a copying device as required by standard versions of the representational theory of mind (see also Bickhard's article). According to Sokol and Chandler, the irony is that 'theory-theory' research on children's reasoning about other people's beliefs and desires in developmental psychology over the last two decades has been committed exactly to representational copying. As such, that research is argued to be simplistic. Instead, their proposal is for a focus on children's capacities to use information in different interpretive ways, notably with diverse attributions of others' beliefs in ambiguous situations.

Equality here refers to the developmental status of the end result. Developmentally equal outcomes will be those that are inherently driven by the developmental processes involved and, once established, will be equally stable and therefore equally likely to remain in operation. Equality in this context does not mean uniformity of outcomes, which are several and open, developmentally speaking. The examples set out both by Fischer and Connell and by Dweck appear to meet the first of these criteria in a relatively straightforward manner. In Dweck's case, the entity conception of ability can be seen to be as complex as the incremental one, while the negative self-images described by Fischer and Connell are certainly no less complex than the positive self-images with which they are contrasted.

However, what of equivalence in terms of adapting to the relevant aspects of the context? Questions of adaptation cannot be addressed without reference to the thing to which the process is said to be, or not to be, adapted. Crucially then, there arises the issue of what one assumes to be the reference point to which things are to be adapted.

It is clear that the interests of the individuals (see Krapp's article) in question are likely to emerge swiftly in any appreciation of these adaptive processes. Fischer and Connell draw a distinction between two different motivational processes: 'epistemic motivation promotes development of skills and knowledge of the world. Self-organization promotes construction and regulation of stable patterns of activities based on long-term goals and representations, especially those involving self and others.' As they go on to note a little later, the circular actions held to be typical of developmental processes require 'a mechanism for appraising whether something is interesting based on the person's long-term goals and knowledge'. Differences in motivational characteristics have often been described as varying in terms of their adaptiveness. The last two or three decades of motivational research have led to a move away from conceptions that compare the strongly motivated with the weakly motivated, those with lots of motivation versus those with little, and instead talks in terms of motivational processes that are adapted or maladapted. A key feature of this latter approach is that one has to specify the reference point. To be well or poorly adapted is to be well or poorly adapted to something, and something in particular.

In constructivism about development, one criterion is temporal transformation of action or thought (cf. Turiel pp. 29-40; see also Moshman, 1999). A different notion of development is used in research on motivation by Heckhausen and Farruggia (pages 85–102). Their argument is that regulation over the life span is interpreted by reference to two types of control; primary control manifest in terms of personal, social and professional goals through the course of life, and secondary control manifest as the use of motivational resources to facilitate goal disengagement and self-protection. A central construct in their argument is that of a 'developmental deadline'. Developmental deadlines are a major opportunity and constraint which interact with both types of regulative control. An open question is the contribution of schooling in making life transitions as well as the differential impact made by academic achievement and intrinsic motivation. The notion of a developmental deadline is an interesting notion, both because of its attendant evidence and because of the intrinsic plausibility of this construct. A currently stronger motivation to do *A* at one point in a developmental cycle may conflict with a motivation to do *B*, which would be unavailable after a particular point in the developmental cycle. The presence of the 'developmental deadline' requires the re-evaluation of actions *A* and *B*. Doubtless, the time at which this re-evaluation is made interacts with its actual content. There is a conceptual distinction at issue here for any joint account of motivation and development. A developmental deadline is a point in time such that a chronological age could well be its criterion, albeit with chronological age often used as a proxy for biological development (e.g. the end of fertility) or socially determined transitions in an educational system (e.g. the move from primary to secondary school; the taking of key examinations relating to qualifications for further education or work). But this is a different notion of development in that, according to constructivism, development is a temporal process of change such that chronological age is its indicator, but not its criterion.

Research methods

It is clear from these articles, and certainly from a broader knowledge of the two areas of enquiry, that one difference between the development and motivation projects is to be seen in the paradigmatic research methods employed. Both camps have engaged in considerable theorizing, and both would be committed to the importance of theory in drawing together the results of empirical labour. However, the empirical traditions have generally been different. Developmental work has largely proceeded by means of the experimental study using assessment tasks in the testing of causal hypotheses interpreted through theoretically important concepts. Motivation researchers, however, have largely invested their energies in the development of questionnaires and scales that have been used to devise reliable, and hopefully valid, insights into the motivations of the target audience.

This divergence of method has two immediate points of interest. First, it can make communication between researchers strongly placed in one of the two traditions difficult. Motivation researchers will need to catch up on the significance of particular paradigmatic experimental manipulations, while developmentalists will have similar problems engaging quickly with the significance of particular profiles of scores on particular tests. However, there is a second, and more important, observation. The two research traditions represent basic assumptions about what is important in the respective field and, notably, when it is important; that is, at which particular point in the life-cycle. The experiment has emerged as the standard procedure in developmental work doubtless for many reasons. However, one such is the argument that young children are not very well able to talk reliably about their experiences. Experimental investigations of what they do under different sets of circumstances become necessary therefore (for the argument that cognitively competent young children are conversational neophytes, see Siegal, 1997). But things are not clear-cut. The contrary argument is that an interview method directed on children's own interpretations and reasoning is both useful and even necessary for access to children's minds on both psychological (Ginsburg, 1997) and epistemological (Smith, 2002) grounds. A complementary interpretation—with substantive and not merely methodological implications—is set out by Sokol and Chandler (pages 125-136). Further, the practice of developmentalists is often opportunistic, minimizing exchanges in some cases and maximizing them in others (see Goswami, 2002).

Education

The interest in educational matters has been an important driver in both fields, perhaps more so in motivation than in development. While noting this, we can also observe the assumption that motivational processes are judged to be educationally more problematic in the later years of formal education, whereas perhaps developmental processes are more problematic in the earlier years. Witness, for example, the enduring concern with the motivational difficulties of the early adolescent and their interaction in many national systems with the transition from primary to secondary phases of education (e.g. Anderman, Maehr, & Midgley, 1999; Galton, Gray, & Ruddock, 1999). The methods adopted by the respective fields have reflected the perceived nature of the phenomena under study, as would clearly be expected, but also the particular issues within those fields that have drawn significant amounts of researcher attention. Adolescence continues to provide a challenge to accounts of cognition and development. One manifestation is the apparently suboptimal levels of achievement of youngsters in otherwise economically successful countries, notably the USA and UK, on international mathematics assessment (Keys, Harris, & Fernandes, 1996; Reynolds & Farrell, 1996; Stigler & Hiebert, 1999; Whitburn, 2000). Another is the requirement for intervention directed on development, rather than instruction directed on learning, to secure real cognitive advances during adolescence across the curriculum subjects of English, Mathematics and Science (Adey & Shayer, 1994; Shayer & Adey, 2002).

Education is a source of multiplicity in several respects. One is brought out in Pintrich's (pages 137-153) discussion of multiple goals and the current debate concerning the possible merits or demerits of performance goals (particularly performance-approach goals) highlighting the importance of the intersection between motivational characteristics and the particular context within which an individual is currently operating. So Pintrich suggests that some educational contexts, particularly those that might be more normative in terms of the ways in which people are judged, will be more likely to bring benefits to those who have performance-approach goals. Pintrich's discussion is primarily couched in terms of variations between different sectors within the educational system, but the contribution of Elliott and Hufton (pages 155-172) reminds us of a second source of multiplicity consisting in cultural variations, which turn out not to be immediately obvious. Recent socio-cultural changes in the breakup of the USSR have led to the re-evaluation of traditional values, notably as relating to academic success. Despite social pressure to work hard in a culture which has traditionally set a high value on high educational standards, and so attested internationally today, the evidence shows that contemporary youngsters have a less positive view of their achievement. <u>Motivation and engagement are not the same thing,</u> and both are differentially interpreted by young people growing up. This points to a dislocation between effort and achievement. The interplay between culture, cognition, motivation and pedagogy is complex, resisting easy generalization. A third source of multiplicity is identified by Boekaerts (pages 173–189) due to learning differences in knowledge domains in particular contexts. Her argument is that learners in educational settings engage in twin-track processing directed both on learning goals as well as on personal well-being within reasonable bounds. These empirically distinct pathways of cold and hot cognition are at the interface between learning opportunities and performance. Emotional outcomes in a learning situation influence the strategies used by that learner. Activated emotions can be overriding over action, even over appropriateness. The mismatch between socio-emotional goals and academic goals is not well identified, still less addressed, in most educational accounts. Crucially as well, emotional goals may be subject to developmental deadlines and time-windows. Top-level goals are mediated by situations in which differences in hierarchical order are constructed by the agent in action.

Many motivational researchers have used the probably apocryphal story of the mathematician (let us call him Brown) in discussing the work of their colleagues. One of us (Rogers) has indeed now done this so frequently that he has quite forgotten the origins of the tale. Nevertheless, for those who are not a part of this circle, it is a story worth repeating.

The story concerns the research students who had come to work with Brown. He, in turn, had made his reputation, which was formidable, by working in the general area of probability theory, and in particular on the MiniMax theorem. His students were devoted, and many of them had made considerable personal sacrifices in order to work with him. They were delighted to have the benefit of his expertise and professional guidance but regretted his lack of sociability. They were pleased then to see him enter a campus coffee bar while they were playing cards. They invited Brown to join them in a few rounds in order both to enjoy his company and to witness his skill in card playing (informed of course by his profound understanding of the relevant probabilities). They offered him a pile of matchsticks being used as gambling chips, and the game commenced. Imagine their distress when Brown proceeded to play a most inept game, losing all of his chips very quickly and then leaving. For a while, each began to doubt the validity of Brown's reputation and the wisdom of their own individual decisions to make so many sacrifices in order to work with him. After a long and uncomfortable pause, one of the students leapt to his feet proclaiming, 'It's alright! I know what he was doing! He wasn't trying to maximize his chips, he was trying to minimize his time!'.

The story is better (believe us) when told live and spun out for all it is worth, however the abbreviated version makes the point. The students had assumed, not unreasonably, that when Brown started to play cards, he was seeking to win—to maximize his chips. Given this assumption, his play was also reasonably judged as inept. The insightful student had had cause to question this intention and had assumed instead that Brown was intending to minimize the amount of time that he would have to spend playing cards with the students. Having allowed himself to be persuaded to partake in the game, Brown quickly came to regret what he saw as a waste of good working time and had rapidly calculated that he could lose the game faster than he could win it (he knew he could do either) and so proceeded to lose—with great skill. The reference point for Brown's behaviour was his desire to get away from the students not to win yet more matchsticks. Against this reappraisal of his intention, the students could be reassured of both Brown's ability and his lack of sociability.

What is at issue here of course is the point of reference for Brown's actions. Appropriate judgments of his actions could only be made against an equally appropriate judgment of the reference point, the intention of the man as he engaged in the game.

Covington (1992, 2000), among others, has drawn on such notions in developing a theory of self-worth motivation. Students are seen to be not unmotivated but differently motivated. While some focus on learning, others develop self-handicapping strategies in order to protect the self from the possible consequences of failure. Within the context of the current volume, such a distinction is captured by the contrast between epistemic motivation and self-organizing motivation. In the above narrative, Brown would have been engaging in forms of self-organizing motivation; he was not concerned about the business of learning to play a meaner game of cards.

Within many now well-known motivational theories, this development of different motivational foci can be readily understood as a function of the different reference points to which the individual in question has come to work. A crucial question remains, then, as to how these various points of reference are acquired. Where there are clear environmental differences from one context to another, any simplistic evolutionary developmental system will be sufficient to enable us to begin to understand how different reference points emerge.

The cases highlighted raise concerns. In educational terms, there would appear to be relatively few clear-cut advantages to having acquired the entity view of ability. In life terms, there would appear to be even fewer advantages in acquiring the negatively valenced self-image described as arising from child abuse. Consistency would appear to be all. Bickhard has argued persuasively that it is stability that in some respects needs to be explained. In developmental terms, change is the norm. Yet, here we are faced with developmental outcomes that do not appear to offer much in the way of advantages other than stability. A stable representation of the self is a vital part of any developed notion of the nature of the world. Relations between the self and the world cannot be managed without it. It is recognized, of course, that the self is probably multi-faceted (Marsh & Yeung, 1997) and that varying facets may come into play at different times. However, the overall structure and the operation of each facet are predicated upon a degree of stability.

Further work into the development of these varying outcomes might help us to understand the different pathways along which people may come to travel. For education, however, the question remains as to which pathway people ought to be encouraged to travel.

A developmental pathway with all travellers experiencing the same press towards the same developmentally 'superior' outcome provides its own system for evaluating the outcome when it comes. The developmentally superior outcomes are the ones that education should encourage. Any bunch of literal scaffolders can know the terrain that they are scaffolding—the wall that needs retaining, the roof that needs to be accessed— only the skilful operators will know how to ensure that the structure they create is adequate for the job and is safe and effective in use. In a developmental world, where the superior outcome is agreed, figurative scaffolders have the same concerns. Given that the developmental outcome is known, the skills are to do with ensuring that just the right kind of support is provided at the right moment. If this shared agreement in outcome is missing, or if there are multiple developmental outcomes, where does the scaffolder start? And where are they heading? Crucially, if development is the education of reason whereby 'each individual is led to think and re-think the system of collective notions' (Piaget, 1995, p. 76), developmental outcomes neither could be, nor should be, predictable. For educators then, the initial task becomes one of determining just what the developmental objectives could and should be in such a way that autonomy is both respected and encouraged (Smith, 2003). What is necessary, then, is to seek out an enhanced understanding of the nature of the process in which motivation and cognition under development are dual aspects. It is also necessary to seek out a better understanding of the varying endpoints that might be reached, together with the forces that determine the destination of any one individual. For example, it is only when we can be clear that it is better to develop an incremental view of ability (or a set of learning goals, or possibly a set of performance approach goals or some combination of these) and by what criteria this is claimed to be so that education can set about the task of determining how to ensure that young people are guided along an appropriate pathway. Should we be naive enough to assume that these are only problems that will beset those charged with the education and support of the young, the argument in Heckhausen and Farruggia's article is here to remind us that there are a number of clearly developmentally relevant judgments to be made throughout the life-cycle. Our excursion into the moral domain also reminds us of the highly value-laden nature of many of the judgments that will need to be made.

Nicholls (1989) argued for the inculcation of 'motivational equity' as a clear goal of educational systems (one which he generally reckoned was not being met within current systems). Nicholls' own developmental analysis was importantly different from that of Dweck in that he had suggested a rather more unidimensional developmental pathway. In this pathway, something similar to entity conceptions of ability emerged as the developmentally later (and superior) outcome. However, motivational equity, he suggests, would be more readily introduced by seeking to counteract this trend and preserving the advantages of the developmentally prior state. To some extent, the paradox of a developmentally superior state being held to be less desirable in educational terms (so well captured by the inclusion in the title of the phrase 'development and its discontents' in one of his articles (Nicholls & Miller, 1984)) opens up the way for the concerns raised here. In suggesting that educational objectives and developmental progression need not always go simply hand in hand, Nicholls made it clear that other criteria will sometimes be needed to determine what the educational outcomes ought to be. The well-known and often rehearsed difficulties implicit in going from statements of what 'is' to statements concerning what 'ought' to be, are a stock part of developmental debates. Multi-pathway developmental accounts do not remove the need for such debates, but they give it a new and interesting twist. When there is more than one 'is', it becomes clear that one should be cautious in simply deriving a single 'ought'.

Many cognitive and interpersonal processes relevant to education can be considered to share the basic pattern of the circular reaction (recall the examples given in Fischer). An example in the interpersonal sphere can be found in the research examining the workings of the self-fulfilling prophecy within school classrooms. The teacher expectancy effect has been closely scrutinized (Blanck, 1993; Dusek, 1985; Rogers, 2002; Rosenthal, 1995; Rosenthal & Jacobson, 1968) since the publication of the classic Pygmalion study. The basic process assumed in most models involves a number of discreet but closely linked events. These would include:

- the development of expectations by the teacher;
- the impact of those expectations upon the teacher's actions;
- the perception of those actions by a pupil;
- the reaction by the pupil to those perceptions;
- in the case of a self-fulfilling prophecy, the movement by the pupil in the direction of the initial expectation.

The latter further confirms the expectation, and so the cycle is strengthened and repeated. On an intra-personal level, many models of self-regulated learning share the same basic pattern of Test–Operate–Test and, eventually, Exit (Miller, Galanter, & Pribram, 1967). Self-regulated learning would be seen by many as an example of just such a pattern (Baumeister, 2000; Zimmerman, 1998). As Zimmerman makes clear, however, there are cycles and there are cycles, and not all such cyclic processes are equally beneficial. Once beneficial cycles are established (and again one needs to be clear as to the criteria by which the benefit will be judged) the very cyclic nature of the process will tend to ensure that further enhancements, and thereby greater benefit, are obtained. However, by the same token, the cyclic process can lead remorselessly downward. For the educator, the objective in working alongside the forces of motivation and development may well be couched in terms of attempting to ensure that the direction of the cycle is judged appropriate.

Initially, a situational interest will be provoked by external stimuli, and this will lead, via a stabilized situational interest, to an individual interest. Krapp highlights the importance of the second stage for education. The initial interest can be formulated in many different ways, for example by a dramatic and attention-grabbing display on an interactive whiteboard, but many of these will simply pass by. The development of longer-term individual interests is, suggests Krapp, as does Boekaerts in a very similar vein, dependent upon both cognitive and 'feeling' strands. The latter are closely related to the central tenets of self-determination theory (Deci & Ryan, 2000, 2002) with an emphasis on needs for competence, self-determination and social-relatedness.

A similar point is made by Pintrich in his discussion of the links between motivational processes and self-regulated learning. Interests provide the reference points by which circular reactions can be judged and thereby directed. However, as Pintrich reminds us, there is a long tradition with motivational research of exploration of both approach and avoidance forms of motivation. Negativity is not always going to follow from the absence of a developed interest in something, but sometimes will follow from the positive development of an avoidance tendency. Pintrich has been primarily concerned here with the distinction between approach and avoidance goals within the scope of a consideration of performance-related goals. Performance goals that encourage approach may yet be seen to be a 'good thing'. However, the interrelationships between approach and avoidance tendencies is due for a considerable revival of research interest, and it is right that this should be predicated on the possibility that both approach and avoidance forms of motivation can have beneficial effects.

The possibility of positive forms of avoidance goals depends on exactly what it is that is being avoided. To illustrate, consider the operation of a simple hand-held navigational device using global positioning satellite (GPS) technology. The coordinates of a target (or waypoint) are entered. The device then simply displays an arrow that will point directly at the waypoint. If one is travelling in the exact direction of the arrow, one is on course for the target. The device enables simple corrections to one's course to be made to ensure that the objective is eventually reached irrespective of the detours that terrain and circumstances may require.

This is a simple and direct form of an approach mechanism, and as Pintrich suggests, it is associated with positive forms of goal-seeking behaviour. However, simple GPS devices can also be programmed with waypoints that one wishes to avoid (for example, when sailing, one can program in areas of barely submerged rocks, difficult currents, etc.). The GPS device is then set to issue a warning whenever one comes within a pre-selected distance of the hazard waypoint. On receipt of such a warning, avoiding action is taken. Once a safe distance is re-established, the monitoring of the hazard waypoint again slips into the background. Similar approaches can be seen without the use of fancy technology. In driving along a busy street, for example, one aims at the objective (the shop at the end of the street) while simultaneously seeking to avoid hitting pedestrians.

In these cases, both approach and avoidance goals are working together in a relatively harmonious manner in order to bring about a combined objective (safe arrival at a chosen destination). They are both associated with positive forms of behaviour designed to achieve a desirable goal. There is minimal conflict between the two. Minimal conflict is not the same as no conflict of course. One could get to the destination faster by ignoring the hazards, but only by enhancing the risk of killing oneself or others in the process.

The classic approach-avoidance conflict explored by Atkinson (Atkinson & Raynor, 1978) concerns situations where approach and avoidance motives directly and immediately conflict. One cannot engage in a task to gain the satisfaction of success while simultaneously avoiding the task in order to avoid the possibility of failure. As Atkinson made clear a few decades ago, the degree to which such conflicts are experienced will depend upon the perceptions of the individual in question. If failure opportunities are barely noticed against the foreground of success opportunities, then little actual conflict is experienced. If one is highly sensitive to both, then a real difficulty arises, and indecision is likely to prevail.

Self- and other inherent representations

So we are back to the nature of the relationship between the ways in which a person represents the world around them and the ways in which they understand themselves. One, of several, messages arising from this collection of articles is that the crucial link between cognition and motivation under development is to be seen in the joint operation of the same processes. How one comes to judge the success of attempts to deal with the world, and the adequacy of the understanding of that world put to use in the process, will in part depend upon what it is that one is trying to achieve. The latter necessarily reflects what it is that one considers oneself to be. Again, as the cross-cultural work of Elliott and Hufton (pp. 155–172) shows us, what one considers oneself to be has to involve an appraisal of the world in which one operates. In this sense, the processes of development and motivation cannot be sensibly considered apart from each other.

Several of our contributors have talked of the importance of inherent processes: an inherent drive towards greater complexity, an inherent need for competence and social connectedness, an inherent need to develop and maintain a stable and coherent self-image and so on. We are clearly not in a position to stipulate the maximum number of inherent processes that it would be sensible for anyone to suggest that human beings have. It is convenient to assume that they exist, and thereby lays a theoretical danger.

Psychology has historically worked with a number of different key constructs that have organized the ways in which psychologists think about the nature of human activity, cognitive and other. There have been times when such constructs have struggled to cover the range of ideas and data to which they were meant to apply. A response has been to increase the number of such constructs. So when one list of instincts appeared insufficient to explain given phenomena, another instinct was invented and added to the list; so too with needs and so too, perhaps, with motivational goals and the inherent processes involved in both development and motivation. We should exercise caution in simply asserting that a given point marks the end of the chain of enquiry due to its clear inherent nature. Detailed research looking at idiographic as well as nomothetic processes, detailed research comparing processes across widely different cultures and subcultures is necessary prior to properly being able to begin to substantiate a claim that a given facet of human activity is inherent in the nature of the beast.

We have, at least, persuaded ourselves that there is inherent good sense in continuing to consider the joint theorizing and researching of development and motivation. Further explorations of the relationships between them, and the extent to which some facets can be convincingly regarded as inherent are undertakings for the future. What we have heard at the conference, and read in this collection, inspires us to believe that such undertakings will be difficult but ultimately highly valuable.

Ways ahead

The primary reason behind the conference at which the articles in this volume were initially presented was to address the question about how to make progress towards a joint model of motivation and development. It is our belief that these papers have made a welcome contribution here. But we are equally mindful of the fact that we are not there yet. What follows now is a frame of reference for charting the way ahead. There are at least three pathways, three routes to take by way of a focus on: analytically distinct concepts, co-instantiated phenomena, and inter-dependent research-programmes. These pathways are not exclusive, and are likely not to be exhaustive of the class.

Analytically distinct concepts

Many accounts of the mind in research generally make the assumption, usually implicitly, that the relationship between motivation and cognition under development is one of independence. Such accounts are dominant in current research, typically dealing with one of these without regard for the other. Under this division of labour, one team deals with cognitive development, and another team deals with motivation. On the successful completion of the work, a complete account of the mind would be composed through additive combination. In outline, the underlying argument can be stated in this way:

(1)   There is no theory of everything.
(2)   On inductive grounds, a restricted focus on each individually enables scientific progress to occur.
(3)   Such progress is a stepwise advance, including the advance from one to the other.

This position seems to make good sense on several counts. First, there is no doubt about the importance of the phenomena (cognitive development, motivation), but these turn out to be exceedingly complex. This complexity is evident in the multiplicity of constructs used in their explanation, and in terms of the multiplicity of operationalizations used in empirical studies. A restricted focus on one of these alone is one way to make progress. Second, different members of the same team adopt different positions in their interpretations. The presence of these alternatives results in controversy. In this context, it makes sense for each team to maintain a restricted focus. But there are also clear and major weaknesses. One is the absence of a check on whether the ideas and evidence available to one team have implications for joint use, still less whether there are fundamental incompatibilities. A 'division of labour' can result in an isolation which amounts to a reciprocal loss. Another weakness is the commitment to an atomistic conception of the mind without due regard for the extent to which the mind is unitary and systemic in its operations and functions. A third weakness is fundamental. It is a fallacy to base a conclusion about the independence of scientific research on a premise stating that two concepts are conceptually distinguishable. This is because the same case can fall under distinct concepts. The concepts of energy, mass and velocity are conceptually distinct. But these distinct concepts are explanatory of one and the same case, such as the release of radioactivity at Chernobyl under the equation $E = mc^2$. A research programme directed on motivation alone or cognitive development alone is liable to be blind, and thereby open to the accusation that 'we have first raised a dust, and then complain we cannot see' (Berkeley, 1962, para. 3). In short, difficulties may well be of our own making.

Co-instantiated phenomena
An alternative approach is to start from the phenomena rather than the concepts under which the phenomena fall. This approach sets out to be inclusive, with the specific intention of assigning a key role to both motivation and cognitive development.

(4)   Motivation and cognition under development are co-instantiated phenomena.
(5)   A joint focus on both enables scientific progress to occur.
(6)   Such progress is dependent on their co-presence in the same account.

This position seems to make sense due to the inclusive focus on motivational and developmental aspects of action and thought. It does not exclude a restricted focus on either aspect alone. But it specifically covers their joint focus as well. Even so, this position is insufficient. First, it represents the start, but not the completion or even the voyage, on a long journey. There are multiple ways in which co-instantiation may occur, including bare correlation, moderation, mediation, unidirectional causality, bidirectional causality and so on. Second, the joint focus on both the motivational and developmental aspects of relevant cases postpones the problem of their interpretation in a joint account. If the impetus for their joint study is due to analytically distinct concepts, the evidence will be under-determining through lack of a unitary model.

Third, the research traditions in these areas severally have their own methods and procedures which are not easily convertible, which we noticed above. All the problems of operationalization and interpretation are implicated here, notably when this matters most in setting out interpretations of multiple evidence. Fourthly, normativity is likely to slip through the net unless its specific inclusion has already been assured in the model. However, the focus on phenomena is no guarantee that this assurance is forthcoming. Co-instantiation is a correlational or causal relation which is external to its terms. But normativity requires there to be a constituting relation internally linked to its terms, operative within the motivating and developmental systems of living minds in action.

Inter-dependent research programme

A third approach is in the making. This requires a distinctive research programme formed by different accounts with a joint ontology and methodology in a productive problem shift (Lakatos, 1974). There are many reasons why little progress has been made towards such a programme. Taking a cue from Wittgenstein (1958) about conceptual confusion in psychology, one main reason is theoretical, and it goes to the core of psychological theory. What exactly is a psychological explanation of human-like? There are at least two main answers to this question (Mischel, 1971; von Wright, 1983). Further, each has a basis in different disciplines. One discipline is normative philosophy and its commitment to the rule-following model whereby an action is related to the agent's goals under that agent's beliefs and desires. The other discipline is empirical psychology and is the mechanist model whereby behaviour is triggered and controlled by independent events. In general, there is an outstanding problem in the cognitive sciences to exploit both (Goldman, 2001). This general problem is well taken. But so are two caveats. One is the avoidance of premature closure in the reduction of either to the other. The other caveat is adequacy, which in this case is the adequacy of psychological explanation.

There are three ways to bring out the difference between these answers. One is to regard rule-following as internal and the control of behaviour as external. But this is misleading, since cognitive and neural processes are internal to the agent and also open to independent control in experimental designs, i.e. external. Further, social rules are rules which are public and objective—try telling your tax-officer that your way of paying taxes is due to your internal constitution to which the nation's taxation laws are irrelevant. A second characterization in terms of external causality as opposed to internal freedom from causality is also misleading. Kant was a champion of freedom of the will, yet his own behaviour in taking an afternoon walk was as regular as clockwork, and his neighbours could set their clocks by his habitual actions. In general, imperatives can function causally just because their content is normative, i.e. rule-governed (Piaget, 1995; von Wright, 1983). A third way is to make reference to norms. Mischel (1971) has argued that Piaget's model of equilibration aspired to be an intermediary between the two approaches, rather than a failed contribution to psychological mechanisms to which it has been regularly assimilated. This is because the motivation behind that model is to show how such norms as consistency and coherence govern and direct the development of human thinking. As Piaget (1965, p. 159; see also Smith, 2002, chap. 7-2) elegantly put this, 'any subject is always "normed"'. A general model of the logic of norms is due to von Wright (1983), central to which is the key notion of the commitments manifest as 'what has to be done' (as opposed to what may be done, what should not be done) and 'what has to be' (as opposed to what can be, what could not be). Under his account, 'normative pressure' is a causal mechanism at work in society in the regulation of behaviour; autonomous normativity is the rule-bound regulation of action. The implication is that a unitary answer can be given to such questions as 'Why are you doing that?', namely 'Because it's right', and 'Why do you think that?', namely 'Because it's true'. To appeal to what is right and what is true requires reference to norms. A fundamental problem for all individuals is in three parts which are to access the norms generally available in their culture, then to constitute specific norms with a binding force on thought and action, and as well as that to forge new norms. None of these can be started, much less completed, without the reciprocal interplay of motivation and cognition under development.

In sum, it is worth reiterating that a commitment to a joint account is, in general, common ground to the chapters in this volume. It is also worth repeating that some key principles—about normativity, developmental pathways for motivated learning, research methods and education—have been set out here. We warmly encourage other researchers and practitioners to think about and then rethink these ideas and evidence, and so continue where this volume leaves off.

References

Adey, P., & Shayer, M. (1994) *Really raising standards*. London: Routledge.

Anderman, E. M., Maehr, M. L., & Midgley, C. (1999). Declining motivation after the transition to middle school: Schools can make a difference. *Journal of Research and Development in Education*, *32*(3), 131-147.

Atkinson, J., & Raynor, J. (Eds.). (1978). *Personality, motivation and achievement*. Washington, DC: Hemisphere.

Baumeister, R. F. (Ed.). (2000). *The self in social psychology: Essential readings*. Philadelphia, PA: Psychology Press.

Blanck, P. D. (Ed.). (1993). *Interpersonal expectations: Theory, research and applications*. Cambridge: Cambridge University Press.

Covington, M. V. (1992). *Making the grade: A self-worth perspective on motivation and school reform*. Cambridge: Cambridge University Press.

Covington, M. V. (2000). Goal theory, motivation, and school achievement: An integrative review. *Annual Review of Psychology*, 171-200.

Deci, E. L., & Ryan, R. M. (2000). The 'what' and 'why' of goal pursuits: Human needs and the self-determination of behavior. *Psychological Inquiry*, *11*(4), 227-268.

Deci, E. L., & Ryan, R. M. (Eds.). (2002). *Handbook of self-determination research*. Rochester, NY: University of Rochester Press.

Dusek, J. B. (Ed.). (1985). *Teacher expectancies*. Hillsdale, NJ: Erlbaum.

Flavell, J. (1999). Cognitive development: Children's knowledge about the mind. *Annual Review of Psychology*, *50*, 21-45.

Flavell, J., Miller, P., & Miller, S. (1993). *Cognitive development* (3rd ed.). Englewood Cliffs, NJ: Prentice-Hall.

Galton, M., Gray, J., & Ruddock, J. (1999). *The impact of school transitions and transfers on pupil progress and attainment*. London: DFEE.

Ginsburg, H. (1997). *Entering the child's mind*. Cambridge: Cambridge University Press.

Goldman, A. (2001). *Pathways of knowledge: Public and private*. Oxford: Oxford University Press.

Goswami, U. (2002). *Blackwell handbook of childhood cognitive development*. Oxford: Blackwell.

Keys, W., Harris, S., & Fernandes, C. (1996). *Third international mathematics and science study. First National Report*. Slough: NFER.

Lakatos, I. (1974). Falsification and the logic of scientific research programmes. In I. Lakatos & A. Musgrave (Eds.), *Criticism and the growth of knowledge* (pp. 91-196). Cambridge: Cambridge University Press.

Marsh, H. W., & Yeung, A. S. (1997). Organization of children's academic self-perceptions: Reanalysis and counter-interpretations of confirmatory factor analysis results. *Journal of Educational Psychology, 89*(4), 752-759.

Miller, G. A., Galanter, G., & Pribram, K. H. (1967). *Plans and the structure of behavior*. New York: Holt, Rinehart and Winston.

Mischel, T. (1971). Piaget: Cognitive conflict and the motivation of thought. In T. Mischel (Ed). *Cognitive development and epistemology* (pp. 311-355). New York: Academic Press.

Moshman, D. (1999). *Adolescent psychological development*. Mahwah, NJ: Erlbaum.

Nicholls, J. G. (1989). *The competitive ethos and democratic education*. Cambridge, MA: Harvard University Press.

Nicholls, J. G., & Miller, A. T. (1984). Development and its discontents: the differentiation of the concept of ability. In J. G. Nicholls (Ed.), *Advances in motivation and achievement: Vol. 3: The development of achievement motivation* (pp. 185-218). Westport, CT: JAI Press.

Pareto, V. (1963). *A treatise of general sociology*. New York: Dover.

Piaget, J. (1965). Genèse et structure en psychologie. In M. de Gandillac, L. Goldman, & J. Piaget (Eds.), *Entretiens sur les notions de genèse et de structure* (pp. 156-159). Paris: Mouton.

Piaget, J. (1995). *Sociological studies*. London: Routledge.

Reynolds, D, & Farrell, S. (1996). *Worlds apart*. London: HMSO.

Rogers, C. G. (2002). Teacher expectations: Implications for school improvement. In C. Desforges & R. Fox (Eds.), *Teaching and learning: The essential readings* (pp. 152-170). Oxford: Blackwell.

Rosenthal, R. (1995). Critiquing Pygmalion—A 25-year perspective. *Current Directions in Psychological Science, 4*(6), 171-172.

Rosenthal, R., & Jacobson, L. (1968). *Pygmalion in the classroom*. New York: Holt, Rinehart and Winston.

Shayer, M. & Adey, P. (2002) *Learning intelligence*. Buckingham: Open University Press.

Siegal, M. (1997). *Knowing children: Experiments in conversation and cognition* (2nd ed.). Hove: Psychology Press.

Smith, L. (2002). *Reasoning by mathematical induction in children's arithmetic*. Oxford: Pergamon.

Smith, L. (2003). Developmental epistemology and education. In J. Carpendale & U. Müller (Eds.), *Social interaction and the development of knowledge*. Mahwah, NJ: Erlbaum.

Stigler, J., & Hiebert, J. (1999). *The teaching gap*. New York: Free Press.

von Wright, G. H. (1983). *Practical reason*. Oxford: Blackwell.

Whitburn, J. (2000). *Strength in numbers*. London: NIESR.

Williams, B. (1996). Truth in ethics. In B. Hooker (Ed.), *Truth in ethics* (pp. 19-34). Oxford: Blackwell.

Wittgenstein, L. (1958). *Philosophical investigations* (2nd ed.). Oxford: Blackwell.

Zimmerman, B. J. (1998). Developing self-fulfilling cycles of academic regulation: An analysis of exemplary instructional models. In D. H. Schunk & B. J. Zimmerman (Eds.), *Self-regulated learning: From teaching to self-reflective practice* (pp. 1-19). London: Guilford.